Architecture for the Poor

Hassan Fathy

Architecture For the Poor

An Experiment in Rural Egypt

The University of Chicago Press
Chicago and London

Architecture for the Poor was originally published in 1969 under the title *Gourna: A Tale of Two Villages,* in a limited edition, by the Ministry of Culture, Cairo.

The University of Chicago Press, Chicago 60637
The University of Chicago Press, Ltd., London

Printed in the United States of America

International Standard Book Number: 0–226–23915–2
Library of Congress Catalog Card Number: 72–95133

Contents

Foreword

At least one billion people will die early deaths and will live stunted lives because of unsanitary, uneconomic, and ugly housing.

Attacked in conventional ways, this problem appears to have no feasible solution. In its study for the World Bank, the Pearson commission provides us with data which show that even in the unlikely event that the world's rich were to give 1 percent of their income to help uplift the world's poor, nearly a third of the world's population would continue to live at levels of grinding poverty. Probably a third of the world's population will continue for the rest of this century to earn in a year less than the weekly salary of today's American factory worker. The capital investment required to provide even minimal housing for a poor family in the United States today is on the order of $20,000. In other words, most years of a man's productive career are consumed by acquiring shelter.

These figures are accurate but they tend to mislead. The cost of housing must be broken down into its component parts. These are, I suggest, three: economic, social, and aesthetic. They are closely related, but each deserves individual attention.

We have been taught to believe that the world economy is divided into two parts, the rich nations and the poor nations. This division is in large part expressed by the contrast between hard currency and soft currency. Hard currency is that which commands advanced technology and so is an object of desire by all peoples. Soft currency is produced by the poor nations whose products are not so eagerly sought by others. Even when a country has ample access to soft currencies, it often cannot acquire those services and goods which it desperately needs or avidly seeks.

But there is another subdivision of economy: the poor within countries. At least a third of the world's population lives below the money economy. From their perspective, there is little difference between hard and soft currencies. Almost anything which they cannot acquire by their own labor from their immediate neighborhood cannot be acquired at all. In many parts of the world, the average income of these people may be as little as one-third of the already pitifully small national average of the poor countries. In the villages of Asia, the yearly income per capita is so small as to be statistically almost meaningless. It is very close to the subsistence level and occasionally dips below it.

In terms of housing, this means not only that structural steel—an item usually imported from hard currency areas—is an impossible luxury but that even the products of urban industry or other regions of a country—cement, timber, glass—are uneconomic or infeasible. Where these materials are pressed into use, their costliness necessarily requires stinginess. This has a crippling effect upon housing, so that government-developed projects often resemble regimented lines of concrete chicken coops.

Traditional villages, sprawling, dirty, and overcrowded to such an extent that the outside observer sees little more than chaos, are often delicate and sensitive expressions of social organization. Ties of kinship and barriers of hostility are often expressed geographically and structurally. However bad the physical housing itself may be, the villager derives some comfort and, indeed, some meaning from its pattern.

This is not an issue alien even to so homogenized a culture as our own. Take the case of the American black community. Its predominant historical experience has been uprooting. Uprooted from tribal societies, Africans were sold into the baracoons of West Africa. There or later, they were often deliberately mixed so that their tribal coherence was destroyed. Even linguistically, the slaves had as much trouble communicating with one another as with their new white masters. This, of course, prevented the possibility of rebellion. Adding to these decisive elements were the criteria of the marketplace. Mothers and children were often parted from one another, so that what had been a society was atomized. Whatever small degree of stability had been attained before the Civil War was again shattered, even if for the better, by emancipation. The rootlessness of the American black community was a function of shanty towns, poverty, and lack of skills. But as social animals, black men, like white, brown, and yellow men, reached out to attempt to touch their neighbors and to reassert two basic urges of all mankind, territoriality and society. Then came renewed turmoil as opportunities afforded by wartime economy were impelled by peacetime depression to cause massive migrations northward into the great cities. The migration was not from point to point but rather from one series of temporary stopping points to another. Many of the black slums in the American cities were originally merely waystations where migrants paused to rest, to attempt to acquire the capital for the next move onward, and to make the mental transition from the rural South to the urban North.

At each of these stages, however, the urges of territoriality in society asserted themselves. Families, even when fatherless and plagued by instability, attempted to assert neighborhood. The feeling was weak, and the growth was ever precarious, but its manifestations were often not to the liking of the more affluent, whether black or white.

Viewing these conditions from the outside, liberal, decent, and well-motivated people attempted to help. A major aspect of this help was urban renewal, better housing laid down on an abstract pattern from the outside. Its relatively simplistic notion was that slums are bad housing. Its solution was to tear down the bad housing and to build good housing. One may quibble about many of its manifestations. It was a bonanza for contractors. It was an architect's boondoggle. It was too expensive for the very poor. These are merely surface issues, however, when viewed in the scale of the real cost of urban renewal: it represented yet a new uprooting of communities whose roots were battered and undernourished. However weak were the ties between neighbors, the process sundered them and forced the individuals to begin all over again in a new, alien, if better physical, environment.

But was the environment socially a better one? Highrise housing developments have been called vertical slums. Many, even the new ones, certainly qualify for this description. The tenants, lacking a sense of territorial identification and ungoverned by ties of neighborhood, follow the pattern we may see even in the primates in despair: they foul their nests. Buildings rapidly delapidate, statistics of crime are appalling, and that sense of lethargy and sullen anger which is the hallmark of "underdevelopment" are evident. It may be, and I suspect it is, a fact that the weaker and the poorer are individuals in societies, the closer they must be to the earth. Whether this is true or not, it is surely evident that people must express their relationships with one another. When thwarted in all other ways, they will do this through the creation of street gangs. Totally thwarted in this expression, they give way to despair. That is the essence of the slum. Ironically, its purest form may not be the sprawling Asian village but the modern urban renewal project.

The third major category in problems of housing is aesthetic. Hard-headed realists may argue that aesthetic considerations are a frill. Viewed in the perspective of sanitation, cost, or net square footage per capita, beauty or ugliness hardly matter. The important thing is to keep out the rain and the cold and to do so at a cost we can afford.

Philosophically, one may argue that men need beauty as much as protection. In any event, mere existence or the attenuation of the passage from the womb to the grave is surely not a proper goal for mankind. For a long time such sentiments were discounted, but there is growing evidence of their centrality. We know that children who are deprived of a visually interesting environment in their early years do not develop brains appropriately "programmed" to deal with many of the problems of maturity. We have seen dozens of examples throughout the world where the provision of all the physical accoutrements of development fail to strike a spark and so fail utterly. The fact is, as we have painfully learned in the process of spending a trillion dollars in the period since World War II, that development occurs in the minds and hearts of men or it does not occur at all. Housing, roads, bridges, dams, are necessary but not sufficient conditions. Development without self-help is an impossibility. But people whose surroundings are ugly and barren are apt to be unproductive and dispirited. This is not the idle speculation of a do-gooder. Any factory manager knows its truth. Workers in bright, attractive surroundings produce more than workers in ugly, drab surroundings. The human spirit is our most precious resource. Its ecology is our greatest challenge.

These are surely awesome if not overwhelming problems—complex economic considerations, a sensitivity to man's social needs and the nourishing of the human spirit. Can they be satisfactorily met?

There surely is no final solution, but occasional men of genius, sensitivity, and deep moral purpose may light our way. The book which follows is a strong and bright beacon.

Grappling with the problems of grinding poverty—poverty on a scale hardly remembered by living Americans—with insensitive bureaucrats, with suspicious people, with unskilled and sullen people, Dr. Hassan Fathy has produced not only answers but inspiration. His solution is of worldwide import. His thought, experience, and spirit constitute a major international resource.

What Dr. Fathy proposes is a new form of partnership. What the poor have to put into the partnership is essentially their labor. In much of the world, they also have the possibility of acquiring, at essentially no cost, only one possible building material, the earth beneath their feet. With these two things, labor and earth, they can do a great deal. But there are technical and other problems which they either cannot solve by themselves or are apt to solve in inappropriate, ugly, or expensive ways. It is here that the architect can make a major contribution. What Dr. Fathy shows us is that it is possible for the architect to guide what is essentially a self-reliant or self-help project. Using his technical skill, the architect can help the people to a cheap solution of the problem of roofing. That is the most difficult building problem and usually creates a demand for extra-village and, therefore, expensive building materials. In many areas, the attempt to solve the roofing problem has led to the creation of enormously heavy and cumbersome roofs, which frequently collapse in earthquakes or after heavy rains. These are generally responsible for the appalling fatalities in Turkey and Iran in severe earthquakes. There is a solution, and in this book Dr. Fathy shows what it is and how it can be quickly learned. There are other issues which affect sanitation, communication, privacy, and other matters of family concern. In all of these matters, the architects can assist people in accomplishing their objectives by their own efforts better and more cheaply than they could without his help. Even in such simple matters as the acquisition of soil from which to make mud bricks, a bit of planning can result in the creation of an economic resource for the village community: a pond in which to raise fish.

All this requires cooperation: without the participation of the architect, the buildings will be ugly, inappropriate, and/or expensive. Without the cooperation of the people, the project will be sterile, unloved, and untended. Ironically, most public housing in the world today is done without the cooperation of either the architect or the people. It is a bureaucratic decision built by contractors, and, whether horizontal or vertical, it almost immediately becomes a slum. It is perhaps the final irony of our age, as Dr. Fathy reminds us, that it costs more to produce this form of ugliness and that we will be driven toward better, more beautiful housing simply because we cannot afford any other kind.

Dr. Fathy embodies what the Adlai Stevenson Institute stands for: an opportunity for a man of vision and commitment to grapple with a great social problem. Even in its failures—and there are aspects of this in Dr. Fathy's work—much may be learned. One thing is clear. There is no substitute even in the world of speed, mass, and abstraction for the gifted individual who cares.

WILLIAM R. POLK
President, Adlai Stevenson
Institute of International Affairs

Preface

This book is an appeal for a new attitude to rural rehabilitation. The standard of living and culture among the world's desperately poor peasants can be raised through cooperative building, which involves a new approach to rural mass housing. There is much more in this approach than the purely technical matters that concern the architect. There are social and cultural questions of great complexity and delicacy, there is the economic question, there is the question of the project's relations with the government, and so on. None of these questions can be left out of consideration, for each has a bearing on the others, and the total picture would be distorted by any omission. Therefore the text deals with the whole complex of problems, each matter falling into its logical place in the exposition (except for certain purely technical information, which I have placed in an appendix), so that all readers, whatever their special interest or qualifications, will be able to grasp the totality of the planning philosophy outlined.

As my proposals chiefly concern the peasant, my book is dedicated to him. I wish that it could have been addressed exclusively to him, and hope the time will soon come when he will be able to read and judge it, but for the time being I must address it to those who have his welfare in trust: to the architect, to the planner, to the sociologist and anthropologist, to all local, national, and international officials concerned with housing and rural welfare, to politicians and governments everywhere, and to everyone who helps to form official policy toward the countryside.

It would not be just to close this preface without making grateful acknowledgment to all those who have helped me in producing this book. In Egypt, Dr. Sarwat Okasha, Dr. Magdi Wahba, Mr. Christopher Scott, Miss Nawal Hassan, Mr. Spiro Diamantis, and Dr. Rowland Ellis. In the United States, I was assisted by a fellowship from the Adlai Stevenson Institute and greatly profited from and enjoyed my association with its staff and other Fellows. At the Institute my ideas found a home, and the spirit so evident there will, I trust, enable me to put them into practice.

HASSAN FATHY

In the Name of God, The Merciful, The Compassionate

We created you, then We shaped you
then We said to the angels, "Bow yourselves
to Adam." So they bowed themselves,
save Iblis—he was not of those
that bowed themselves.
Said He, "What prevented thee to
bow thyself, when I commanded thee?"
Said he, "I am better than he; Thou
createst me of fire, and him Thou
createst of clay."
Said He, "Get thee down out of it;
it is not for thee to wax proud here,
so go thou forth, surely, thou art
among the humbled."
Said he, "Respite me till the day
they shall be raised."
Said He, "Thou art among the ones
that are respited."
Said he, "Now for thy preventing me,
I shall surely sit in ambush for them
on thy straight path;
then I shall come on them from before them
and from behind them, from their hands
and their left hands; Thou wilt not find
most of them thankful."

—The Koran

1 Prelude
Dream and Reality

Paradise Lost: *The Countryside*

If you were given a million pounds, what would you do with them? A question they were always asking us when we were young, one that would start our imagination roaming and set us daydreaming. I had two possible answers: one, to buy a yacht, hire an orchestra, and sail round the world with my friends listening to Bach, Schumann, and Brahms; the other, to build a village where the fellaheen would follow the way of life that I would like them to.

This second wish had deep roots, going back to my childhood. I had always had a deep love for the country, but it was a love for an idea, not for something I really knew. The country, the place where the fellaheen lived, I had seen from the windows of the train as we went from Cairo to Alexandria for the summer holidays, but this fleeting experience was supplemented by two contrasting pictures, which I had got respectively from my father and my mother.

My father avoided the country. To him it was a place full of flies, mosquitoes, and polluted water, and he forbade his children to have anything to do with it. Although he possessed several estates in the country, he would never visit them, or go any nearer to the country than Mansoura, the provincial capital, where he went once a year to meet his bailiffs and collect his rent. Until my twenty-seventh year I never set foot on any of our country property.

My mother had spent part of her childhood in the country, of which she preserved the pleasantest memories, and to which she longed to return right up to the end of her life. She told us stories of the tame lambs that would follow her about, of all the animals on the farm, the chickens and pigeons, of how she made friends with them and watched them through the year. The only animals we saw close up were the lambs bought for Kurban Bairam, which as soon as we had made friends with them were taken to be killed, or the herds of young calves being driven through the streets to the slaughterhouse. She told us how the people produced everything they needed for themselves in the country, how they never needed to buy anything more than the cloth for their clothes, how even the rushes for their brooms grew along the ditches in the farm. I seemed to inherit my mother's unfulfilled longing to go back to the country, which I thought offered a simpler, happier, and less anxious life than the city could.

These two pictures combined in my imagination to produce a picture of the country as a paradise, but a paradise darkened from above by clouds of flies, and whose streams flowing underfoot had become muddy and infested with bilharzia and dysentery. This image haunted me and made me feel that something should be done to restore to the Egyptian countryside the felicity of paradise. If the problem appeared simple to me at that time, it was because I was young and inexperienced, but it was and is a question that has occupied the greater part of my thoughts and energies ever since, a problem whose unfolding complexity through the years has only reinforced my conviction that something should be done to solve it. Such a "something," though, can only work if inspired by love. The people who are to transform the countryside will not be able to do it by large directives issued from office desks in Cairo; they will have to love the fellah enough to live with him, to make their homes in the country, and to devote their lives to practical work, on the spot, toward the improvement of rural life.

Because of this feeling of mine for peasant life, when I left secondary school I was led to apply for admission to the School of Agriculture. There was, however, an examination for students aspiring to enter this school. Now, my practical experience of farming was strictly limited to what I had seen out of the train windows, but I thought I could probably make up for my shortcomings by studying up on the theory of agriculture from textbooks. I carefully learned all about each separate crop and went to face the examiners (it was an oral exam). The examiner asked me: "If you had a field of cotton and wanted to plant rice in it, what would you do?" "What a silly question," I thought, and answered, "Simple. I would pull up the cotton and plant the rice." He said nothing, but asked me how long it takes maize to grow. Misremembering, instead of six weeks, I said six months. "Are you sure?" asked the examiner. "Wouldn't seven months be nearer?" I thought about it. I had noticed from the train that maize fields could be very big, and I had never seen anyone in them. It must take a long time to harvest maize. "Yes," I said, "perhaps seven months." "Even eight months?" "Well yes, I suppose so." "Or nine?" It began to occur to me that perhaps he was not treating my answer with the respect it deserved. They dismissed me politely, and I did not get into the School of Agriculture.

I went instead into the Polytechnic, where I chose to study architecture. After I graduated I went one day to supervise the building of a school at Talkha. Talkha is a small country town on the river in the north of the Delta, opposite Mansoura. The site for the school was outside the town, and after the first day or two I made a deliberate detour to avoid going through the town. I was so disgusted at the sight and smell of the narrow streets, deep in mud and every kind of filth, where all the garbage from the kitchens—dirty water, fish scales, rotting vegetables, and offal—was regularly thrown, and so depressed at the appearance of the squalid little shops, fronts open to the smell and the flies in the street, displaying their few wretched wares to the poverty-stricken passersby, that I could not bear to pass through the town.

This town haunted me; I could think of nothing but the hopeless resignation of these peasants to their condition, their cramped and stunted view of life, their abject acceptance of the whole horrible situation in which they were forced to put up with a lifetime's scrabbling for money amid the wretched buildings of Talkha. The revelation of their apathy seized me by the throat; my own helplessness before such a spectacle tormented me. Surely something could be done?

Yet what? The peasants were too sunk in their misery to initiate a change. They needed decent houses, but houses are expensive. In large towns capitalists are attracted by the returns from investment in housing, and public bodies—ministries, town councils, etc.—frequently provide extensive accommodation for the citizens, but neither capitalists nor the state seem willing to undertake the provision of peasant houses, which return no rent to the capitalists and too little glory to the politicians; both parties wash their hands of the matter and the peasants continue to live in squalor. God helps those who help themselves, you might say, but these peasants could never do that. Hardly able to afford even reeds to thatch their huts, how could they hope to buy steel bars, timber, or concrete for good houses? How could they pay for builders to put the houses up? No. Abandoned by God and man, they dragged out their short, diseased, and ugly lives in the dirt and discomfort to which they had been born. Their state is shared by millions in Egypt, while over the whole of the earth there are, according to the U.N., 800,000,000 peasants—one-third of the population of the earth—now doomed to premature death because of their inadequate housing.

It happened that one of our farms was near Talkha, and I took the opportunity of going to look at it. It was a terrible experience. I had had no idea until then of the horrible squalor and ugliness amid which the peasants on a farm lived. I saw a collection of mud huts, low, dark, and dirty, with no windows, no latrines, no clean water, cattle living practically in the same room with people; there was not the remotest connection with the idyllic countryside of my imagination. Everything in this wretched farm was subordinated to economics; the crops came right up to the thresholds of the huts, which were crowded into their own filthy farmyard so as to leave the maximum room for money-making crops; there was no shade, for the shade from trees would inhibit the growth of the cotton; nothing had been done out of consideration for the human beings who spent their lives there.

This picture supplanted that earlier one of a rural paradise with muddy streams. Yet perhaps it was fortunate that the farm belonged to us, for it brought home to me that we ourselves were responsible. The first bit of the country I saw was one of our family's farms, and we had been content to live in ignorance of the peasants' sickening misery.

Of course, I urged my parents to rebuild the farm, and they did. But, besides the farm building and peasants' houses themselves, I was most interested in getting a house built there for our family. I felt that the chief cause of the farm's disrepair was that none of us ever visited it, and the best guarantee of its continued well-being would be to have members of our family living there as often as possible. Luckily there was a little two-room rest house there, which I was able to repair and remodel, although my parents thought I was mad, and it did in fact prove so pleasant that my brother stayed there and brought guests, so that it was almost always occupied.

Mud Brick—*Sole Hope for Rural Reconstruction*

> *The highest goodness, water-like,*
> *Does good to everything and goes*
> *Unmurmuring to places men despise;*
> *But so, is close in nature to the Way.*
> Lao Tze

Surely it was an odd situation that every peasant in Egypt with so much as an acre of land to his name had a house, while landowners with a hundred acres or more could not afford one. But the peasant built his house out of mud, or mud bricks, which he dug out of the ground and dried in the sun. And here, in every hovel and tumbledown hut in Egypt, was the answer to my problem. Here, for years, for centuries, the peasant had been wisely and quietly exploiting the obvious building material, while we, with our modern school-learned ideas, never dreamed of using such a ludicrous substance as mud for so serious a creation as a house. But why not? Certainly, the peasant's houses might be cramped, dark, dirty, and inconvenient, but this was no fault of the mud brick. There was nothing that could not be put right by good design and a broom. Why not use this heaven-sent material for our country houses? And why not, indeed, make the peasants' own houses better? Why should there be any difference between a peasant's house and a landowner's? Build both of mud brick, design both well, and both could afford their owners beauty and comfort.

So I started to design country houses in mud brick. I produced a number of designs, and in 1937 even held an exhibition in Mansoura and later in Cairo, when I delivered a lecture about my conception of the country house. From this lecture came some chances to build. These houses, mostly for rich clients, were certainly an improvement on the old town type of country house, but largely because they were more beautiful. In spite of their economical mud brick walls, they were not so very much cheaper than houses built of more conventional materials, because the timber for the roofs was expensive.

Mud for Roofing, Bahtim: *Trial and Error*

Soon afterwards the war started, and all building stopped. Steel and timber supplies were completely cut off, and the army requisitioned such materials as were already in the country. Yet, still obsessed by my desire to build in the country, I looked about for ways of getting round the shortage. At least I still had mud bricks! And then it occurred to me that, if I had mud bricks and nothing else, I was no worse off than my forefathers. Egypt had not always imported steel from Belgium and timber from Rumania, yet Egypt had always built houses. But how had they built? Walls, yes. I could build walls, too, but I had nothing to roof them with. Couldn't mud bricks be used to cover my houses on top? What about some sort of vault?

Normally, to roof a room with a vault, the mason will get a carpenter to make a strong wooden centering which has to be removed when the vault is made; this is a complete wooden vault, running the full length of the room, held up by wooden props, and on which the courses of the masonry vault will rest while being laid.

But besides being elaborate and requiring special skill to insure that the voussoirs are pointing toward the center of the curve, this method of construction is beyond the means of peasants. It is the kind of thing used in building a bridge.

Then I remembered that the ancients had built vaults without such centering, and I thought I would try to do the same. About this time I was asked to do some designs for the Royal Society of Agriculture, and I incorporated my new ideas in these houses. I explained my wishes to the masons, and they attempted to put up my vaults without using centering. The vaults promptly fell down.

Repeated attempts brought no more success. It was clear that, if the ancients had known how to build vaults without centering, the secret had died with them.

My elder brother happened at that time to be a director working on the Aswan Dam. He heard of my failure, listened sympathetically, and then remarked that the Nubians were, in fact, building vaults that stood up during construction without using any support at all, to roof their houses and mosques. I was immensely excited; perhaps, after all, the ancients had not taken their secret to their provoking vaulted tombs with them. Perhaps the answer to all my problems, the technique that would at last let me use the mud brick for every part of a house, was awaiting me in Nubia.

Nubia—*Survival of an Ancient Technique of Vaulting*

One morning in February 1941 I got off the train at Aswan, in company with a number of students and teachers from the School of Fine Arts. The students were making a study tour of archaeological sites, and I had seized the chance of going with them to see what was to be seen in Nubia.

My first impression was of the extremely undistinguished architecture of Aswan itself. A small provincial town, looking like a seedy Cairo transplanted to the country; the same pretentious façades, the same gaudy shop fronts, the same poor-relation, apologetic, would-be metropolitan air. A depressing little eyesore, spoiling the lovely and dramatic scenery of the Second Cataract. There was nothing in Aswan for me; certainly no sign of the rumored techniques I had come in search of. I was so disappointed that I nearly decided to stay in my hotel.

However, I made the trip across the river, for my brother had told me that I must look at the villages of the district rather than Aswan itself. On entering the first village, Gharb Aswan, I knew that I had found what I had come for.

It was a new world for me, a whole village of spacious, lovely, clean, and harmonious houses each more beautiful than the next. There was nothing else like it in Egypt; a village from some dream country, perhaps from a Hoggar hidden in the heart of the Great Sahara—whose architecture had been preserved for centuries uncontaminated by foreign influences, from Atlantis itself it could have been. Not a trace of the miserly huddle of the usual Egyptian village, but house after house, tall, easy, roofed cleanly with a brick vault, each house decorated individually and exquisitely around the doorway with claustrawork—moldings and tracery in mud.

1–2

I realized that I was looking at the living survivor of traditional Egyptian architecture, at a way of building that was a natural growth in the landscape, as much a part of it as the dom-palm tree of the district. It was like a vision of architecture before the Fall: before money, industry, greed, and snobbery had severed architecture from its true roots in nature.

If I was delighted, the painters who had come were in ecstasies. At every corner they sat down, unwrapped canvases, put up easels, seized palette and brush, and set to. They started, exclaimed, pointed; it was a gift in a million for an artist. Meanwhile, I tried to find somebody who could tell me where the builders lived who had created this village. Here I was less lucky; all the men seemed to live away from the place, working in towns. There were only women and children there, and they were too shy to talk. The girls simply ran away giggling, and I could get no information at all.

Back in Aswan, with my appetite whetted but by no means satisfied, I continued my search for a mason who knew the secret of building these vaults. In the hotel I chanced to talk to the waiter about my quest, and he told me that there were indeed masons living in Aswan, and he would put me in touch with one. There was not much work for a professional builder of mud brick houses, it seemed, because every man in a village, whatever his usual job, was able to run up a vaulted house for himself, so these few masons were employed by the inhabitants of the provincial towns like Aswan, who had lost the knack of building in the traditional way. However, there were a very few masons who built the vaults, and the waiter said he would introduce me to *moallem* Boghdadi Ahmed Ali, the oldest of them.

The next day our party went to see the Fatimid Cemetery at 3 Aswan. This is a group of elaborate shrines, dating from the tenth century, built entirely in mud brick, where vaults and domes are employed with splendid assurance and style.

There is also, close to Aswan, the Monastery of St. Simeon, a 4 Coptic building of the same period. Here too mud brick domes and vaults are employed, but the simplicity and humility of the monastic ideal is revealed in the architecture, which thus proves able to accommodate equally well the contrasting inspirations of the Moslem and Christian religion. Among other things, I noticed with great surprise and interest that the refectory held a broad gallery, supported entirely upon an ingenious system of main and secondary vaults to avoid a heavy filling between the curved surface of the vault and the horizontal floor above it. This showed argument that mud brick buildings could go up to two stories and still be strong enough to survive for a thousand years. I was getting more and more confirmation of my suspicions that the traditional materials and methods of the

Egyptian peasant were more than fit for use by modern architects, and that the solution to Egypt's housing problem lay in Egypt's history.

There still remained, though, to learn how the local vaulting was done. I had been promised a meeting with this master mason, but he did not show up. Not till the very last moment of our visit, when we were actually on the platform waiting for the train, did Boghdadi Ahmed Ali finally arrive, and there, with the train shrieking impatiently, amid a hissing of steam and the clanking of coaches, the shouts of guard and passengers and lookers-on, we had just time to shake hands and exchange addresses before I was borne away to Luxor.

[5] This architectural excursion was, for me, a hunt after mud brick vaults. After Aswan, we went to Luxor, where I was especially pleased to examine the granaries of the Ramesseum—long vaulted storehouses, built of mud brick 3,400 years old. It seemed to be a fairly durable substance.

[6] From Luxor we went to Touna el Gebel, where I found more vaults, 2,000 years old, one supporting an excellent staircase.

It is curious that in one short tour I had seen standing proof of the prevalence of vaulting throughout Egyptian history, yet, from what we had been taught in the School of Architecture, I might never have suspected that anyone before the Romans knew how to build an arch. Archaeologists confine their attention to broken pots and effaced inscriptions, their austere discipline being enlivened from time to time by the discovery of a hoard of gold. But for architecture they have neither eyes nor time. They can miss architectural statements placed right under their noses—there are books which state that the Ancient Egyptians could not build domes, and I have seen an Ancient Egyptian dome in the tomb of Seneb, right in the middle of the cemetery at Giza. There can be no question but that the technique of building vaults and domes—in mud brick, too—was perfectly familiar to Egyptians in the twelfth dynasty.

The Nubian Masons at Work—*First successes*

When I was back in Cairo, I wrote immediately to Aswan for masons. There was no time to lose, for the Royal Society of Agriculture's farm was still roofless after the collapse of our first attempt at vaulting. In a few days I had met Abdu Hamed and Abdul Rahim Abu en Nur—masons from Aswan—and the next day they were working on the farm. From the very first moment that I met them, they gave promise of a new era in building, for when they were asked how they would prefer to be paid, by the day or by the job, they were too simple to see any difference. Now the average workman much prefers to be paid by the day, for then he can take frequent rests, refresh himself with coffee every half hour or so, and spin out the work so that it will continue to be a source of income to him for many weeks. It never occurred to these Aswani masons, though, that there could be two times for finishing a job, dependent upon the method of payment, and they simply said they would roof a room for 120 piastres. When asked how long it would take, they said "One and a half days." One hundred twenty piasters is L.E. 1.4.0. The bricks cost about L.E. 1.0.0., two laborers to help them another L.E. 1.0.0; so for L.E. 3.4.0. we had a room 3 m × 4 m built in one and a half days. In concrete it would cost about L.E. 16, in timber L.E. 20.

And in fact when they started working it took them exactly one and a half days to roof one room. The terms agreed, the masons asked us to make them the special kind of bricks they used for vaults. These were made with more straw than usual, for lightness. They measured 25 cm × 15 cm × 5 cm (10 in. × 6 in. × 2 in.) and were marked with two parallel diagonal grooves, drawn with the fingers from corner to corner of the largest face. These grooves were very important, for they enabled the bricks to stick to a muddy surface by suction. So we made the bricks and dried them, and a week later went down to the site. On our way down I noticed that the masons had no tools except for their adzes. I asked them, "Where are your trowels?" "We don't need trowels," they said, "the adze is enough."

At the scene of our failure the walls were still standing although our attempt at a vault had collapsed. In each room there were two side walls, three meters apart, and an end wall somewhat higher against which the vault was to be built. The masons laid a couple of planks across the side walls, close to the end wall, got up on them, took up handfuls of mud, and roughly outlined an arch by plastering the mud onto the end wall. They used no measure or instrument, but by eye alone traced a perfect parabola, with its ends upon the side walls. Then, with the adze, they trimmed the mud plaster to give it a sharper outline.

7–8

9–18

Next, one at each side, they began to lay the bricks. The first brick was stood on its end on the side wall, the grooved face flat against the mud plaster of the end wall, and hammered well into this plaster. Then the mason took some mud and against the foot of this brick made a little wedge-shaped packing, so that the next course would lean slightly towards the end wall instead of standing up straight. In order to break the line of the joints between the bricks the second course started with a half-brick, on the top end of which stood a whole brick. If the joints are in a straight line, the strength of the vault is reduced and it may collapse. The mason now put in more mud packing against this second course, so that the third course would incline even more acutely from the vertical. In this way the two masons gradually built the inclined courses out, each one rising a little higher round the outline of the arch, till the two curved lines of brick met at the top. As they built each complete course, the masons were careful to insert in the gaps between the bricks composing the course (in the extrados of the voussoirs) dry packing such as stones or broken pottery. It is most important that no mud mortar be put between the ends of the bricks in each course, for mud can shrink by up to 37 percent in volume, and such shrinkage will seriously distort the parabola, so that the vault may collapse. The ends of the bricks must touch one another dry, with no mortar. At this stage the nascent vault was six brick-thicknesses long at the bottom and only one brick-thickness long at the top, so that it appeared to be leaning at a considerable angle against the end wall. Thus it presented an inclined face to lay the succeeding courses upon, so that the bricks would have plenty of support; this inclination, even without the two grooves, stopped the brick from dropping off, as might a smooth brick on a vertical face.

Thus the whole vault could be built straight out in the air, with no support or centering, with no instrument, with no drawn plan; there were just two masons standing on a plank and a boy underneath tossing up the bricks, which the masons caught dexterously in the air, then casually placed on the mud and tapped home with their adzes. It was so unbelievably simple. They worked rapidly and unconcernedly, with never a thought that what they were doing was quite a remarkable work of engineering, for these masons were working according to the laws of statics and the science of the resistance of materials with extraordinary intuitive understanding. Earth bricks cannot take bending and sheering; so the vault is made in the shape of a parabola conforming with the shape of the bending moment diagrams, thus eliminating all bending and allowing the material to work only under compression. In this way it became possible to construct the roof with the same earth bricks as for the walls. Indeed, to span three meters in mud brick is as great a technical feat, and produces the same sense of achievement, as spanning thirty meters in concrete.

The simplicity and naturalness of the method quite entranced me. Engineers and architects concerned with cheap ways of building for the masses had devised all sorts of complicated methods for constructing vaults and domes. Their problem was to keep the components in place until the structure was completed, and their solutions had ranged from odd-shaped bricks like bits of three-dimensional jigsaw puzzles, through every variety of scaffolding, to the extreme expedient of blowing up a large balloon in the shape of the required dome and spraying concrete onto that. But my builders needed nothing but an adze and a pair of hands.

Within a few days all the houses were roofed. Rooms, corridors, loggias were all covered with vaults and domes; the masons had solved every problem that had exercised me (even to building stairs). It only remained to go out and apply their methods throughout Egypt.

It happened that I had a friend, Taher Omari, who had a farm at 19–20 Sedmant el Gabal on the edge of the desert of Fayum. It was in a lovely situation and just perched on the clifflike edge of a kind of plateau overlooking the Bahr Youssef Canal and the Nile Valley. Unfortunately it was rather off the beaten track, so that my friend could not keep a constant eye on it, and consequently the local peasants, who coveted the wood, had stolen all the roofs in the farm. There were a number of buildings all gaping and open to the sky—a perfect subject for my masons' next demonstration.

Now that roofing was proved to be so cheap, we could afford to spread ourselves. All we needed was mud, of which we had quite enough; so there was no need to be niggardly with roofed space. We set to and put roofs over stables and storehouses and houses for the workers—we worked in a high state of exhilaration and covered the whole farm in no time at all with fine mud roofs. Taber Omari was delighted. One building, intended as a storehouse and roofed with a noble dome, so pleased him that he took it for a music room. But all the buildings were pleasing to the eye. Whether for donkeys or men or just for stores, they all had a satisfying curving rhythm that seemed to come without asking when we designed for vaults but which straight lines and flat roofs hardly ever produce. And this is the second great point about mud brick housing with vaulted roofs. Besides being cheap, it is also beautiful. It cannot help being beautiful, for the structure dictates the shapes and the material imposes the scale, every line respects the distribution of stresses, and the building takes on a satisfying and natural shape. Within the limits imposed by the resistance of materials—mud—and by the laws of statics, the architect finds himself suddenly free to shape space with his building, to enclose a volume of chaotic air and to bring it down to order and meaning to the scale of man, so that in his house at last there is no need of decoration put on afterward. The structural elements themselves provide unending interest for the eye. The vault, the dome, pendentive, squinches, arches, and walls give the architect unlimited scope for a justified interplay of curved lines running in all directions with a harmonious passage from one to the other.

Just outside Cairo, in Marg, lived another friend of mine, Hamed Said. He was an artist and lived with his wife in a tent, partly in order to be near to nature, which he greatly loved, and partly because he could not afford a house. When he heard of the Royal Society of Agriculture farm at Bahtim and how little it had cost to build, he grew most interested, for he had for some time been wanting a studio.

He went to look at the buildings, and when he saw the singular quality of the light in a vaulted loggia there, he immediately decided to build a similar loggia for himself. Some relatives of his had a farm, on which we put up a studio consisting of one large domed room, with a vaulted bed alcove, built-in cupboards, and an open-ended loggia giving onto the fields and an uninterrupted view of acre after acre of palm trees. He had the bricks made on the spot—the soil was sandy, so he didn't need even straw—and the masons built the house for just L.E. 25. We picked up some very beautiful old wooden grilles for the windows and some cast-off doors for the cupboards, all long since discarded in favor of shiny European-style fittings. Altogether he got a charming little cottage studio for about L.E. 50.

Ezbet el Basry: *Iblis in Ambush*

There was another little village, or hamlet rather, of some twenty-five houses, situated outside Meadi about nine miles from Cairo; it was called Ezbet el Basry and was inhabited largely by thieves. Very justly, it was quite swept away by a sudden flood, such as occurs every twenty years or so, and the Egyptian Red Crescent undertook to rehouse the homeless families. This flood showed the hand of God most plainly, for not only did it punish the unrighteous, but it restored to at least one of their victims his stolen property. This victim was Amin Rustum, who had had two tires stolen from his car at a time when tires were quite unobtainable honestly and fetching L.E. 80 to L.E. 100 each dishonestly. He knew the culprit—and the tires—to be in Ezbet el Basry, but the police would not do anything about it. However, on the day of the flood there was a swirl of water, and Rustum's two tires came sailing merrily into the police station, where they obligingly ran aground, and he collected them.

The Red Crescent had a Ladies' Committee, which provided an outlet for the charitable impulses of Cairene wives, and it was this committee that had charged itself with the responsibility for rebuilding Ezbet el Basry. Through Mrs. Sirry Pasha, the president, I came to offer my services for the project. I went to look at the devastated village, which proved to have been built of mud bricks, but most incompetently. The houses had, at ground level, a mud wall only one brick thick, which naturally could not be expected to resist a torrent of water. The walls had just crumbled away and the houses had collapsed. However, this was no argument against employing mud bricks on that site. With an adequately thick wall and a stone foundation, mud brick houses would survive even Noah's flood.

I prepared my designs and estimates. The cost, for twenty houses, worked out at L.E. 3,000. Full of enthusiasm, I submitted them to the committee. How many afternoons we spent, drinking tea and smoking cigarettes and talking intermittently about the village. Meeting after meeting, resolution after resolution, objections, suggestions, evasions, bright ideas and serious doubts, until we could have built ten villages with our own hands in the time we wasted.

22

My masons were ready, the inhabitants were still living in tents, and nothing seemed to be getting done! At last, in the middle of a meeting, when I had begged to be allowed to build at least one house just to show it could be done, Mrs. Aboud Pasha suddenly said, "You seem to be a practical sort of man. Here, take my checkbook. Write what sum you like, take the money and go and build us your house." I took it; I already knew that I could build a house for L.E. 150, and so I had told the committee. But at this moment another architect, who was sitting on the committee on behalf of the Ministry of Social Affairs, whispered to me: "Don't be a fool, put down more. You will never do it for that." "I know exactly what I am doing. I have built before for this much, and I know it can be done," I said.

With this money assured me from a private source, I could go ahead, and the committee could not very well procrastinate any further. Within forty days the house was complete. It was a very handsome building, with two large rooms, sleeping alcoves as before, built-in cupboards, generous storage space, a big loggia, an enclosed courtyard. Altogether it cost exactly L.E. 164.

23–25

Having been so successful, I naturally expected to be given the job of completing the other nineteen houses wanted, but soon after this Mrs. Sirry Pasha came and explained to me that as the committee had their own architect, who would have to design the houses for them, they could not give the commission to me. I concealed my disappointment and gracefully accepted her regrets. Still, the house was there, and it came in very useful for the committee; we even held one or two parties in it, and many people came to see and admire it.

I used to admire it myself as I passed it every day in the train between Cairo and Meadi. I could see it out of the window in the distance, and I always made a point of looking out for it every time

I went past. Then one day, as I looked out of the window, the house was not there. I looked again, I asked myself if I had made a mistake, if this was not the place, or if I had got into the wrong train, but I was quite right. The house had just gone. I went round to the site to see what had happened, and there was my beautiful house, in bits all over the ground. Even at that moment I found time to notice how strong it was, and how the vault had come down in big pieces, like segments of an eggshell, tough and homogeneous as pieces of leather, for the mud bricks had set into a single monolithic shell.

They told me, with apologies, that it had unfortunately been necessary to demolish the house because it did not harmonize with the houses designed by their own architect, but they were sure I would understand. Their architect had sent one of his assistants, a young man hitherto chiefly distinguished for having put up a faithful copy of a Swiss chalet among the palm trees and camels on the road to the Pyramids, and he had produced his own version of cottages fit 26 for peasants to live in. I saw his plans later, and they showed a row of twenty concrete houses, each consisting of two square rooms and a corridor ninety centimeters wide with a water closet at the end of it. There was not even a kitchen, let alone requirements like sleeping recesses and cupboards, and the buildings were no more inspiring architecturally than a row of airraid shelters. I quite saw that my house didn't harmonize with them.

Some time later I discovered a further reason that had made the committee's architect reluctant to invite comparisons. His twenty houses were erected at a total cost of L.E. 22,000.

Still, even if this little house had a short life and even if it failed to achieve its principal purpose of impressing the Red Crescent, it did succeed in impressing other people. It led to a commission from the Chilean Nitrate Company for some rest houses in Safaga, on the Red Sea. This gave me an opportunity to expand my team of masons and to get to know their capabilities better. So well did we do there that Boghdadi Ahmed Ali, the chief mason, was even able to save up enough to go to the Hejaz and become a Hadji. We got to know one another like members of the same family, and I found my respect for these men growing daily as I worked with them.

A Tomb Robbery Begets a Pilot Housing Project

In its short life, the house at Ezbet el Basry was also seen by certain people working for the Department of Antiquities, not indeed out of antiquarian interest, but with a view to fulfilling a very practical and interesting need. In Egypt, as may readily be supposed, the

Department of Antiquities is among the more important government offices, and it had recently been involved in a great scandal.

Among the ancient monuments for which it is responsible is the old Cemetery of Thebes situated at a place called Gourna, across the river from Luxor which itself is built on the site of the ancient town of Thebes. This cemetery comprises three main parts: the Valley of the Kings to the north, the Valley of the Queens to the south, and the Tombs of the Nobles in the middle on the hillside facing the agricultural land.

The village of Gourna is built on the site of these Tombs of the Nobles. Here there are very many graves, some known, cleared, and cleaned, and some still unknown to the department and consequently full of objects of great archaeological interest.

There are seven thousand peasants living in Gourna crowded into five clusters of houses, built over and around these tombs. Seven thousand people living quite literally upon the past. They—or their fathers—had been attracted to Gourna some fifty years before by the rich graves of their ancestors, and the whole community had ever since lived by mining these tombs. Their economy was almost wholly dependent on tomb robbing; the farmland around could not support anything like seven thousand people, and anyway it belonged mostly to a few rich landowners.

Although the Gournis had become unrivaled experts in spotting hidden tombs, and were most sly and successful robbers, yet they had not handled their industry very wisely. They had mined recklessly, exhausting the richest treasure long before the antiquities fetched a really high price. Hakim Abu Seif, an inspector of antiquities, told me that in 1913 a peasant had offered him a whole basket of scarabs for twenty piasters, and he had refused it! Today scarabs fetch at least L.E. 5 each.

Not that the loot was confined to scarabs, nor indeed were all the peasants so simple. At the time of the discovery of the tomb of Amenophis II—an intact eighteenth-dynasty tomb—a sacred boat was stolen by one of the guards, who set himself up in forty acres of land on the proceeds.

Yet the operations of these tomb robbers should not be viewed too lightheartedly. For all their skill, for all their likableness, and in spite of their undeserved poverty, the damage they do is measureless. They excavate and sell, and no one knows the provenance of their finds, which means a big loss to Egyptology. Sometimes they do worse: if by chance one of these robbers finds treasure made of gold, he melts it down. Jewelry, plate, statuettes—masterpieces of workmanship, beyond price in any market—go straight into the pot and are turned into sordid ingots, to be sold for the current price of gold. From the surviving works—the treasures of Tutankhamon's tomb, the lovely figured dish recently found at Tanis—we can get some idea of the wicked destruction that has been going on. Mrs. Bruyère, the wife of one of the archaeologists, has seen in a peasant's house crude bars of gold that must once have been treasures that would take pride of place in any museum in the world.

Of course the peasants had fallen a natural prey to the dealers in the city, who, being alone able to communicate with unscrupulous foreign buyers, were able to exploit the Gournis' delicate position and buy their valuable produce for far less than its real value. The peasants took all the risks, developed the skill, and did the hard work; the dealers sat in perfect safety, encouraging the vandalism, and grew fat on the Gournis' hard-won loot.

Eventually, the diminishing returns from tomb robbing forced the inhabitants to ever greater risks and ever more audacious forgeries, (for the forgery of antiques was an incidental skill that their situation had developed in them) until at last there was an unparalleled scandal. A whole rock carving in one of the tombs—a well-known and classified ancient monument—was cut out of the living rock and stolen. It was as if someone had stolen a window from Chartres or a column or two from the Parthenon.

This robbery caused such a stir that the Department of Antiquities had to take some positive action over the problem of Gourna. There was already a royal decree expropriating the land on which the Gournis' houses were built and annexing the whole area of the necropolis to the government as public utility land. This decree gave the Gournis the right to continue using the existing houses, but prohibited any further additions or extensions. So now another ministerial decree had to be issued expropriating the houses too, with the intention of clearing the whole antiquities zone of its undesirable squatters.

A decree, however, is one thing, its execution quite another. Where were seven thousand people to be moved to? If their houses were bought at current valuation, the Gournis would not receive enough money to buy new land and build new houses. Even if they were compensated generously, they would only spend the money to marry more wives and would then become landless and penniless vagabonds. The only solution was to rehouse them, but hitherto this had been far too expensive a proposition. One million pounds was the estimate for an exactly similar village which was being built for the workers at Imbaba, just outside Cairo. It was then that my buildings came to the notice of the Department of Antiquities.

It so happened that the same idea occurred independently to Osman Rustum, the head of Engineering and Excavations, and to M. Stoppelaere, the head of the Restoration Section in the Department of Antiquities, so that they each suggested to the Abbé Drioton, the director-general of the department, that I be approached about the new village of Gourna.

They had seen my two examples of mud brick building, the houses for the Royal Society of Agriculture and the house for the Red Crescent, and had been impressed alike by the potentialities of the material and the low cost of using it. Accordingly Drioton came to see these buildings and approved the suggestion, with the result that I was granted leave of absence from the School of Fine Arts for three years to build a village. So I was going to fulfill my childhood wish—I hoped somewhat more cheaply than for L.E. 1,000,000.

Birth of New Gourna—*The Site*

To choose a site for the new village, a committee was convened, consisting of representatives of the Department of Antiquities (the head of the Inspectorates Section, Osman Rustum, and the chief inspector of Luxor), the Mayor of Gourna and the sheikhs of the five hamlets, and myself. This committee had to find a site well away from all ancient remains, which meant that it could not set the new village upon the hills above the river valley, as would seem most sensible, for these hills were thick with tombs for a distance of some three and a half miles along the front of the agricultural land belonging to the village, from the Valley of the Queens to the Valley of the Monkeys. Finally we settled upon a patch of agricultural land close by the main road and the railway line, low down in a *hosha*—a permanently dry field kept free from floodwater by a system of dikes. The land was bought by compulsory purchase from its owner, Boulos Hanna Pasha; there were fifty acres and it cost L.E. 300 per acre.

However attractive may have been the project of at last building a whole village, it was also somewhat daunting to be presented with fifty acres of virgin land and seven thousand Gournis who would have to create a new life for themselves there. All these people, related in a complex web of blood and marriage ties, with their habits and prejudices, their friendships and their feuds—a delicately balanced social organism intimately integrated with the topography, with the very bricks and timber of the village—this whole society had, as it were, to be dismantled and put together again in another setting.

To tell the truth, my delight had from the beginning been flavored with more than a dash of incredulity. It was uncanny enough that a whole village should be projected without reference to the State Building Department, but it was even more unnerving to find myself with the sole responsibility for creating this village, and free to do what I liked with the site.

27 It needed a very self-confident architect to start building there, **28** within sight of the Temple of Deir el Bahari and the Ramesseum, **29** under the minatory eyes of the Colossi of Memmon gazing coldly over the countryside toward our site.

2 Chorale
Man, Society, and Technology

Architectural Character

Every people that has produced architecture has evolved its own favorite forms, as peculiar to that people as its language, its dress, or its folklore. Until the collapse of cultural frontiers in the last century, there were all over the world distinctive local shapes and details in architecture, and the buildings of any locality were the beautiful children of a happy marriage between the imagination of the people and the demands of their countryside. I do not propose to speculate upon the real springs of national idiosyncrasy, nor could I with any authority. I like to suppose simply that certain shapes take a people's fancy, and that they make use of them in a great variety of contexts, perhaps rejecting the unsuitable applications, but evolving a colorful and emphatic visual language of their own that suits perfectly their character and their homeland. No one could mistake the curve of a Persian dome and arch for the curve of a Syrian one, or a Moorish one, or an Egyptian one. No one can fail to recognize the same curve, the same signature, in dome and jar and turban from the same district. It follows, too, that no one can look with complacency upon buildings transplanted to an alien environment.

Yet in modern Egypt there is no indigenous style. The signature is missing; the houses of rich and poor alike are without character, without an Egyptian accent. The tradition is lost, and we have been cut off from our past ever since Mohammed Ali cut the throat of the last Mameluke. This gap in the continuity of Egyptian tradition has been felt by many people, and all sorts of remedies have been proposed. There was, in fact, a kind of jealousy between those who regarded the Copts as the true lineal descendants of the Ancient Egyptians, and those who believed that the Arab style should provide the pattern for a new Egyptian architecture. Indeed, there was one statesmanlike attempt to reconcile these two factions, when Osman Moharam Pasha, the Minister of Public Works, suggested that Egypt be divided into two, rather as Solomon suggested dividing the baby, and that Upper Egypt be delivered to the Copts, where a traditional Pharaonic style could be developed, while Lower Egypt should go to the Moslems, who would make its architecture truly Arab!

This story goes to show two things. One is the encouraging fact that people do recognize and wish to remedy the cultural confusion in our architecture. The other—not so encouraging—is that this confusion is seen as a problem of style, and style is looked upon as some sort of surface finish that can be applied to any building and even scraped off and changed if necessary. The modern Egyptian architect believes that Ancient Egyptian architecture is represented by the temple with its pylons and cavetto cornice, and Arab by clustered stalactites, whereas Ancient Egyptian domestic architecture was quite unlike temple architecture, and Arab domestic architecture quite different from mosque architecture. Ancient Egyptian secular buildings like houses were light constructions, simple, with the clean lines of the best modern houses. But in the architectural schools they make no study of the history of domestic buildings, and learn architectural periods by the accidents of style, the obvious features like the pylon and the stalactite. Thus the graduate architect believes this to be all there is in "style," and imagines a building can change its style as a man changes clothes. It was thinking like this that led some architect to ruin the entrance to the classrooms at Gourna school by transforming the original archway into an Ancient Egyptian-style temple doorway complete with cavetto cornice. It is not yet understood that real architecture cannot exist except in a living tradition, and that architectural tradition is all but dead in Egypt today.

As a direct result of this lack of tradition our cities and villages are becoming more and more ugly. Every single new building manages to increase this ugliness, and every attempt to remedy the situation only underlines the ugliness more heavily.

Particularly on the outskirts of provincial towns where the most recent building has been taking place the ugly design of the houses is emphasized by the shoddy execution of the work, and cramped square boxes of assorted sizes, in a style copied from the poorer quarters in the metropolis, half finished yet already decaying, set at all angles to one another, are stuck up all over a shabby wilderness of unmade roads, wire and lines of washing hanging dustily over chicken runs. In these nightmarish neighborhoods a craving for show and modernity causes the house owner to lavish his money on the tawdry fittings and decorations of urban houses, while being miserly with living space and denying himself absolutely the benefits of real craftsmanship. This attitude makes the houses compact and outward-facing, so that the family has to air bedding over the public street, and air itself exposed to the neighborhood upon its barren balconies; whereas if the owners were less cheap-minded they could take advantage of the only house type that can make life tolerable in these places, the courtyard house, and enjoy both space and privacy. Unfortunately this suburban architecture is the type that is taken by the peasants as a model of modernity and is gaining ground in our villages; on the outskirts of Cairo or Benha we can read the approaching fate of Gharb Aswan.

To flatter his clients and persuade them that they are sophisticated and urban, the village mason starts to experiment with styles that he has seen only at second or third hand, and with materials that he cannot really handle with understanding. He abandons the safe guide of tradition, and without the science and experience of an architect tries to produce "architects' architecture." The result is a building with all the defects and none of the advantages of the architect's work.

Thus the work of an architect who designs, say, an apartment house in the poor quarters of Cairo for some stingy speculator, in which he incorporates various features of modern design copied from fashionable European work, will filter down, over a period of years, through the cheap suburbs and into the village, where it will slowly poison the genuine tradition.

So serious is this situation that a thorough and scientific investigation of it becomes quite imperative if ever we are to reverse the trend toward bad, ugly, vulgar, and inefficient housing in our villages.

Sometimes I have despaired at the size of the problem, and given it up as insoluble, the malign and irreversible operation of fate. I have succumbed to a feeling of helplessness, sadness, and pain for what was becoming of my people and my land. But when I found myself having to deal with the actual case of Gourna, I pulled myself together and began to think more practically about the problem.

The Process of Decision Making

Culture springs from the roots
And seeping through to all the shoots
To leaf and flower and bud
From cell to cell, like green blood,
Is released by rain showers
As fragrance from the wet flowers
To fill the air.
But culture that is poured on men
From up above, congeals then
Like damp sugar, so they become
Like sugar-dolls, and when some
Life-giving shower wets them through
They disappear and melt into
A sticky mess.

It seemed to me that we could not cure the general crisis in Egyptian architecture simply by building one or two good model houses as examples, nor even a whole village. Rather we should have to try to diagnose the disease, to understand the root causes of the crisis, and to attack it at these roots. The cultural decay starts with the individual himself, who is confronted with choices that he is not equipped to make, and we must cure it at this stage.

Building is a creative activity in which the decisive moment is the instant of conception, that instant when the spirit takes shape and all the features of the new creaton are virtually determined. While the characteristics of a living creature are irrevocably settled at the moment of fertilization, the characteristics of a building are determined by the whole complex of decisions made by everyone that has a say in the matter, at every stage of its construction. Thus the instant of conception on which the final form of a living creature rests becomes for a building a multiplicity of such instants, each playing a decisive part in the total creative process.

If we can identify and seize these instants, then we can control the whole process of creation.

The deliberate exercise of choice—the making of decisions—is the central activity of life, and as the occasions for an exercise of choice by an organism increase, the higher in the scale of life may that organism be placed. From the simplest known organisms, the rotifera, whose whole existence consists in discriminating between the edible and the inedible, to the most complicated, man, every hour of whose life is replete with decisions made or demanding to be made, there is no organism that does not spend all its time choosing. To be alive is to make decisions. The decisions a man has to make are far more subtle, and require the conscious assessment of far more factors, than those that simpler animals make.

Furthermore, man's decisions are different in quality from those of other animals, for man has the ability to affect the world around him by his decisions and to change its appearance and nature quite radically. Since man's decisions have such great potentialities for both good and evil, his responsibility is grave indeed. This is, in fact, one of the most important aspects of the human predicament, that all man's decisions change the world, that he cannot escape the decisions, and that he is conscious of the good or the evil he does, the beauty or the ugliness he creates.

Once upon a time, it is said, God called the angels and offered them this responsibility of decision making; they very wisely declined, preferring to remain in their unchanging perfection of harmony with the universe. God then asked the mountains to accept responsibility, and they too refused, being content to be passively subject to the forces of nature. But when God offered man the gift of responsibility, the ignorant creature accepted it because he didn't realize what it entailed. So now, like it or not, man is saddled with the responsibility that frightened both the angels and the mountains, and has the chance to prove himself greater than either.

Let us not forget, though, that he accepts the risk of defeat, and that if defeated he will be seen to be the most presumptuous and contemptible animal in creation. The world at any moment is a blank page awaiting our pencil; an open space may hold a cathedral or a slagheap.

Because no two men make the same decisions in similar circumstances, we say that men's characters differ. Decision making, choosing, is another word for self-expression—or, perhaps better, is the necessary prelude to all self-expression.

A conscious decision may be reached either by consulting tradition or by logical reasoning and scientific analysis. Both processes should yield the same result, for tradition embodies the conclusions of many generations' practical experiment with the same problem, while scientific analysis is simply the organized observation of the phenomena of the problem.

The most subtle decisions are called for when a man makes something. In one's daily life many apparently conscious decisions are simply the operation of habit, but in making some object one has more scope for decision than in performing the functions accessory to living. Certainly one may make something according to habit—it will then be living and beautiful only by the residual virtue of the decisions one took when first trying to make that kind of object, and by virtue too of the minor decisions taken in the act of making the habitual movements of fabrication. Yet the best way to create beauty is not necessarily to make an odd or original design. How true this is even in the work of God, who does not have to change the design concept in order to produce individuality in men, but can span the whole scale of beauty between Cleopatra and Caliban simply by adjusting the position or the size of the elements in a face.

It is interesting to observe that habit may in fact release a man from the need to make many less interesting decisions so that he can concentrate on the really important ones of his art. One brain cannot make more than a limited number of decisions in a given time; so it is just as well that some can be relegated to the unconscious. A carpet weaver has learnt to work so fast and surely with her hands that she no longer thinks of each separate movement but can concentrate on the design as it grows beneath her fingers. She is like a musician, whose whole attention is given to his rendering of a piece and who scarcely follows each finger as it produces a note.

Tradition's Role

It may be that what we call modern is nothing but what is not worthy of remaining to become old.
Dante Alighieri

Tradition is the social analogy of personal habit, and in art has the same effect, of releasing the artist from distracting and inessential decisions so that he can give his whole attention to the vital ones. Once an artistic decision has been made, no matter when or by whom, it cannot profitably be made again; better that it should pass into the common store of habit and not bother us further.

Tradition is not necessarily old-fashioned and is not synonymous with stagnation. Furthermore, a tradition need not date from long ago but may have begun quite recently. As soon as a workman meets a new problem and decides how to overcome it, the first step has been taken in the establishment of a tradition. When another workman has decided to adopt the same solution, the tradition is moving, and by the time a third man has followed the first two and added his contribution, the tradition is fairly established. Some problems are easy to solve; a man may decide in a few minutes what to do. Others need time, perhaps a day, perhaps a year, perhaps a whole lifetime; in each case the solution may be the work of one man.

Yet other solutions may not be worked out fully before many generations have passed, and this is where tradition has a creative role to play, for it is only by tradition, by respecting and building on the work of earlier generations, that each new generation may make some positive progress toward the solution of the problem. When tradition has solved its problem and ceased developing, we may say that a cycle has been completed. However, in architecture, as in other human activities and in natural processes, there are cycles just beginning, others that have been completed, and others at all stages of development in between, that exist simultaneously in the same society. There are, too, traditions that go back to the beginning of human society, yet which are still living and which will exist perhaps as long as human society does: in bread making for example, and in brick making.

There are, on the other hand, traditions which, although they have appeared only recently and ought to be in an early phase of their cycle, were in fact born dead. Modernity does not necessarily mean liveliness, and change is not always for the better. On the other hand there are situations that call for innovation. My point is that innovation must be a completely thought-out response to a change in circumstances, and not indulged in for its own sake. Nobody asks that an airport control tower be built in some peasant idiom, and an industrial structure like a nuclear power station may force a new tradition upon the designer.

Once a particular tradition is established and accepted, the individual artist's duty is to keep this tradition going, with his own invention and insight to give it that additional momentum that will save it from coming to a standstill, until it will have reached the end of its cycle and completed its full development. He will be relieved of many decisions by the tradition, but will be obliged to make others equally demanding to stop the tradition dying on his hands. In fact, the further a tradition has developed, the more effort the artist must expend to make each step forward in it.

Tradition among the peasants is the only safeguard of their culture. They cannot discriminate between unfamiliar styles, and if they run off the rails of tradition they will inevitably meet disaster. Willfully to break a tradition in a basically traditional society like a peasant one is a kind of cultural murder, and the architect must respect the tradition he is invading. What he does in the city is another matter; there the public and the surroundings can take care of themselves.

Let him not suppose that this tradition will hamper him. When the full power of a human imagination is backed by the weight of a living tradition, the resulting work of art is far greater than any that an artist can achieve when he has no tradition to work in or when he willfully abandons his tradition.

One man's effort can bring about an altogether disproportionate advance, if he is building upon an established tradition. It is rather like adding a single microscopic crystal to a solution that is already supersaturated, so that the whole will suddenly crystallize in a spectacular fashion. Yet it differs from the physical process in that this artistic crystallization is not a once-and-for-all occurrence, but an act of reaction that has to be perpetually renewed. "Completeness without completion is useful. Fulfillment without being fulfilled is desirable" (Lao Tze).

Architecture is still one of the most traditional arts. A work of architecture is meant to be used, its form is largely determined by precedent, and it is set before the public where they must look at it every day. The architect should respect the work of his predecessors and the public sensibility by not using his architecture as a medium of personal advertisement. Indeed, no architect can avoid using the work of earlier architects; however hard he strains after originality, by far the larger part of his work will be in some tradition or other. Why then should he despise the tradition of his own country or district, why should he drag alien traditions into an artificial and uncomfortable synthesis, why should he be so rude to earlier architects as to distort and misapply their ideas? This happens when an architectural element, evolved over many years to a perfect size, shape, and function, is used upside down or enlarged beyond recognition till it no longer even works properly, simply to gratify the architect's own selfish appetite for fame.

For example, it has taken men very many years to arrive at the right size for a window in various architectural traditions; if an architect now commits the gross error of enlarging the window till it takes up a whole wall, he is at once confronted with a problem: his glass wall lets in ten times as much radiation as did the solid wall. If now to shade the window he adds a brise-soleil, which is nothing more than an enlarged Venetian blind, the room will still receive 300 percent more radiation than one with a solid wall. Furthermore, when the architect enlarges the width of the slats of the Venetian blind from 4 centimeters to 40, so as not to upset the scale of the glass wall, what is the result? Instead of admitting a gentle diffused light, as a shutter or Venetian blind does, it dazzles the eye of anyone in the room with a pattern of broad black bars against a brilliant glare of light.

Not only that, but the view, the securing of which was the initial object of the glass wall, is permanently spoiled by these large bars cutting it up; the brise-soleil has not even the virtue of folding away, as have the shutter and the Venetian blind. Even in a cool climate like that of Paris, the glass wall can prove to be an unmanageable extravagance; during the hot summer of 1959 the temperature inside the UNESCO building, due to the "greenhouse effect" of its glass walls, and despite the labors of the air conditioning machinery, rose so high that many of the employees fainted. Superfluous then, to comment on the introduction of glass walls and brise-soleils in tropical countries; yet it is hard to find an example of modern tropical architecture that does not employ these features.

If the architect walks soberly in the tradition of his culture, then he must not suppose that his artistry will be stifled. Far from it; it will express itself in relevant contributions to the tradition and contribute to the advance of his society's culture.

When the architect is presented with a clear tradition to work in, as in a village built by peasants, then he has no right to break this tradition with his own personal whims. What may go in a cosmopolitan city like Paris, London, or Cairo, will kill a village.

Any man's mind is so complex that his decisions are always unique. His reaction to the things around him is his alone. If in your dealings with men you consider them as a mass and abstract and exploit the features they have in common, then you destroy the unique features of each.

The advertiser who plays upon the common weaknesses of mankind, the manufacturer who satisfies the common appetites, the schoolmaster who drills the common reflexes, each in his way kills the soul. That is, each, by overvaluing the common features, crowds out the individual ones. To some degree the individual must be sacrificed to the mass; otherwise there can be no society, and man dies of isolation. But all people should ask themselves how, in human personality, the common and the individual factors should be balanced. Inexorably and largely unchallenged, the promoters of sameness have prevailed and have eliminated from modern life the tradition of individuality.

Mass communications, mass production, mass education are the marks of our modern societies, which, whether communist or capitalist, are in these respects indistinguishable.

A workman who controls a machine in a factory puts nothing of himself into the things the machine makes. Machine-made products are identical, impersonal, and unrewarding, as much to the user as to the machine minder.

Handmade products appeal to us because they express the mood of the craftsman. Each irregularity, oddity, difference is the result of a decision made at the moment of manufacture; the change of design when the craftsman gets bored with repeating the same motif, or a change of color when he runs short of one color or thread, witness to the constant living interaction of the man with his material. The person who uses the object thus made will understand the personality of the craftsman through these hesitations and humors, and the object will be a more valuable part of his surroundings for this reason.

Saving Individuality in the Village

Once, when a man wanted to build a house, he would launch into some of the most complex and prolonged decision making of his life. From the first family discussion of the idea to the day when the last workman left the completed house, the owner would be working with the builders—not with his hands, perhaps, but suggesting, insisting, refusing—maintaining a running consultation with them and making himself responsible for the final shape of the house. Indeed, this continuous interest of the owner in his house would continue indefinitely, for there was a superstition to the effect that once a house was quite finished, its owner would die; so the prudent householder would go on for ever altering and adding to the structure and putting off the laying of the fatal last brick.

The men who worked on the house would all be craftsmen, knowing what they could do and knowing their own limitations. Probably they would be from the same neighborhood as the owner, and would know him well, so that he would have no difficulty in explaining what he wanted, while the building contractor would understand very well how much the owner could afford to spend and what he could get for his money. As the work progressed, the owner would choose the various fittings: with the carpenter he would talk about *mushrabiyas,* doors, and cupboards, with the stone carver about sideboards and ornaments round the door if he were poor, with the marble cutter about mosaic sideboards, fountains, wainscoting, and floors if he were rich, and with the plaster cutter about stained glass windows. He would be a real connoisseur in these objects; it would be impossible to fool him; he would know what he wanted and make sure that he got it.

Each craftsman would show him in practice what was possible, and the owner would choose between subtle variations in three-dimensional design that could never be represented on an architect's plan.[1]

The one man missing in this building venture was the architect. The owner dealt directly with the men who did the work, and he could see what he was getting. For their part, the craftsmen were free to vary their designs within the limits of tradition and subject to the owner's approval. If an architect had come between owner and craftsmen, he would have produced plans that neither could understand, and, unable to escape from his drawing boards, would have remained quite ignorant that the variations of detail possible in a design make all the difference between a good house and a bad one.

I once talked to moallem Mohammed Ismail, a craftsman who makes windows out of stained glass set in plaster. This was once a

1. Once, the head architect in the Ministry of Works, which is responsible for building and maintaining mosques, had to prepare some plans that included a capital with stalactites in the customary Arab pattern. It proved extremely difficult to draw the elevation of the capital with these intricate stone pendants, and the architect had been wrestling with the problem for several days, in no good temper, when one of the plasterers came into the office and peered at the plan. He asked what the architect was doing, and on being told he said, "But this is perfectly simple. I will make you one of these capitals in plaster and bring it tomorrow morning." And so he did, perfectly modeled, so that the architect was able to draw his plans from the model and then pass them solemnly on to the same plasterer to make the capitals from. In fact many features of great architectural beauty can no more be represented by geometrical projections on a plan than can a great piece of sculpture.

common decoration in a city house, but when I asked Ismail how many others apart from himself practiced the craft, he could think of only one man, moallem Loutfy. I asked Ismail if he was teaching his craft to his children. He said, "My elder son is a mechanic and I have sent the younger one to school." "So after your generation there will be nobody left to carry on the tradition?" "What do you want me to do? Do you know that we often don't have anything to eat. No one wants my work today. There's no room for a stained glass window in this new architecture of yours. Think of it, once even the water bearer used to decorate his house and would engage me. Today, how many architects even know of our existence?" "And if I brought you ten boys," I said, "would you teach them the craft?" Ismail shook his head. "I wasn't taught in a school. If you want to revive the trade, then give us work. If we have work, then you will see, not ten schoolboys here, but twenty apprentices." (I was able to give him a commission, and his work attracted the attention of other architects, so that his elder son, the mechanic, was drawn back to the craft, and has now surpassed his father in skill.)

The modern advance in technology which has given us new materials and methods in building has also necessitated the intrusion of the professional architect, a specialist who has been taught the science of working in these materials. This architect with his expertise has taken all the pleasure of house building away from his client, who is unable to catch up with the rapidly advancing techniques. Now, instead of the unhurried, appreciative discussions with the craftsmen as the house is being built, the owner has the opportunity to exercise his choice over marks on a plan in the architect's office. He doesn't understand the idiom of architectural drawing nor the architect's jargon, so the architect despises him and browbeats him[2] or else deceives him into accepting what the architect wants by adding specious trees and motorcars.

The architect feels that his own technical knowledge—his ability to talk of stresses and bending moments—puts him in a class above

2. Quelles sont par ordre d'importance vos préoccupations quand vous avez à construire un logement? (de Lauwe questioning Le Corbusier).

Answer: D'abord de quoi s'agit-il? De la clientèle privée, ou de l'homme en général? La clientèle privée est généralement loufoque, abêtie, avec des manies acquises au cours de la vie. Elle ne m'intéresse pas beaucoup. (*Famille et Habitation,* by Paul Chombart de Lauwe [Centre National de la Recherche scientifique], p. 197.)

To appreciate the participation of the ordinary citizen in the culture of his city today, we may contrast Le Corbusier's regard for his client with the relationship between the patrons and craftsmen of the past. Let us remember that a "patron" could be as humble a person as Mohammed Ismail's water bearer. The responsibility for this degeneration of the patron to the status of client lies squarely upon the architect, who has himself degenerated from an artist to a professional.

his client, and the client, being overawed, acquiesces in his own deposition. Ironically enough, though, few architects can handle the new forms artistically, and simple engineering replaces architecture, to the progressive uglification of town and country.

So the rich man who can afford an architect is deprived of much of his former power to decide for himself. The poor man, you might suppose, is more fortunate. Sometimes perhaps he is, when left to himself, but when the government decides to build for him, then he is far worse off than any rich man bullied by an architect. For the government architects, even when they don't dismiss the poor as too ignorant to be taken into consultation, say that they have no time to deal with each family separately. "We have a million houses to build, we have little money and little time. Please be realistic. How can we possibly send architects to wrangle with a million families? Quite Utopian. Housing is hard politics—we have done very well—we have tabulated our families according to size, composition, income, estimated change. By statistical analysis we have discovered that there are five kinds of family, and we have designed the ideal house for each. We are now going to build 200,000 of each kind of house. What more can we do?" And so the government's architects produce their irrefutable argument and build their million identical houses. The result is hideous and inhuman; a million families are bundled into these ill-fitting cells without being able to say a word about the design, and however much science is applied to the grading of families and the matching of them to their dwellings, the majority are bound to be discontented.

By applying statistical averages to housing, these architects ignore an elementary warning to all amateur wielders of statistics. The statisticians themselves tell us that though the characteristics of a whole population are stable, the individuals in this population vary unpredictably.

Statistical averages might be of great value to a life insurance company in estimating the average life span among its policy holders, but not even an insurance company, let alone a statistician, can tell us when any given individual will die. For a government department, lacking architects, to mass-produce designs for the different families on the basis of statistical averages, would be like an insurance company, lacking accountants, deciding for each one of its policy holders his allotted life span and then sending round its agent with a pistol to tidy the client away and thus keep its books in order.

The architect who undertakes this wholesale massacre of individuality would be indignant if asked to design a hundred different houses for a hundred private clients in a month. Not only indignant, but ill; he would collapse after designing twenty. Yet when designing a million houses for the poor, so far from collapsing is he that he is ready to take on another million the next month. He designs one house and adds six zeroes to it.

In doing this he is multiplying something that, properly, cannot be multiplied. When a house is built, various kinds of work go into the building. These labor processes can be classified as follows: (1) creative labor (the design); (2) technical labor (the engineering calculations); (3) administrative and organizational labor (accounting, recruiting workers, etc.); (4) skilled labor (masons, carpenters, plumbers, etc.); (5) semiskilled labor (concrete layers, etc.); (6) unskilled labor. Each of these classes of labor makes up a certain proportion of the total amount of labor, and the ratio between them should be fairly constant. If any one class is missing, the final building will be affected in some way or another, and the role of architecture in the cultural development of the country will be diminished.

If the unskilled labor is missing, then obviously the building will not get built! For this reason one cannot economize on unskilled labor. One can economize, however, on some of the other classes. With less skilled labor, the quality of work will suffer. With less administrative labor, your building project will get into a muddle. So usually, since authorities building for poor people are determined to economize somewhere, they economize in creative and technical labor. The engineering work may perhaps be done once and multiplied, but the creative work cannot be skimped. It is difficult to understand why authorities should be so niggardly in giving good professional service to individual families, and why architects comply with their dictates. Truth to tell, the mistake is not so much with the authorities as it is with the technicians; in medicine no one expects the doctor when dealing with the poor to try to mass-produce operations. Why then, when a passing infirmity like a sore appendix is honored by careful personal treatment, should a permanent necessity like a family house be accorded any less? If you chop off appendixes by thousands with a machine, your patients will die, and if you push families into rows of identical houses, then something in those families will die, especially if they are poor. The people will grow dull and dispirited like their houses, and their imagination will shrivel up.

The government architect, or the government itself, in fact, might excusably inquire now whether I am suggesting that the million families be left in their picturesque discomfort just as if there were no alternative to mass design. A rhetorical question, to be sure, but the government will follow it up by asking, with a triumphant smile, how a million families can be housed for the little money at the government's disposal. Not even architects work purely for love, and builders of all descriptions want paying once a week. Materials cost a lot, so does machinery. We must cut down costs, they say, by rationalizing our programs, streamlining the whole process, and economizing in the way indicated by industrial mass production. How else can we house millions except by standardizing the houses?

But none of these apostles of mass production and prefabrication seems to realize just how poor an Egyptian peasant is. There is no factory on earth that can produce houses these villagers can afford. The average income of the Egyptian peasant is L.E. 4 per year. A survey of fourteen typical villages in Upper and Lower Egypt showed that 27 percent of the total number of rooms had no roof. Now the usual form of roofing today is reed stalks laid over one or two light wooden poles. The peasants are often too poor to afford reed stalks (10 PT per camel load) and the prefabricators expect them to buy reinforced concrete! How can people so poor that they cannot even afford to buy ready-baked bread, but have to make their own to save the baker's profit, even dream of a factory-made house? To talk of prefabrication to people living in such poverty is worse than stupid, it is a cruel mockery of their condition.

Well, we cannot house them cheaply even when we do standardize, and we cannot house them with any semblance of human dignity unless we destandardize, which is said to be expensive. It is a pity that government authorities think of people as "millions." If you regard people as "millions" to be shoveled into various boxes like loads of gravel, if you regard them as inanimate, unprotesting, uniform objects, always passive, always needing things done to them, you will miss the biggest opportunity to save money ever presented to you.

For, of course, a man has a mind of his own, and a pair of hands that do what his mind tells them. A man is an active creature, a source of action and initiative, and you no more have to build him a house than you have to build nests for the birds of the air. Give him half a chance and a man will solve his part of the housing problem—without the help of architects, contractors, or planners—far better than any government authority ever can. Instead of one architect in an office sitting up all night to find out how many houses of each size will best fit the masses to be housed, each family will build its own house to its own requirements, and will inevitably make it into a lively work of art. Here, in each private person's longing for a house, in his eagerness to make one himself, is the alternative to the disastrous mass housing schemes of so many governments.

And the architect? If he has no time to spend in individual consultation, if he is not offered enough money to make the job worth his while, then the job is not for him. Let him go and hawk his expertise to people who will pay for it, and leave the poor to design their own houses. To take the other alternative, to design one house and multiply it by a thousand, as a road engineer designs a section of road and unreels it for any number of miles, is to betray his profession, to sacrifice the artistic nature of a house to money, and to abandon his own integrity.

The government would still have a very big part to play in a building revival stemming from the individual family. It would have to create the conditions for such a revival to flourish; clearly the conditions do not exist now, or there would be no problem. It would have to remove the various obstacles to private building, it would have to give a great deal of guidance to the completely inexperienced people (the overall planning of a village or town is authority's proper field, as is the provision of services, the training of people in the craft of building, and the giving of material help at the right points). The special training that authority would have to provide would necessarily be extended to architects in Egypt trained in the problems of rural architecture.

All this is well within the resources of any government. If only the government will change its attitude to housing, will remember that a house is the visible symbol of a family's identity, the most important material possession a man can ever have, the enduring witness to his existence, its lack one of the most potent causes of civil discontent and conversely its possession one of the most effective guarantees of social stability, then it will recognize that nothing less will do than the utmost a man can give in thought, care, time, and labor to the making of the house he will live in. It will recognize that one of the greatest services a government can render to its people is to give each family the chance to build its own individual house, to decide at every stage how it is to be, and to feel that the finished building is a true expression of the family's personality.

If anyone doubts the practicability of letting the people build their own houses, he should go to Nubia. There he will see standing proof that uninstructed peasants, given the necessary skills, can do far better than any government housing scheme has ever done. Indeed, the same evidence of imagination, ingenuity, and enthusiasm can be seen in many a shanty town where homeless people have constructed delightful buildings out of packing cases, gasoline cans, and other such rubbish. Of course these districts have no drainage, no paved streets, and the houses themselves are leaky, noisy, overcrowded, and prone to catch fire. But the buildings do look nice, because the people in their irrepressible artistry have made each one different, have seized on the only possible decoration—bright color-wash and flowers—and because the materials impose an overall harmony on the sites. In Jordan refugees from Palestine have built themselves such a city, in Athens refugees again have built many districts that today form the only presentable domestic architecture in the city, while in Peru something happened that is a lesson to all planners everywhere. In 1959, 100,000 people living in the slums of Lima decided to build a complete new suburb for themselves on empty land some way outside the city. Knowing that the authorities would be unsympathetic, these people planned the whole operation in secret, like a military maneuver; they divided themselves into four groups, each with its own leader and each to have a district in the new suburb; they drew up plans, laying out the suburb with roads, squares, schools, and churches; and on the night of 25 December they marched, carrying materials with them. They reached their target, and between 10 p.m. and midnight put up a thousand temporary houses, sited according to their plan, and each quarter had a church. By midnight the authorities had noticed what was going on, and police were rushed out to stop the squatting. Despite this, 5,000 people (out of a planned 100,000) stayed and are still living there, at Ciudid de Dois, ten miles from Lima. The moral scarcely needs pointing: if 5,000 people can house themselves in one night, in a well-laid-out suburb planned by themselves and in the teeth of official opposition, what might they not do with official encouragement?

What a hunger for housing this story shows, and what a will to work and build and help one another!

It would, however, be as well to enter a warning here. It must not be supposed that all peasants will naturally produce fine building as soon as they are given the materials and shown how. Most poor people envy the rich and try to copy the possessions of the rich. Therefore, when a peasant gets enough money to build a house, he often builds a copy—cheaper and nastier in every way—of the houses of the local rich, which in their turn are copied from the villas of Europe.

Thus a peasant who is allowed to indulge his own taste will end up with a clumsy copy of a copy. Even the remote original will have been a house erected by one of the unbalanced and stupid European clients turned down by M. Le Corbusier, for the Egyptians are by no means the only people who equate modernity with excellence. Yet there does exist in Egypt a potential ability to create beautiful designs. Some years ago Mr. Habib Gorgui and Mr. Ramses Wissa Wassef taught a group of village children to weave tapestries, and left them to make their own designs. They produced work so beautiful that it could bear comparison with the loveliest Coptic tapestry;

when exhibited in Europe it attracted the admiration of every artist and critic who saw it.

Traditional Village Crafts Restored

In Luxor and the villages around there used to be a very interesting kind of carpentry. Because timber is scarce and poor in quality, a carpenter who made a door would construct it out of many small boards nailed together in a pleasing and original pattern. A few such doors still exist, particularly in the village of Nagada, but their owners are busily destroying them and replacing them with doors of the familiar European type with four panels, which is admiringly termed *malakan* (American).

When we came to put doors on our houses in Gourna, my carpenter, Ibrahim Aglan, contemptuously refused to make these traditional *sabras* doors, and when I pressed him he said that he was a proper carpenter, town-trained, and didn't know what they might botch up in a village. It so happened that we had a village carpenter who had come to make a beam for a mill, so I asked this man—who worked with an adze only—if he could make sabras doors. He said, "Of course," whereupon, in front of Ibrahim Aglan, I embraced him, called him a true artist, a man I could understand, a real Egyptian, and I smiled at him and patted him on the back. At the same time I frowned furiously at Aglan, called him a man with no feelings, no art, a copyist, a fake, not an Egyptian but a Malakan, no craftsman, a clumsy woodchopper who wasn't worthy of his tools, until I had got him into a fine state of furious indignation. Then I said, "Very well, if you want to show that you are really better than this village carpenter, there are nine doors to be made for the shops. Go and make them, and make every one different. Go away and don't come back till you've shown me that you can make sabras better than this man." And he did. Once he was forced back to the native tradition he too grew enthusiastic about it, and before long was producing the most ingenious and beautiful patterns, the best of which is the great door of the mosque.

With the masons, too, I used the same approach, telling them to fill in the windows of the market building with different patterns of claustra; the result is a much more interesting surface than could have been obtained with identical patterns.

30–35
36

Thus we see that traditional crafts can be quickly restored—it is more a matter of giving them prestige than of teaching them again. The artist—in our case the architect—must set his authority against the glamor of the Malakan; he must find out the hidden and dying crafts and bring them to light, revive them, give the craftsman back his lost confidence, and encourage the craft to spread by giving new commissions.

Unhappily, almost nothing is done in this direction. Most architects, including those who pay lip service to the charm of tradition, say that such craftsmanship is out of date and cannot survive under modern conditions—even when they see it surviving in front of their eyes. It is fashionable to say of crafts as if self-evident, "Ah yes, but of course we can't go back to that," or to talk of modes of production not viable in a fully interlocking economy, etc. Claptrap, to fend off awkward inquiries and hide the fact that most architects are acquainted only with industrial materials and could not do as well as the local craftsmen, given the same materials.

This patronizing attitude comes out too in the way officials and experts will assure you that the peasants don't like peasant crafts and that they all want concrete buildings. This is in the first place an evasion of responsibility, because peasants, in Egypt, at any rate, will have to wait five hundred years if they want concrete; the experts postulate alternatives that they know don't exist. In Nigeria I saw a public relations display—two panels, one showing the worst African hovels photographed from unflattering angles, the other showing clean European-type buildings in concrete and aluminum, and the question "This or that?" The officials there confessed that these were not real alternatives at all; the country could afford only mud and straw.

But apart from the dishonesty of implying that expensive solutions are practicable, it is also libelous to father your own depraved taste on the peasants. Like all people, peasants are awed by authority and importance, and when told what they ought to want, they do their best to comply. And even if peasants really wanted ugly buildings, it would be our duty as architects to guide them toward an appreciation of beauty, and certainly not, by pandering to their taste, to lend our authority and approval to it.

The truth is, though, that peasants do like good architecture when they see it, and with a little encouragement can make the most perceptive criticism of bad architecture. When we started to build the 37 school at Fares, the villagers objected to mud brick and said they wanted a concrete school—this although not one of the houses in the village had any concrete in it and many of them had probably never even seen concrete. But when the school was finished, the mayor came to see me one day, glowing with pride, and said that the pilgrims who came every year to celebrate the birthday (*mouled*) of a holy man and visit his tomb there had this year gone to see the school instead, and that all the village was very proud of it.

Again, I once took two of my masons (Boghdadi Ahmed Ali and

Oraby) to lunch in Cairo and, wanting to find a place where they could feel at ease, I took them to a restaurant called Hati, which is rather gaudily decorated with gilt mirrors, chandeliers, and so on. At first they were terrified of the vulgar place, and tried to run away, but I hauled them back and told them not to be children, and that they were as good as anyone else there. They said it was much too grand for them; so I exploded at them: "Grand! You dare to call this cheap imitation grand, you who can build better than this with your eyes shut!" And, taking courage, they came in and started to discuss the place, making such sound and telling criticisms as even many architects might not.

The Use of Mud Brick an Economic Necessity

We are fortunate in being compelled to use mud brick for large-scale rural housing; poverty forces us to use mud brick and to adopt the vault and dome for roofing, while the natural weakness of mud limits the size of vault and dome. All our buildings must consist of the same elements, slightly varied in shape and size, arranged in different combinations, but all to the human scale, all recognizably of a kind and making a harmony with one another. The situation imposes its own solution, which is—perhaps fortunately, perhaps inevitably—a beautiful one.

Whatever the peasant may want to do, whatever rich men's villas he may wish to copy, he won't be able to escape the severe restraint imposed upon him by his material. Whether, when he has lived in a truly beautiful and dignified village, he will still hanker after imported modernity, we shall have to wait and see. Perhaps, when he has no reason to envy the rich man anything at all—his wealth, his culture, and his consequence—then too he will cease to envy him his house.

Normally, a peasant has only one big chance in the whole of his life to choose for himself what sort of house and furniture he wants. Only when he marries can he make any major change in his surroundings, for it is only for this occasion that he brings together enough money to make such a major decision. The custom is for the bridegroom to give the bride a sum of money, the *mahr,* which is a kind of dowry, while she is expected to provide furniture, kitchen utensils, and linen. All these goods are collected in the house of the bride's parents and then carried in procession with great ceremony to the couple's new home. The procession goes all round the village, displaying the goods, so as to show everyone that the new couple are well provided and able to take their place as an independent family among their neighbors. These household goods will have to last them for the whole of their life, and their purchase decides the beauty or ugliness that will surround the couple and their children for years ahead.

Another critical step is taken when a family builds a house for itself. This, indeed, may determine the surroundings not only for one lifetime but for generations to come.

If it is only once in a lifetime or once in several generations that the individual has a chance to make any big change in his environment, how often does it happen that a whole village is presented with such an opportunity? Here, on an enormous scale, was exactly the same chance, exactly the same freedom to choose between beauty and ugliness, and the decision, once made, would determine the visual environment of thousands of people for a century or more to come. The importance of the decisions taken at this time is perfectly obvious. No care, no skill, no exercise of sensibility can be superfluous at this moment.

In Gourna a thousand families were going to take this step of getting a new house. Each family deserved the chance to make its house as efficient and beautiful as possible, and each family deserved to have a say in the design of the house. Because each family differs from all others, it would be necessary to design each house individually.

If each family were to have its individual house carefully adapted to its needs and the way of village life, then it would take a long time to design them all. This, I thought, was perfectly satisfactory. I did not at all care for the method of designing the village arbitrarily and as a whole at the very beginning of the project, and then, in the three years given for its completion, simply supervising the construction. Besides being too rigid and inhuman a method, it would be very boring

Gourna was to house nine hundred families, which implied building at the rate of thirty houses a month. Thirty houses would be, at the most, three family neighborhoods, and certainly the design of three such blocks could easily be completed in one month. However, when we came to the actual building, I found that even the working drawings lost much of the importance they usually have. The masons were master craftsmen to whom every detail of the work had become familiar over many years, for it was their own technique. They knew by heart the proportions of the various rooms and, given the height of a dome or vault, could tell immediately where to begin the springing. In fact, they would even watch me while I was drawing, and tell me not to bother with these dimensions. Between us, the masons and I had restored the creative relationship between designer and craftsman and brought together two members of the dispersed trinity;

that the third member, the client, did not play a full part in Gourna was not our fault, and I am sure that in any future project the three members will cooperate harmoniously and fruitfully as once they used to.

Reestablishment of the "Trinity": Owner, Architect, and Craftsman

In official building projects, the design department prepares all the shop drawings and hands them over to a contractor, who has to follow them to the letter, under the supervision of architects in the field. At Gourna, however, we were our own designers, supervisors, and contractors, while the masons were as conversant with all the processes of construction as the architect himself. Thus all I had to draw were the ground plans of the individual houses and, to give them the heights, silhouettes of the family neighborhood blocks.

One of the great advantages of using traditional building methods and bringing the craftsman back into the team is that by so doing the architect is relieved of the work that he had unnecessarily taken over from the craftsman. In this method of construction the unit of design is the room; the masons can be trusted to supply it in standard quality and all sizes almost as if it came prefabricated from a factory. Such economy could never be obtained with concrete or other alien materials and techniques.

Ideally, if the village were to take three years to build, the designing should go on for two years and eleven months; right up to the last moment I should be learning, modifying, and improving my designs and making them fit more perfectly the families that would live in them. In spite of these good intentions, however, I found at Gourna that it was very difficult to interest the peasants in their new houses. This indifference was, indeed, largely due to their reluctance to do anything which might later be construed as an acceptance of the plan for removing them, but it also sprang from their inability to put into words their needs and fancies. One sheikh told me that so long as his cattle were properly accommodated he didn't want anything else, and this was a pretty general sentiment. I changed their minds only by showing them that, if they devoted their attention only to cattle and regarded their houses as a kind of annex to the stable, their city-educated sons would be too ashamed to visit them. They agreed that it was worth while bestowing some attention on the house, but they said that they would leave it to me to design whatever I liked. This carte blanche made the problem even more perplexing. How could I possibly learn all the details of the domestic life of a Gourni peasant and understand what he wanted in a house?

Possibly this indifference of the men toward their houses arose from the fact that the house is the province of the woman, not the man. It would have been a great help if I could have consulted the women, but it was unfortunately impossible because they were kept jealously out of the way. Later, when certain ladies of my acquaintance came to Gourna, we did manage to take the ideas of some of the village women.

Anticipating this difficulty of getting the Gournis to take a constructive part in the planning of their houses, very early on I built some twenty houses to show them the kind of architecture we were proposing, as they couldn't understand plans. I hoped, too, to observe the families actually living in them, and thus, as it were, "consult" them by seeing their needs in practice.

This may seem a lot of trouble to take, and the reader may wonder whether the Gournis ever did make any contribution in their role as clients. I believe, though, that the contribution the client makes to a design, however ignorant or even suspicious he may be, is something we cannot do without. Not only did we have a duty to these poor peasants to restore to them their position as patrons of a craft—whether or not they themselves had surrendered such right, and whether or not they resented the idea of the project—but we owed it to ourselves as architects not to try to design without the indispensable help of the client. Certainly the Gournis' somewhat unrewarding attitude to us arose only because they saw us as agents of the government which was intruding all unasked into their lives. A Gourni having a house built for himself with his own money would have quite a different attitude, and would play a far more positive part in the building than he wanted to with us. It was an attitude of busy interfering concern in every stage of the building that I wanted to encourage in our clients the Gournis.

The intelligent participation of the client is absolutely essential to the harmonious working-out of the building process. Client, architect; and craftsman, each in his province, must make decisions, and if any one of them abdicates his responsibility, the design will suffer and the role of architecture in the cultural growth and development of the whole people will be diminished.

The Gournis could scarcely discuss the buildings with us. They were not able to put into words even their material requirements in housing; so they were quite incapable of talking about the style or beauty of a house. A peasant never talks about art, he makes it.

The peasant art of Gourna is not particularly striking. It occupies the place one might expect on the scale between the high style of Nubian peasant building and the complete degeneration of the Delta. If you travel by train from Aswan to the sea you will observe that the level of folk art steadily declines; plotted on a graph, it would produce a curve roughly following the profile of the river. Gourna is situated about halfway along the river between Nubia and Lower Egypt.

Vernacular Architecture of Old Gourna

Thus, although Gourna has nothing of the colorful and imposing architecture of Nubia to show, nor perhaps the same pride in really beautiful craftsmanship, yet there are occasional buildings that show a certain purity of form, that are at least free from the artistic corruption that thickens about all village life as one proceeds northward.

No people anywhere is entirely devoid of artistic creativeness. However repressed by circumstances, this creativeness will always show through somewhere. In Gourna it is not so much in their houses, where they are open to bad influences, but in their various little domestic constructions that the villagers allow themselves to mold the most individual and beautiful plastic forms. In the old village there are beds like large mushrooms where the children can 38 sleep safe from scorpions (from which they derive their name *beit el agrab*); there are imposing, monumental pigeon towers with a very particular dignity of their own; there is a simple, grand, and beautiful bed raised by a peasant in his house, as central and important as the 39 bed of Odysseus; there are even one or two whole houses showing the same flow and plasticity of line that the beit el agrab has. These houses, as it happens, are among the very poorest in the village. Their owners were forced by their poverty into genuine design. Because they could afford in their houses neither the rather tasteless elaborations that their richer neighbors affected, nor the help of a paid builder, they had to contrive every part of their dwelling themselves. Thus the plan of a room or the line of a wall would not be a dull, square, measured thing but a sensitively molded shape, like a pot. In many of these very poor houses, if one can see past the incidental mess and dirt, the lines of the building present an instructive 40 lesson in architecture. Look at the photograph of the little house in Gornet Moraï; here there is no taint of architectural snobbery, no straining to climb into a "higher" social station, but a straightforward adaptation of the materials to the purposes of the peasant's life; each detail was built because he wanted it and where he wanted it, in the most convenient shape and size, without any thought of impressing other people. The result is in fact quite impressive. The house has the quiet self-sufficiency of any artifact produced by a competent professional.

This particular kind of plasticity and informality cannot be reproduced from a drawing board. It is conceived as it is built, like a piece of modeling in clay, and flat drawing has no part in the process. Such a house must be built by the owner, for every irregularity and curve is a reflection of his personality. But just because of this personal stamp that the house carries, it can exist only in a village where building is a leisurely and unsophisticated process. As soon as a project such as ours is launched, the building process jumps to a quite different level, becomes organized, time-conscious, and generally more "professional." Such a jump from the "modeled" house to the "engineered" one is a natural stage in the evolution of building, following an increase in the villagers' wealth. If the change takes place naturally, the new architecture will grow into a tradition. It was not, indeed, my task in Gourna to create the tradition that the Gournis ought to have had, for even if it were possible to do for a man what he must do for himself, to get inside his skin, to be his artistic conscience for him, such presumption would destroy his artistic initiative and integrity and defeat its own end.

Yet I could not flatly ignore all that the Gournis had done, erase every vestige of their own creativeness, and plump down my own designs on the site thus cleared of embarrassments. Such of the traditional construction as could be incorporated I had to use, and as much as possible of the spirit of the Gournis I had to bring out in the new designs.

Certain constructions were easily incorporated, and they helped us greatly from the beginning by providing a keynote in the design. The pigeon towers of the old village, for example, were entirely 41–42 original and spontaneous peasant forms, not suggested from elsewhere but dictated wholly by the villagers' taste, their own inventive answer to the problem of keeping pigeons. Such a structure went with no sense of strain into the setting of the new village. The same hands made it, the peasant mason built the old pigeon tower for the new village, and it is just as right today as it was yesterday.

Then again, we found a very interesting *maziara* in the old village. 43–44 A maziara is the place that holds the water jar called *zeer,* and in this case it took the form of a vault that shaded the water jar from the sun, a somewhat crude arrangement, but quite pretty. In the new village the vault supporting the staircase offered a suitable situation and really deep shade, while we were able to complete the arrangement by adding a claustra—a kind of mud brick mushrabiya—to act as a natural air filter.

45 In the mosque too, we were able to preserve an important part of the Gourni tradition. One of the old mosques of Gourna made use of a straight external staircase slanting up to the minaret, a form which 46 dates from the earliest years of Islam and is still found in Nubia and Upper Egypt. Although the mosque in the new village had to be far

larger, since it would serve the entire population, now concentrated into one village, yet it was well worth while making the effort to adapt the old design, including the external staircase, to the new scale.

It is important to understand that this search for local forms and their incorporation in the new village was not prompted by a sentimental desire to keep some souvenir of the old village. My purpose was always to restore to the Gournis their heritage of vigorous locally-inspired building tradition, involving the active cooperation of informed clients and skilled craftsmen.

Change with Constancy

At all costs I wanted to avoid the attitude too often adopted by professional architects and planners when confronted with a peasant community, the attitude that the peasant community has nothing worth the professionals' consideration, that all its problems can be solved by the importation of the sophisticated urban approach to building. If possible I wanted to bridge the gulf that separates folk architecture from architect's architecture. I wanted to provide some solid and visible link between these two architectures in the shape of features, common to both, in which the villagers could find a familiar point of reference from which to enlarge their understanding of the new, and which the architect could use to test his own work's truth to the people and the place.

An architect is in a unique position to revive the peasant's faith in his own culture. If, as an authoritative critic, he shows what is admirable in local forms, and even goes so far as to use them himself, then the peasants at once begin to look on their own products with pride. What was formerly ignored or even despised becomes suddenly something to boast about, and moreover, something that the villager can boast about knowingly. Thus the village craftsman is stimulated to use and develop the traditional local forms, simply because he sees them respected by a real architect, while the ordinary villager, the client, is once more in a position to understand and appreciate the craftsman's work.

Yet, to arrive at a positive decision on the kind of architecture for the new village, further investigation was necessary.

Besides the man-made environment of Gourna, with which the new village would have to harmonize, there is the natural environment of landscape, flora, and fauna. A traditional architecture would have accommodated itself to this natural environment, both visually and practically, over many centuries. The new village would have to tone with this environment from the very beginning, and its buildings must look as if they were the product of centuries of tradition. I had to try to give my new designs that appearance of having grown out of the landscape that the trees of the district have. They should look as much at home in the fields as the date-palm and the dom-palm. Their inhabitants should live in them as naturally as they wore their clothes. But it was a very heavy task for one man; could I think myself into the experience of generations of village masons, or conceive in my mind all the slow modifications caused by climate and environment?

Yet we can seek the help of our elders to obtain such knowledge. The Ancient Egyptians had penetrated the soul of this land and had represented its character with an honesty that carries across to us over the intervening millennia. In their drawings—simple lines painted on the walls of the tombs—they convey more of the essential character of nature than do the most elaborate confections of color and light and shade by the most celebrated exponents of modern European-style painting.

As an architect's plans are all line drawings, I thought that I could place against my designs drawings of the flora and fauna of the district, done simply, like Ancient Egyptian drawings, and I was certain that these pictures of palm tree or cow as seen in the Tombs of the Nobles would set off the honesty or show up the falsity of the buildings. I did all my renderings of the test designs like this; carefully avoiding the professional slickness of many architects' plans, which often distort natural forms in order to make the setting match the buildings, I did not try to produce effects of depth, nor bring in 47 convenient oak trees to balance a massing, but executed my drawings in plain lines and set about them sketches of the animals and trees and natural features of Gourna. These were: the hill above Gourna, which, with its natural pyramid on top, has always been a sacred rock; the cow, for the cow-goddess Hathor was the protectress of the cemetery of Gourna, and Gourna was in a district where there were many cows and where the ubiquitous buffalo of Egypt was not seen; the two trees, the date-palm and the dom-palm, for these are the trees of Upper Egypt; a certain character shown in the massing of some of the houses in old Gourna, with their loggias on top.

All these shapes I put against my first tentative, exploratory rendering, to act as a standard of comparison. I felt that in Gourna it was our duty to build a village that should not be false to Egypt. The people's style had to be rediscovered; or, rather, refelt from the sparse evidence of local crafts and local temperament. We had a technique from Nubia; we could not build Nubian houses here. Being faithful to a style, in the way I mean it, does not mean the reverent reproduction of other people's creation. It is not enough to copy even the very best buildings of another generation or another locality. The method of building may be used, but you must strip from this method all the substance of particular character and detail, and drive out from your mind the picture of the houses that so beautifully fulfilled your desires. You must start right from the beginning, letting your new buildings grow from the daily lives of the people who will live in them, shaping the houses to the measure of the people's songs, weaving the pattern of a village as if on the village looms, mindful of the trees and the crops that will grow there, respectful to the skyline and humble before the seasons. There must be neither faked tradition nor faked modernity, but an architecture that will be the visible and permanent expression of the character of a community. But this would mean nothing less than a whole new architecture. Change would certainly come to Gourna anyway, for change is a condition of life. The peasants themselves wanted to change, but they did ont know how to. Exposed as they were to the influence of the meretricious buildings in the provincial towns round about, they would probably follow these bad examples. If they could not be saved, if they could not be persuaded to change for the architecturally better, they would change for the worse.

I hoped that Gourna might just hint at a way to begin a revived tradition of building, that others might later take up the experiment, extend it, and eventually establish a cultural barricade to stop the slide into false and meaningless architecture that was gathering speed in Egypt. The new village could show how an architecture made one with the people was possible in Egypt.

Climate and Architecture

The climate of Upper Egypt is characteristic of a hot, arid zone, with a very wide difference between day and night temperatures. Because of the almost complete absence of cloud screening, the ground by day receives a great amount of solar radiation, while by night it radiates a great amount of heat out to the sky again. Thus any surface exposed to direct sunshine, such as the ground or the walls and roof of a building, heats up enormously during the day, and has to lose its heat during the night.

Therefore the comfort of people inside buildings in this district depends largely upon the thermal properties of the walls and roof. The best materials are those that do not conduct heat.

Sun-dried earth brick is, fortunately, one of the poorest conductors of heat. Partly because of its very low natural conductivity (.22 calories/minute/cm^2/unit thickness for bricks with 20 percent fine sand, .32 calories/minute/cm^2/unit thickness for bricks with 80 percent coarse sand, as against .48 for baked bricks and .8 for hollow concrete blocks), and partly because mud is weak and necessitates thick walls, the mud brick houses of Upper Egypt do remain remarkably cool for the major part of the day. At Kom Ombo, the concrete houses built by the sugar company for its employees proved too hot to live in during summer and too cold in winter, and the employees preferred to live in the mud houses of the peasants.

Yet thick mud brick walls are not a perfect means of keeping cool, for although mud is a poor heat conductor, it retains heat for a long time. Thus the wall that keeps you cool all morning has actually been taking in and storing up all the heat that falls upon it, and all through the night it will radiate this heat out again, partly into the room. For this reason it is much hotter at night inside a mud brick house than outside.

The obvious solution is to live downstairs during the day, protected by the thick structural walls of the house, and the roof, and at night to move up onto the roof to sleep in the cool night air. There would in fact be a need for a very light structure around and over the upstairs area to keep as much sun as possible off the downstairs part, and also to preserve the sleeper from mosquitoes. The principle is to shelter behind very thick mud wall by day, and to sleep on the roof under a tent, or something equally thin, at night. At Gourna the downstairs rooms of a house might reach their maximum temperature at about seven in the evening, some five hours after the maximum in the open air, while at eight in the morning, when the rooftop would already be unpleasantly hot, the downstairs rooms would be refreshingly cool.

This temperature regime may be modified if the house is built round a courtyard. The courtyard acts as a well into which the cooler air from the roof sinks, and so the downstairs rooms cool more rapidly during the night.

The second factor governing people's comfort inside a house in Upper Egypt is air movement. As the air is so dry, any breeze at all helps to evaporate sweat and so to cool the body. Thus it is most important to pay close attention to the ventilation of houses here.

The prevailing wind is north-northwest and is relatively cool. If this wind is to ventilate a house, it must be admitted through openings. The question is, Where should these openings be?

When I first went to Gourna, in the middle of the summer, I visited M. Stoppelaere, who was staying in Howard Carter's rest house, which was unbearably hot. It was so unpleasant that I preferred to go out in the sun, and suggested to my friend that we go and look at some tombs. He took me to the tomb of Nefer-Renpet, at Khokha, and when we arrived there we found it locked. While waiting for the keys to come, we sought shade in a nearby *madyafa*. But inside the loggia of this madyafa there was such a cool and refreshing draught 48 that we immediately looked to see why. The loggia was built with its back to the prevailing wind, and opened downwind. In the back wall and high up were pierced two rows of small openings, facing the wind. Now in common architectural practice one would always have the bigger opening facing the wind, if the object were to catch as much breeze as possible. Yet in fact this madyafa was cunningly arranged according to the best precepts of aerodynamics. As my brother explained to me later, a loggia opening to leeward, with only small openings to windward, will have a steady airflow through it because the airflow *over* and *round* it creates low pressure within it, so air is pulled in a steady stream through the small openings. A loggia with a large opening to windward, on the other hand, with no openings or only a small one to leeward, will soon fill up with air, so that fresh air passes over the loggia instead of through it, leaving the inside air stale.

This effect, which is quite easy to understand in general terms, has recently been given more precise expression in the following formula.

The rate of air-flow through the building, in cubic ft. p.h.	=	3,150 (area of inlets in square ft.) (wind speed in m.p.h.).

This formula holds if the wind in the immediate vicinity of the inlet is at right angles to the plane of the wall. If it is not, then the assumed rate of airflow must be reduced accordingly: at wind direction 45 degrees to an elevation of the building, the airflow should be reduced by 50 percent.

Further, if there is an appreciable difference between the areas of the outlets and of the inlets, then the expression must be adjusted to allow for this difference. The adjustment consists in substituting another value for the figure 3,150 in accordance with the following table, in which the values in the first column are the ratios of the total outlet area to the total inlet area:

If the areas are the same size, then:

	Value
$\frac{\text{Area of outlet}}{\text{Area of inlet}} = 1$	3,150

If the outlet is larger than the inlet, then:

$\frac{\text{Area of outlet}}{\text{Area of inlet}} = 2$	4,000
$= 3$	4,250
$= 4$	4,350
$= 5$	4,400

If the outlet is smaller than the inlet, then:

$$\frac{\text{Area of outlet}}{\text{Area of inlet}} = \tfrac{3}{4} \qquad 2{,}700$$

$$= \tfrac{1}{2} \qquad 2{,}000$$

$$= \tfrac{1}{4} \qquad 1{,}100$$

Thus we see clearly that the greater the ratio of outlet area to inlet area, the greater the airflow through the building.

Orientation of Houses Determined Partly by Sun, Partly by Wind

The positioning of rooms in order to keep them cool is also a matter that requires careful thought.

A shaded area with a through draught will always be relatively cool. The point is, from what should the room be shaded? Direct sunlight, certainly, but also from reflected radiation, which can sometimes make a room even hotter than the sun can. For every south-facing wall reflects the sun off its dazzling white surface straight into the rooms across the road. Even the stones and surface irregularities of the ground reflect the sun off their southern faces, so that they act like a radiator in a central heating system.

But the rooms which get all this reflected radiation smack in their faces are rooms which face north. Therefore it is essential to examine the immediate surroundings of the house before uncritically applying the usual principle "Living rooms should face north." Certainly a north-facing room will benefit from the cool northerly breeze, and provided we can be sure that there is no reflected radiation, north is the best aspect for the room. But if there are other houses nearby, it will be probably cooler to face the living rooms south, in spite of the usual practice. For then there can be no reflected radiation, and direct radiation from the sun, which will be very high in the sky when it bears on this wall, can be cut off by an overhang to the roof. Even the northrly breeze can be induced to flow through the living-rooms by the planning of the rooms.

In Iraq the peasants normally build their living room to the south, and back it with a north-facing loggia. The living-room is roofed with a dome which has a hole in the top, so that air heated in the ovenlike dome continually escapes, and cool air is continually drawn in from the shady loggia. The only drawback to the Iraqi design is that it has no overhang to shade the southern wall from the sun, because the Iraqis have little timber.

Every house in our village would be provided with a guest room, in addition to the family-neighborhood madyafa, which was also entitled to be used as the family living room and was not to be preserved as a "best" room for receiving strangers.

Its design followed the principle of the *ka'a.* The central square *dorka'a,* roofed with a dome, had *iwans* leading off it in which people could sit. It was a very high room—one and a half normal stories plus the height of the dome—to allow for high openings above the roofline of the ground floor. Hot air would thus rise and escape through these high openings, producing an inflow of air lower down to cool the room.

The orientation of buildings would be determined partly by the sun and partly by the wind. The best orientation for the sun would be with the long axis of the building lying east-west, a common principle of architecture.

But we would like to have the wind blowing onto as large an area of the walls as possible, to go through the house and cool it. The prevailing wind comes from the northwest, so ideally the house should be northeast to southwest, perpendicular to this wind. Should we compromise, bisect the angle between the two indicated orientations, and set the house east-northeast to west-southwest, as is the usual architectural practice? No, because the dilemma is a purely artificial one, created by our unthinking attitude to the window.

The Malkaf, or Wind Catch

In Europe, where heat control is not of prime importance, the window serves three purposes: it lets in air, it lets in light, and it lets you see out. But these three functions are not inseparable, and, in fact, builders in the Middle East used to separate them. In old Cairene houses the function of ventilation in the principal halls (ka'as) is performed by a device called the *malkaf* that catches the wind high up, where it is strong and clean, and by a special design of the room, with the central part (*dorka'a*) very high, that lets hot air escape at the top. Such a wind catch may be set at precisely the right angle to catch the wind, irrespective of the orientation of the house.

49–51

The wind catch as used in the schools we built in Gourna consisted of a chimneylike air passage with a large opening high up facing the prevailing wind. Set inside it was a sloping metal tray filled with charcoal that could be wetted by a tap; the air flowed over this baffle and was thus cooled before entering the room. This device is reminiscent of the *salsabil* that stands in the halls and iwans of old Arab houses—this is a slab of marble curved with a wave pattern, with fountain water trickling down it. In future applications of the wind catch principle the cooling baffle might be left visible and made of some absorbent material like asbestos with a pleasing pattern on it, like a salsabil. At Gourna the wind catch produced a drop in temperature inside the classroom of 10° C.

52 The function of providing a view is discharged by the mushrabiya —a kind of oriel window built out from the wall in which is fixed a latticework screen of turned wood which suitably tames and softens the harsh Egyptian light before letting it into the room. Behind this mushrabiya the ladies of the house may sit and comfortably watch the street, in perfect seclusion—without, incidentally, the need to peek out from behind curtains or to cross over the room to see out; the mushrabiya, in fact, does everything a glass wall does and more.

We then could use the wind catch to free us from the need to orientate the house for the wind, and could consider simply the solar orientation. In fact, even this would be in some degree subservient to the exigencies of the plan, for if every building were arranged in the same way the plan would become monotonous. Moreover, every deviation from the general idea would imply individual consideration of each house and an individual solution of its particular problems, which is artistically desirable.

Society and Architecture

Although I believe that the appearance of a building has the most profound effect upon its inhabitants, yet one cannot house men in the Parthenon. One's beautiful designs must serve the humble everyday needs of men; indeed, if these designs are true to their materials, their environment, and their daily job, they must necessarily be beautiful.

The new village could be true to its function, however, only if we knew precisely what this function would be. We should have to uncover the everyday life of the Gournis and reveal it, perhaps even more minutely than they themselves knew it.

A man has a set of habits in action, thought, and reaction which, when we wish to differentiate him from other men, we call his individuality. When we consider a society, we see that it is a pattern of such individualities and, more important, that each individuality is the creation of all the rest—each idiosyncracy in action, thought, or reaction has developed under pressure from the many other idiosyncracies that adjoin it and under the demands of climate, work, and trade. Individuality is not an abstract and mysterious "quality" but the sum of many tangible details: what time a man gets up, whether he shaves, the clothes he affects, his habits of speech, the people he is servile to and those with whom he is masterful. More than anything else, it is his house.

This, a magnification of himself and his most lasting monument, agrees in size, in aspect and in luxury with the other details of his individuality. It is, of course, adapted to his economic needs and determined, up to a point, by his economic means, but it has all the incidental characteristics of his temperament too. In Cairo the loftiness of the ka'a in the palace Katkhoda with its austere simplicity and dignity reflects the princely hauteur of the emir for whom it was built, while the comparatively squat and lavishly decorated hall in the house of Gamal-Eddin Elzahaby fits the florid commercial soul of this Master of the Merchants.

Placid people live in tranquil houses, in a village of beggars the walls cringe and whine, and haughty people's houses stare coldly over your head. The house is fully conscious of its social status, too; as the man knows who are his betters and whom he may look down upon, so the house takes a site that fits its station, and displays in the size and the luxury or poverty of its fittings a most delicate adjustment to the stratification of society. In Egypt, a villager considers it a sign of high distinction to own a house with timber floors, which he calls *Masri,* that is, "Cairene," and would boast of his acquisition to his fellow villagers who have just straw and reeds for roofs.

Thus a village, after many generations have lived in it, comes not only to fit its inhabitants' routine of work and recreation, but grows to reflect the oddities of its community, bricks and mortar growing into a living whole with harvest and planting, with weddings and funerals, with buying and selling, with craft, with trade, with the feelings of family for family and class for class. The buildings take on the many-dimensioned shape of the society, as an old shoe takes the peculiar shape of one man's foot, or rather as some growing plant constantly adapts itself to its environment.

A shoemaker may take pains to fit his customer, by measuring his foot and shaping the shoe carefully so that it is just right for him —or he may, like an army bootmaker, produce a standard size of shoe and let the customer's foot adapt itself as best it can. The same thing in Gourna: I had a living society in all its complexity and I could either force it into a few standard-size dwellings, leaving it to experience all the cramps and blisters of a recruit getting used to his boots, or I could measure it and produce a village that would accommodate it in all its irregularities and quirks, which would be rather like taking a snail out of one shell and inserting it in another.

A village society takes long to measure and needs more subtle instruments than a tape measure. One thing was clear from the start: that each family must be designed for separately. So at the very least we should have to consult every family in Gourna, and we should have to find out many things that were rather difficult to elicit from the suspicious and strict Gournis.

We had a kind of guide in an earlier survey of the old village that listed the houses and described their areas, number of rooms and roofing materials; but this survey had been made ten or fifteen years before, and even if it had not been out of date, it would not have given the sort of information that I wanted. Some social research was urgently needed, but social workers were hard to come by, and, even if they could be obtained, I knew from experience that the questions they would ask would be crude "yes or no" ones designed not to reveal a society but to produce statistics. Such statistics tell very little of value to the architect; they can only tell me how many children Zeid has or whether Ebeid has a donkey, and cannot reveal whether Zeid and Ebeid get on well together.

The customary questionnaire could never bring to my notice such an important social fact as the way architecture can break up a family. If a boy wins his way from a peasant hovel, through school and university, to become a lawyer, doctor, teacher, or officer, as more and more peasant boys are bound to, then he will be ashamed of his old home and will not come back to the dirt and ugliness where his parents live. Out of seven thousand Gournis, only one had graduated, and he was now a lawyer who practiced in Cairo and never set foot in his native village. With the spread of education under the new law, a whole new generation of children would be taught—quite rightly—to despise the squalor of their homes; but—wrongly—they would come to look upon the flashy modernity of urban dwellings as the true sign of progress and civilization. The kind of questions asked in the usual surveys could not reveal how quickly country life was changing. One might never realize how the old traditional pattern of isolation and ignorance of the outside world was being smashed to pieces by the country bus and taxi; once upon a time a man might live and die in a village and never go so far as the nearest town, but today the face of Egypt is scored with thousands of bus tracks, and all sorts and classes of people crowd into rickety motor vehicles just for the ride.

Parliamentary government, too, with its propaganda, election speeches, and posters, brings the city right into the village. The radio in the café has long since replaced the folktale and the fable. Universal education is opening new horizons to our children. Western communications have done for the village what Copernicus did for the Earth—the village is now seen as a small part of the universe, not its center, while the Western world, the factories of Czechoslovakia and Italy with their goods which are specially designed in crude and conspicuous colors to meet the corrupt taste of the peasant, increasingly comes to seem like the sun, the only source of life. The overwhelmed peasant, seeking progress, has abandoned the cultural traditions safeguarding his taste before acquiring the faculty of discrimination necessary to replace them.

The ever more shiny products of Europe and America, the lustrous metal cups and gold-spangled glasses, the dazzling colored-glass jewelry and gilt furniture, have conquered the defenseless markets of the villages, and forced into ignominious hiding the beautiful sober handiwork of local craftsmen. The peasant, his eyes opened to the opulence of city life, takes as his arbiter the urban civil servant and the police captain, for whom anything European is good. There is no God but God; there is no civilization but Western civilization. The debased and greedy taste of the middle-class townsman dictates the fashion to millions of peasants. Just as the rest of Egypt's living history is in full retreat up the Nile, so her craftsmanship is disappearing before the attack of shiny tin and gaudy cloth.

The visual character of a village, like the habits of its population, may change beyond recognition while to the undiscerning eye of the statistician it remains exactly the same. Statistics will completely miss such vital information as how the people celebrate personal and religious feasts. By remaining ignorant, for example, of the custom which obtains in some villages of Upper Egypt, whereby anyone who has come back from Cairo stays the first night not in his own house but in the mayor's madyafa, to give out news, an architect would fail to make provision for the custom.

To find out what customs and rituals obtained and to map the hierarchy of the community, we should have to talk to the elders of the village, and watch the village life for many months. To find out how the people went about their work, and how they used their houses, we should have to observe and invite suggestions.

Indeed, we should really have subjected the village to a thorough socio-ethnographic and economic investigation, conducted with the utmost scientific rigor, since we wished for reliable information on which to base our planning. The social ethnographer is not generally recognized as an essential contributor to town and regional planning; yet to my mind he is as important as the demographer. Today nearly all planners are dealing with communities in the process of change, and no planner can claim from his own limited experience and untrained observation to understand the changes in culture that are taking place even in his own society. Far less can he claim to understand an alien society, as planners often have to. Only a social ethnographer can provide this understanding, which may prove vital to the success of a plan. It should be as unthinkable for town planning to do without a socio-ethnographic survey as to do without a demographic record of the community.

The authorities never accorded us such a professional assistance;

so we had to manage with our own knowledge and intuition, based on a sympathetic understanding of peasant life. A good doctor may often make a more accurate diagnosis by direct observation than an inexperienced one can with a whole battery of scientific aids; telling myself this, I hoped that even the scanty data we had collected, supplemented by our experience, might suffice for a successful prescription in the case of Gourna! Points such as that remarked on before, which an incomplete statistical survey would miss, should if intelligently interpreted provide a clue to the correct solution of the architectural problem.

The first big architectural problem in New Gourna was the layout of the village. What character the streets should have and how the houses were to be related to one another was a question of the first importance.

Kinship Structure and Local Custom

There are many possible ways of arranging a number of houses and of varying the way in which the village meets the country. In Europe, for example, the village and the landscape interpenetrate, and the houses are not only open to the landscape but are part of it, just as the trees and fields are part of the village.

In Egypt, where the character of cultivation is different and the appearance of farmland less attractive, the villagers prefer to pack their houses close together into almost a monolithic mass. This is partly because of the hostile nature of the countryside, partly for protection, and partly because of the high cost of farmland, which they don't want to waste. The need for protection from nature and other men, both for themselves and for their cattle, is reflected in the way the houses and villages open inwards toward the center and turn their backs on the outside world.

This is true especially of those villages built actually on farmland. In Upper Egypt, where the river valley is narrow, the villages tend to be built on the flanking hills, where they can afford to take up more space. Old Gourna is in fact a particularly sprawling village, partly because each house has been built to take in as many tombs as possible.

Now most architects when replanning a village arrange the houses in straight, orderly streets, parallel to one another. This is easy, but dull. In fact, when these parallel streets consist of uniform, minimum-standard houses unrelieved by vegetation or other features, the effect is sordid and depressing. Yet there is no need to arrange houses like this. Exactly the same houses can just as easily be grouped round a small square. This is fully as economical as the straight rows of houses, and has several advantages.

First, a square keeps the customary inward-facing orientation of village houses. Second, it brings to the village something of the grace and urbanity of the rich man's life in the town. The pasha's palace was always built around a courtyard or series of courtyards, which gave it a very special atmosphere of calm and beauty. Unfortunately there has grown up among architects a prejudice against courtyards, because, when the pashas abandoned their palaces and the people moved in, these courtyards were used as building space and choked with small, insanitary dwellings. Thus, what had been a spacious and calm courtyard became a teeming warren of ill-ventilated hovels. But we can restore the courtyard to the people while ensuring that it won't meet the fate of the pasha's courtyard. By grouping their houses round courtyards or small squares, we can give them all the beauty the pasha enjoyed and at the same time accommodate them neatly and cleanly. The courtyard, of course, will be no longer closed, but will communicate with the street so that it becomes public property, and can never be built up, while at the same time clearly attaching to one group of houses.

53–56

I feel that the square and the courtyard are particularly important architectural elements in Egypt. Open spaces like this, within buildings, are part of the character of all Middle Eastern architecture—are found, in fact, from Morocco right through the desert lands to Syria, Iraq and Persia, and reach perhaps their finest expression in the town houses of Old Cairo. It is worth digressing for a moment to consider the meaning of the courtyard and the square to those who live in the Arab world.

In enclosed space, in a room or in a courtyard, there is a certain quality that can be distinctly felt, and that carries a local signature as clearly as does a particular curve. This felt space is in fact a fundamental component of architecture, and if a space has not the true feeling, no subsequent decoration will be able to naturalize it into the desired tradition.

Let us look at the Arab house as an expression of Arab culture. In what ways have the environmental forces that have molded the Arab character affected domestic architecture?

The Arab comes from the desert. The desert has formed his habits and outlook and shaped his culture. To the desert he owes his simplicity, his hospitality, his bent for mathematics and astronomy, to say nothing of his family structure. Because his experience of nature is so bitter, because the surface of the earth, the landscape, is for the Arab a cruel enemy, burning, glaring, and barren, he does not find any comfort in opening his house to nature at ground level. The kindly aspect of nature for the Arab is the sky—pure, clean, promising coolness and life-giving water in its white clouds, dwarfing even the expanse of the desert sand with the starry infinite of the whole universe. It is no wonder that for the desert dweller the sky became the home of God.

European pagans had gods in rivers and in trees, or disporting themselves on mountain tops, but no god of theirs lived in the sky. God in heaven comes to the world from the shepherds and camel drivers of the desert, who could see no other place fit for Him; for them the surface of the earth was productive only of jinns and demons who rolled about in sandstorms.

This instinctive and inevitable tendency to see the sky as the kindly aspect of nature gradually developed, as we have seen, into a definite theological proposition, in which the sky became the abode of the deity. Now with his adoption of a settled life the Arab began to apply architectural metaphors in his cosmology, so that the sky was regarded as a dome supported by four columns.

Whether or not this description was taken literally, it certainly gave a symbolic value to the house, which was considered to be a model or microcosm of the universe. In fact, the metaphor was extended further to the eight sides of the octagon that supports, on squinches, a dome symbolizing the sky; these eight sides were held to represent the eight angels who support the throne of God. Because the sky is for the Arab at once the home of the holy and the most soothing face of Nature, he naturally wants to bring it into his own dwelling. Just as in Europe men try to make their houses one with the landscape and its vegetation, either through gardens or through plate glass walls, so in desert countries men try to bring down the serenity and holiness of the sky into the house, and at the same time to shut out the desert with its blinding, suffocating sand and inhospitable demons.

The means of doing this is the courtyard. The house is a hollow square, turning blind, windowless walls to the outside, with all its rooms looking inwards into a courtyard from which only the sky can be seen. This courtyard becomes the owner's private piece of sky. The space enclosed by the rooms of his house can, at its best, alone induce a feeling of calm and security that no other architectural feature can, while in every case the sky is, as it were, pulled down into intimate contact with the house, so that the spirituality of the home is constantly replenished from heaven.

The serenity of an enclosed courtyard is not imaginary, it is not a piece of far-fetched symbolism, but a fact to be experienced by anyone who walks into an Arab house or into the cloister of a monastery or college. The value of the enclosed space was recognized not only by the desert dwellers but all along the Mediterranean seaboard, by the Ancient Greek and Roman villa builders, by the Spaniards with their patios, as much as by the Arab architects in the mosques of Cairo and the houses of Damascus, Samarra, and Fustat.

57 Yet, to the Arab especially, the courtyard is more than just an architectural device for obtaining privacy and protection. It is, like the dome, part of a microcosm that parallels the order of the universe itself. In this symbolic pattern, the four sides of the courtyard represent the four columns that carry the dome of the sky. The sky itself roofs the courtyard, and is reflected in the customary fountain in the middle. This fountain, or basin, is in fact an exact projection of a dome on squinches. In plan it is precisely the same, basically a square with, at a lower level, the corners cut off to form an octagon; from each of the new sides thus formed a semicircle is scooped out, so that the whole basin is an inverted model of a dome, just as if a real dome were mirrored in the water.

The inward-looking Arab house, open to the calm of the sky, made beautiful by the feminine element of water, self-contained and peaceful, the deliberate antithesis of the harsh world of work, warfare, and commerce, is the domain of woman. The Arabic name *sakan,* to denote the house, is related to the word *sakina,* peaceful and holy, while the word *harim,* which means "woman," is related to *haram,* "sacred," which denotes the family living quarters in the Arab house.

Now it is of great importance that this enclosed space with the trembling liquid femininity it contains should not be broken. If there 58 is a gap in the enclosing building, this special atmosphere flows out and runs to waste in the desert sands. Such a fragile creation is this peace and holiness, this womanly inwardness, this atmosphere of a house for which "domesticity" is so inadequate a word, that the least little rupture in the frail walls that guard it destroys it. That is why the patio, open on one or two sides, which perhaps is pleasant enough in Spain where the countryside is comparatively tame, would never do in the Middle East, where the fierce desert will jump in like a jinn and devastate the house. If even one side of the courtyard is a simple wall, the atmosphere will be spoiled. The sakina is disturbed. Only rooms that are really lived in can hold the magic in place, and this is because, of course, it is not a substance—we can only talk in parables—but a feeling, and it is created exactly by this turning inward of the room.

For these reasons, then, principally, I planned each house around a courtyard. But not only does each house contain its own courtyard;

each group of houses is also arranged to enclose the larger, semi-public common courtyard or square, the "pasha's courtyard" that I have already talked about. Each of these squares, with the houses around it, was intended to serve one family group, or *badana*.

The badana is a tightly related knot of people, consisting of some ten or twenty families, with a recognized patriarch and a close sense of corporate allegiance. The families live in adjoining houses and, though there are differences of wealth and status between the individual families, they follow a communal way of life.

The larger badana has its own café, and no one ever goes to another; it has its own barber and its own grocer; when bread is baked by one family, all the neighboring families in the badana may use the oven to heat their old bread, and families take turns to provide this service; at feasts and celebrations at the reception of guests the badana as a whole provides the banquet and the entertainment. In several important respects the badana is the principal socio-economic unit of the peasant. I had to take account of this, to make sure that each badana was housed together and given facilities for pursuing all the communal activities to which it was accustomed.

59–60

This was an additional reason for planning the houses round squares, in which the badana could receive guests and hold the festivities connected with weddings and circumcisions (a madyafa or guestroom was provided for the common use of each badana in its square), while it would also be convenient for more practical purposes such as the temporary storing of fuel and hay, which otherwise would clutter up the public street. But more important, because of the focus it will give to the group of houses, all turned inward and looking onto it, the square will create something of the same atmosphere for the badana as the courtyard of the private house does for the individual family.

Thus it will help to cement together the family group by a constant gentle emphasis on its oneness, and in numerous practical ways, as by facilitating the established practice of warming one's bread in the oven of whichever of one's neighbors happen to be baking, and by providing a place for children to play where they will be under the eyes but not under the feet of their mothers.

Yet more important, to me, than these considerations is the effect on the person who comes from a room in his house, through the house courtyard, into the larger, but still enclosed, square, and only then into the public street. Whether in a village or a town, this gradual contraction is more peaceful and more soothing than an abrupt plunge from the small privacy of one's room into the bustle of the street or the hugeness of the field.

Exactly the same units can be arranged in a variety of ways—on a gridiron plan or any other form—but quite the best arrangement is a well-proportioned square. Notice, though, that it is vitally important that the houses should face inward, into the square, just as it is essential that the courtyard of the house should be bounded by inward-facing rooms.

Quite often we see so-called squares that are, in effect, simply accidental spaces defined by the ends of house rows, by a school wall, or the back of a factory. When all the buildings turn their backs on a square, or at best present it with a cold shoulder, how can we expect the people to use the space as a real square? Not only does the atmosphere leak out; it is never put in in the first place, and such melancholy spaces soon become garbage dumps and meeting grounds for gangs of juvenile delinquents.

Village receptions are a very important part of the villagers' life. A family ceremony or a religious feast demands a big gathering, and all the neighbors lend a hand with the catering. The guests are grouped according to their rank, the head of the group of families—the oldest and most respected man in the badana—taking the place of honor in the madyafa, where, together with the other most favored guests, he is served with a meal. More distant relatives sit a little farther away under the covered loggias, and the crowd of casual acquaintances and passersby gathers outside in the square.

The private squares could be seen in most vigorous use for this kind of entertaining at the time of the Prophet's anniversary, which is the equivalent of Christmas. The celebrations last for twelve nights, on each of which a different family entertains, and the people of the neighborhood gather to hear the Koran read and to take part in the "utterance" (*zikr*) or rhythmic movement and chanting of the name of God.

Socioeconomic Considerations

We had to learn more about the Gournis than their social grouping and their customs, however. More important were the true facts of the villagers' economic life, from which we could gauge the effect of the move upon their ability to earn a living. Although our commission was simply to build a new set of houses, we could not conscientiously ignore this question of the Gournis' livelihood after the transfer. How villagers earn their living must affect the design of their houses and the provision of public buildings.

The first fact that became apparent was that the Gournis could never hope to live from the land around the village. The total amount of farmland available to Gourna is only 2,357 feddans (a feddan = 1.038 acres), while the population at the 1947 census was 6,394. Since 2,357 feddans can support only 3,000 people, there would be at least 3,000 surplus population who would have to support themselves in some other occupation. Gourna had grown up to serve the antiquities trade, and its inhabitants had been employed mostly as laborers on the excavations and had made a lot of money too by tomb robbing and selling things to tourists. At the outbreak of war in 1939 the population must have been about 9,000, but the halting of all excavation and the drying up of the tourist trade caused many Gournis to leave the village, while in 1947 a severe epidemic of malaria *gambia* killed about a third of the remaining population. Nevertheless, even this reduced population could not find enough work to live, in spite of the recommencement of excavations, while their old occupation of tomb robbing was growing ever less rewarding because of the increased vigilance of the authorities and the exhaustion of the tombs. Moreover, when they moved, the Gournis would find it more difficult and more expensive to live, for whenever a community is uprooted and all its little conveniences of life disrupted, those people who just managed to scrape along before will starve, everyone's resources will seem smaller.

Now the Department of Antiquities assumed that the population would continue to shrink, which was a natural inference from the actual economic situation of the village at the time. Yet there were —and still are—two possible ways in which a growing population could support itself. One was to replace the various occupations dependent on antiquities by crafts and to turn Gourna into a center of rural industry. This is feasible as shown by the example of Negada, a nearby town whose twenty thousand inhabitants support themselves by weaving. If the Gournis became mostly craftsmen, the population could be stabilized at its present figure and would then begin to grow at a natural rate of increase.

The other possibility for growth rested upon Gourna's proximity to Luxor and to the antiquities zone. The new village would become a tourist base for visits to the valleys of the tombs; already the roads from the Nile ferry to the antiquities past Gourna are macadamized, and a small bridge has been built over the Fadleya Canal. There is even talk of building a bridge over the Nile to link Luxor with the west bank. Gourna is much closer than Luxor to the majority of the important monuments, and a tourist hotel there would provide a great deal of work, both directly and indirectly. In fact, as communications improve, the value of the land will go up and the village may even become a suburb of Luxor.

Thus it seems highly probable that Gourna will grow. The plans for the new village provide for the replacement of every house in the old village, whether inhabited or not, by a new one, so that New Gourna should be able to accommodate almost the original population of 9,000. If the population exceeds 9,000, there is room to expand north and west until the *hosha* is filled up: at present only one-fifth of it is taken up by New Gourna. The public buildings are big enough to handle a considerable increase in population, except for the primary schools; new ones would have to be built at the rate of one to every 2,000 new inhabitants.

So a vital part of the project was to extend the resources of the Gournis by giving them trades that would earn money. They already had a few; I have mentioned their remarkable skill in faking antique statuary and scarabs, and besides this they used to turn alabaster vases, weave some very fine woolens, and make pottery. They also supported a number of silversmiths, but silverwork was little wanted now and the trade was dying.

The work on the new village would provide a splendid chance to introduce the various trades connected with building. Indeed, without abundant local skill, the village could not be built. I wanted to teach the Gournis brickmaking, quarrying, brick and lime firing, bricklaying, plumbing, and plastering. Then, to furnish their new houses, I wanted to preserve and perhaps modify traditional designs of furniture that would suit the houses.

Once these trades were learnt, the villagers could sell their skill and their products to other villages round about. But if these, why not other trades too? The local kind of woven cloth should find a market. They could be taught to make straw mats, baskets, rugs, and tapestries. I very much wanted to discover some simple, low-temperature glaze for crockery, so that they might make, and sell, good tableware. Jewelry, too: there was a custom of saving money in the form of silver brooches, anklets, bangles, necklaces, and other sorts of jewelry—hence the silversmiths. I thought that it was nicer to have your savings where you could see and admire them than to keep them in a bank, and so I wanted to encourage the silversmiths' trade to revive. Souvenirs might also be made for tourists (some scope here for the antiquity fakers). We even thought of establishing a small workshop for making stained glass windows.

If all these new activities started in the village, it would immediately give the people a more satisfying life. Their personal possessions would multiply and their houses become more beautiful, they would earn more money and grow out of their long habit of wretchedness.

Civilization is to be measured by the kind of accessories to living and the kind of habits a people has, not by the costliness of their possessions. A man may own an electric razor, but he is no more civilized than one who has an old-fashioned one; both shave, and that is enough. The silken prince in his private library, amid the bound and crested first editions, is not a scrap more civilized because of that than the threadbare workman studying the thumbed and dirty volumes in a public reading-room. With simple but adequate houses, sufficiently furnished, provided with sanitary facilities, and decorated with the excellent local manufactures, with education, with money coming in from trade, with increasing contact with travelers, tourists, and teachers from outside, the standard of life in the village would be greatly raised. The people would be healthier, happier, more comfortable, and more secure, and even the tables of the statisticians would show fewer deaths and more children.

The economy of New Gourna had perforce to depend upon manufacture and "export." We had the chance to choose whatever trades seemed most profitable, and we should enjoy all the advantages of a strong trading community over our weaker agricultural neighbors. These neighbors might well feel jealous to see the Gournis, as a reward for fifty years of thieving, presented with the means of growing richer still, at the honest farmers' expense, and certainly there was no justification at all for favoring the Gournis, in particular. If they got all the markets, it would be difficult later on to vary the trades and raise the living standard of the other villages.

In fact, a village cannot exist by itself and should not be considered an isolated entity. At all points it should fit into the overall pattern—not merely in space, but in the various dimensions of social and economic growth, so that as it evolves and its work, trade, and way of life develop, it will help to maintain rather than disrupt the ecological stability of the region. We should have had a long-term regional plan, allotting village industries so as not to produce impossible pressures of competition, but we didn't. However, this was not an immediate worry; in the present state of the country, so great is the lack of every kind of manufacture, of the most elementary necessities for civilized life, that there is more than enough room for all the villages in Egypt to multiply their production many times.

Rural Crafts in Gourna

In the matter of rural crafts in Gourna, I must explain that except for the building crafts I had never intended to develop them myself; it was not my job. But we made some experiments, sampling the soil, as it were, to see if crafts could grow in Gourna.

The most important craft would have been the making of textiles. This would have been a permanent asset to the village and have commanded a steady market. There were already two local weaves of great interest in Gourna, the *berda* and the *monayar,* while a nearby village, Nagada, known as the "millionaire" village, produced a very intricate and expensive weave called *ferka,* which I wanted to introduce into Gourna. Besides these, all woolen cloths, there was a cotton weave for scarves and the like that was very pretty indeed with its delicately proportioned stripes; this, however, was not of very good quality because of the bad yarn and dyes.

Textiles

In the course of our efforts to start a textile industry we made some experiments in dyeing, with the help of the village weaver, Iskander. The local vegetable dyes were once very beautiful, but they had been abandoned in favor of cheap chemical dyes, which are used with very vulgar effect on the traditional weaves of cloth. If the vegetable dyes could be reintroduced, Gourna cloth should sell well. We intended to revive the techniques of vegetable dyeing, because these dyes are faster and softer-colored than chemical ones. But until we could start producing vegetable dyes in a large way, we had to rely on aniline dyes, and we made a number of experiments to render these dyes more gentle and harmonious. Among other things, I thought of subduing the harsh contrasts of the anilines by mixing each dye in the dirty water from its complementary color, and also of choosing the original wool carefully, so that a naturally dark brown wool would be dyed red, a light brown wool yellow, a black wool black, and so on. This would soften the bright colors while making the somber ones glow. In these experiments we were greatly helped by Imperial Chemical Industries, Ltd., who took an interest in the work and let me have dyes in small quantities, contrary to their usual practice.

The improved and dyed Gourna weaves were most attractive. It happened that M. Boudin, a director of Janssen's in Paris, saw these cloths and liked them so much that he offered to buy every meter of the colored monayar that we could produce.

The Minister of Commerce and Industry, Mr. Mamdouh Riaz, visited the village and was also interested in the weaving and dyeing experiments. He encouraged us greatly by promising to send us an expert in textile making to establish the crafts.

This man soon arrived. He was Mohammed Talha Effendi, a very kindhearted and socially-minded person, and very enthusiastic about his work. Overnight, he collected into the khan a gang of twenty little children to be taught weaving. The first thing he did was to give them all a good wash; then he set them down to wind threads, set up the loom and so on. It was astonishing to see how some of them took to tapestry weaving with the naturalness of spiders, as if the craft were in their blood.

When Shafik Ghorbal, the Undersecretary, came to visit us, he was very impressed by these little weavers; he noticed, though, that they looked thin and hungry, and he suggested that they be given a bowl of lentil soup every day. It was a sensible and practical suggestion that everyone applauded (especially the children), until the ministry asked what budget to put the soup on. It turned out that there was no appropriate heading under which lentil soup might be charged, unless indeed we could start the primary school working, put the children in it, and charge the one piastre or so a head to the school meals account. It seemed an expensive way of getting a bowl of soup, to build a school and engage a staff of teachers. The problem resolved itself, however, when the ministry fell almost immediately afterwards and Talha Effendi was removed. The children were turned out and left to roam around the antiquities zone begging for baksheesh from all the tourists.

After this setback I thought that the textile crafts would be more firmly rooted if the crafts school could be built and put into operation. Therefore I hastened to get it built. It was intended to be both a training center and a communal workshop, with looms and dyeing facilities. It was provided with six troughs for dyeing, each trough with its own boiler worked by an oil-and-water-drop furnace—a very effective device that will boil up a whole barrelful of water in a quarter of an hour. The crafts school had room for ten horizontal looms for the native weaves and a number of upright looms for ordinary cloth.

As soon as it was finished I wrote to the Ministry of Commerce and Industry offering them the crafts school. The ministry already had a handicrafts center at Quena, but this was hidden away in a second-floor rented flat; so I thought they would welcome the chance to put their crafts teaching into these well-equipped permanent premises, especially as they were offered free. But the director-general wrote back to me saying that I was trying to force my ideas on the ministry and that they wouldn't accept the offer. From his tone it seemed almost as if I was trying to take something from him instead of giving him something free. Thus the weaving experiment died away, entirely through active governmental discouragement.

Pottery

Besides weaving, I wanted to give the Gournis a practical way of making glazed pottery, for reasons explained earlier.

The problem involved in making tiles is that there is, or was, no suitable glaze that melts at the temperatures obtainable in ordinary peasant kilns. So we had either to find a low-temperature glaze or a cheap and practical high-temperature kiln. I was told by the Japanese sculptor Isamu Negutchi that someone at the University of California had made a glaze that would run at 600°C, but although I have asked many people, no one else seems to have heard of it.

I did, however, design a kiln, worked on the oil-and-water-drop principle, for firing bricks and lime.

There is also, for anyone interested in this matter, the native pottery and ceramics industry of Rosetta, where once the most beautiful ceramic tiles were made, tiles that may still be seen in the old houses of Rosetta and Damietta.

Father de Montgolfier, a priest who ran a small dispensary at Garagos, across the river to the north of Luxor, saw that I was interested in improving the local pottery. He invited his nephew, who was a potter, from Paris to come, and we built a very beautiful workshop at Garagos for him. Unfortunately the pottery his nephew produced, though very fine, was not what I needed. It was far too artistic, whereas what the peasants needed was very straightforward, simple, usable pottery and tiles. Above all, we needed a technique that the peasants could easily copy, something as cheap and simple as mud brick building.

61

I should like to bring Isamu Negutchi and de Montgolfier together to see if they couldn't produce something between them.

All these new trades would have to be taught to the Gournis. On the principle that you cannot send a greybeard back to school, I thought that we should concentrate on producing our new tradesmen from among the children of the village.

Knowing that schoolrooms are apt to be insulated from reality by a good wadding of chalk and examination papers, and that children fidget and look out of the window, despite the best intentions of their teachers, I resolved not to teach these new trades in a school. Much better to make use of a system of apprenticeship. The learners would work in the shop of a master craftsman, and from their first day under him would be plunged into the atmosphere of the trade. They would learn all the knacks and tricks, they would see in hard cash the use of their knowledge—for from the beginning they could sell their work—and there would be none of that bewilderment that afflicts most students when they try to relate the abstractions of the classroom to the realities of life outside. They would grow into the job, understanding all its snags and earning not praise from a schoolmaster but money from a customer when they did good work. My apprentices would never be like those students discharged from a school with a certificate in their hands, looking greenly for an opening and jumping at the first chance into some office job.

The Crafts Khan

The common practice in apprenticeship would have to be speeded up. We could not have boys kept for three years cleaning the master's tools and winding balls of string. So we should have to invite craftsmen from other parts, assess the length of time they would need to stay, and pay them a salary and accommodate them while they were with us. To this end I planned, as one of the most important public 62–64 buildings in the village, a hostelry where each master craftsman could stay, together with his family, with workshops where he could practice and teach his trade and shops where he could sell his wares. In this khan, as I called it, the new trades that would set up the economy of New Gourna would be taught.

The khan was to be the main instrument by which the supply of fresh craftsmen was to be regulated. The idea of the building grew out of Gourna's need for new trades and from the fact that a school organization would be very uneconomical for our purpose.

In the normal course of life a community can absorb only a limited number of craftsmen in any one trade. When boys learn a trade as apprentices, the master craftsman takes care that he does not have too many skilled journeymen in his shop, for they have to be paid, and so he keeps many of his apprentices for a long time doing harmless jobs about the shop, admitting them very circumspectly to the mysteries of the craft and only when he really needs them. In this way, too, he makes sure that the market is never overburdened with competing master craftsmen, and so assures his own living. Thus the apprenticeship system is an excellent natural means for conserving the balance of crafts in a community.

It is, however, conservative. When a change in the work pattern seems desirable, when many more craftsmen are needed in some particular craft, then the apprenticeship system cannot apply so well. To restock Gourna with craftsmen, we needed some system that would combine the large output of a school with the flexibility and low cost of the apprenticeship system, and we found it in the khan. The building itself, cheap in the first place, would house a succession of master craftsmen, each invited to come and pass on his skill as quickly as possible until our needs in that particular trade should be met. He would then go back home, and his rooms could be taken over by another craftsman who would teach some other necessary craft.

There would be no classes, the craftsmen would sell their work, the apprentices would learn rapidly (for their masters, being there only temporarily, would have no reason to hold them back), and if ever the village should be fully supplied with flourishing crafts, the building could be turned into something else. Pupils, having successfully learned their craft, would practice in the village, not in the khan, and take on apprentices for themselves in their turn. Thus one trade after another would be "sown" in the village from the khan, whereupon it could continue to grow by itself. The trades to be taught by this system would be those for which there was a fairly limited demand: jewelry making, wood turning, carpentry, fancy weaving, cabinet making, the (now respectable) reproduction of antiques, and so on.

Other trades, notably weaving and dyeing, would have a large and constant market. There would be a continuous demand for cloth, hence a continuous need for weavers and dyers. These would be taught in the crafts school, the second biggest teaching building in the village, where it was worth while setting up a permanent organization. It was intended that as boys learned the trades taught there, they should practice them in the same building, which would become a little cloth factory that trained its own craftsmen.

There would, of course, also be two primary schools where all the children in the village would learn to read and write, and from which, with luck and application, they might eventually proceed to high school and university.

The Crafts Exhibition Hall

The permanent exhibition of crafts was of some interest as an uncommon provision in a village. Here we intended to keep on show samples of all the products of New Gourna's new craftsmen, so that visitors and tourists might conveniently inspect our wares. It would

65 be placed on the main road from the Colossi of Memnon to Luxor, and the better to entrap tourists, we should pay a small commission on sales to their car drivers and dragoman. Another public building was to house the women's social center and dispensary. At the dispensary treatment would be available for minor injuries and illnesses, a clinic could be held by a visiting doctor, and maternity services could be provided. Attached to this and communicating directly with the dispensary would be the women's social center, where women could be instructed in hygiene and the care of children. This center would have workrooms where they could do handiwork together and a kitchen where they could learn the elements of good cooking and which would incidentally serve the dispensary. There would also be a turkish bath, an open-air theater, and even a little church for the hundred or so Copts in the village.

In short, I wanted in the public buildings of Gourna to provide for all the communal needs of the villagers—for their work and trade, for their education, for their amusement, and for their worship.

I included a description of these proposed buildings in a report to the Department of Antiquities. Besides simply describing the buildings, this report explained the system of work we had decided upon, and also the principles of compensation for the families that were to move.

Because of the unfamiliar techniques we would be using, we could not hand over the job to a contractor. No contractor had any experience of mud brick roofing, so we should be quoted quite impossible sums if we invited tenders. If we had commercial firms making our bricks, transporting materials and building, it could not possibly cost us less than L.E. 1,000,000. We had L.E. 50,000

The only way so much work could be done for so little was by adapting not only the peasant's methods of construction but also his methods of work when he builds on his own. The main difference would be that we should have to pay for work that the peasants would ordinarily give for nothing.

We could build the whole village ourselves. We would not depend upon commercial sources for any of our materials; we would make every single article which could possibly be made on the spot; it would be an entirely (though paid) "do-it-yourself" operation. We would make our own mud bricks, we would build kilns, quarry stones, burn lime, bake bricks for sanitary units, etc. We would employ no one except the masons from Aswan and the Gournis themselves. In this way the whole project could become a vast technical school where the villagers would learn the various building trades, to go with the others that would be taught to them in the khan and the crafts school.

The new houses were to be designed individually, allowing each family the same number of rooms and the same area as it was already occupying. This was more realistic than trying to assess the value of the existing houses and designing new houses at the same cost, for in a large-scale project like this any figure for the individual cost of a house would be largely meaningless. Furthermore, basing the new accommodation on the old made it easier to lay down a minimum standard—two rooms and sanitation—so that the poorest families, who inhabited literally worthless properties (in some cases simply a fenced-in grave), should be properly housed.

I explained these principles of family housing in my report. However, I chose to begin work on the public buildings for two important reasons. First, from my experience of government departments I suspected that once there was a good number of dwelling houses up, the government would say, "Thank you very much; that is very nice indeed," would rush the peasants into the houses, and would cut off all further money for anything else, so that the public buildings would never get built and the new village would remain a huddle of houses with no center. Second, I wanted to allow myself time to observe the villagers and to talk with them about their own personal houses. I did not need their advice on the design of the mosque or the schools, but I wanted to make each house just right for the family that was to inhabit it.

Although I had been given a site and a free hand, the department had not been so lavish with its money. The sum allotted me was based upon an arbitrary assessment of the value of the houses in Old Gourna, and was in no way related to the probable cost of building the new village. The peasants were to be expropriated and had been allotted L.E. 50,000 as compensation. This money was to be turned over to me to build a complete village of nearly one thousand houses. Unfortunately it hadn't occurred to the department that a village needs more than just houses, and, though L.E. 50 per house was a reasonable estimate (provided we used the method I had developed on the previous buildings under normal conditions), there was nothing left over for roads, schools, mosque, and the other necessary public buildings and services.

I was supposed to finish the village in three years, and for the first season's work I was given L.E. 15,000! At about the same time, for that other project at Imbaba where a thousand houses were to be built, all exactly the same and each one cramped enough to be fitted inside the guestroom of one of my houses, the government had granted L.E. 1,000,000.

However, I managed to conquer my diffidence and got down to designing. There was no point in grumbling about the money. Let us put up some buildings, do as much as we could, and trust that more could be provided later to finish the village. If I asked for more there would be arguments, delays, and we should never get started at all.

Not only this, but I had taken on about the stiffest sociological challenge in Egypt. I felt that if I was to prove beyond question that the principles advocated were right, I should have to prove it under the most challenging conditions, and certainly no one could complain that in the rehousing of the Gournis I had chosen an easy problem. The Gournis themselves were solidly opposed to the idea. They had no inclination to move from the village they knew and the trade they had grown up in, nor to populate a new village and engage in new and arduous employment just to prove a theory of building. Still less did they fancy relinquishing the profitable income from their private excavations or *kehita* as they call them, which made them richer than the general run of fellaheen, in order to earn their bread in the sweat of their brows like everyone else.

The report went up to the Department of Antiquities, and I heard no more about it. I do not know if it was ever read, but I took the absence of comment for an indication that it was approved and went ahead with the design.

The Plan of New Gourna

The site was bounded on two sides by a light railway that curved round at the southeast corner. Here there was a little halt, which obviously determined the location of the market, for the traders and peasants would want to bring and send their goods by train. The market occupied a large square area here, and provided the main entrance to the village. Visitors would cross the railway, enter the market through a gate, and then go through a second arched gateway on the opposite side of the market into the village proper. From this gateway the main thoroughfare wound through the middle of the village like a snake, in three curves, ending in the opposite corner at a small artificial lake and park. Halfway along, this thoroughfare became much broader and, together with a wide street leading south at right angles to it, formed the main square of Gourna.

Around the square were disposed the mosque, the khan, the village hall, the theater, and the permanent exhibition hall. The other public buildings were further away from the center; the boys' primary school, for example, was situated by the park at the northwest end of the main thoroughfare, where it was cool and quiet (to catch 66 the prevailing northeast breeze in the vicinity of the park). The girls' school occupied a similar position but rather more to the east. The crafts school I put by the market, partly to encourage its sales and partly to let the dyers drain away their waste water into an adjacent ditch.

Two other main streets curved away in crescents, one from each end of the middle part of the main thoroughfare, forming a similarly winding thoroughfare connecting the northeast with the southwest corner of the village. On this thoroughfare were, south, the little Coptic church, and north, the turkish bath, the police station, and the dispensary.

This layout of the main streets separated the four "quarters" of the village. In each of the quarters was to be housed one of the main tribal groups of Old Gourna. Here I must explain that besides the grouping of families into badanas there was a larger grouping into tribes or clans; in Old Gourna the five-tribal groups that made up the population lived in four quite distinct hamlets. In the new village I planned to keep this physical distinction by settling the tribal groups into the four well-marked quarters, which were allotted as follows:

The Hassassna and Atteyat, who had lived in Assassif (the hamlet lying in the middle of Old Gourna), were to be housed in the middle of the new village, to the north of the square. The Hassassna are a very old clan; their name derives from Al Hussein, the grandson of the Prophet, from whom they are descended. Because of this ancestry, they have always been respected as a pious and learned people, and at the time in question they included Sheikh el Tayeb, a very holy old man who was venerated all over the region. Therefore it seemed fitting to group the Hassassna around the buildings that represented religion and learning; the mosque, the two primary schools, and the women's social center attached to the dispensary. With the Hassassna, in the same quarter, I put the Atteyat. This tribe has always been associated with the Hassassna, and lived with them in the same hamlet of Old Gourna. Their name derives from the word for a gift. The Hassassna and Atteyat occupied a semicircular quarter to the north of the square.

South of the main road, and embracing this semicircle, lay the large quarter of the Horobat. Their name means "the warriors," and they were in fact an active group that included the most prominent tomb robbers. So their quarter included the marketplace, the khan, the village hall, the theater, the crafts school, the exhibition hall, and the police station.

The Ghabat, the third tribe, take their name from the word "forest." Their quarter, therefore, adjoined the artificial lake and the park.

There was a fourth tribe, the Baerat, which lived mainly in the neighboring village with this name, while a small number of families lived in Gorent Mora, one of the hamlets of Old Gourna. They had always kept themselves rather apart from the Gournis, and in fact came under the mayor of Baerat. These were housed at the extreme western end of New Gourna, separated by a broad street from the rest of the village.

The broad streets separating the quarters were intended as main traffic routes connecting all the public buildings and meeting in the square. To ensure good ventilation and insulation of the blocks of houses, as well as to facilitate movement and to mark off the quarters, these streets were all at least ten meters wide.

67–73

By contrast, the streets giving access to the semiprivate squares of the different badanas were made deliberately narrow—no more than six meters wide—to provide shade and a feeling of intimacy, and included many corners and bends, so as to discourage strangers from using them as thoroughfares. On the plan they appear to be interlocking, as they are meant to facilitate intercommunication between the member families of the neighboring badanas.

I did not give the streets this crooked plan simply to make them quaint or because of some love for the Middle Ages. If I had adopted a regular plan like a gridiron, the houses would have been forced into a uniform design too. In long, straight streets, and even in symmetrical curves, the houses must all be exactly the same if the general appearance is not to be messy; yet the families who live in these houses will not be all the same.

Furthermore, however convenient the gridiron layout may be in large cities where the planner's chief concern is to achieve the optimum speed and volume of motor traffic, in a small village whose peasants will probably never possess even bicycles, such a pattern is positively harmful. To have a little village cut up by its streets into small rectangular blocks, one next to the other without any interconnection, is to make a kind of civilian barracks of it, whereas it is the architect's job to make his village as charming as possible. If the architect is to offer any excuse for his arrogance in dictating what his fellow men shall live in, that excuse must be that he can surround them with beauty. It would be grossly discourteous of an architect whose imagination had been enriched amid the loveliness of Sienna or Verona, or the Cathedral Close of Wells, to scamp his work and fob his clients off with something less than the most beautiful architecture he can create.

There is still less excuse for an Egyptian architect, who ought to know the beautiful streets of Old Cairo, deliberately to add to the weight of bad building that burdens Egypt today. He should go and look at Darb el Labana street with its seventeenth-century houses leading to the gate of the mosque placed just in the corner where the street makes an L-turn, or he should examine again the group of mosques and buildings round the Saladin Square, or the precinct of the Citadel itself. He should go to Dardiry Street and see how the architect has turned a difficult problem to good account: having to set his rectangular upstairs rooms on a curved street, he has set each one slightly askew on its bottom story, so that one end of it juts out more than the other, and supported it on brackets of varying sizes and depths to suit the amount of overhang. He should recollect all those places—villages, whole towns, quarters, squares, streets—that he longs to visit again and again, those rare achievements of beauty, civility, and culture which by their existence somewhere on the surface of the earth shore up our confidence in civilization and raise our esteem for humanity, and in the spirit of their designers he should go to work on his own task.

In designing a village the architect has need of the greatest artistic care if he is to create a unity, character, and beauty that will even approach the natural beauty that the peasants create unconsciously in their villages that have grown slowly and naturally. It is no courtesy to them to make the price of good plumbing the loss of all delight to the eye. Yet what rules should he apply, upon what principles proceed, to achieve his object? Certainly the magical effects produced in those few masterpieces of composition did not come by chance, but unfortunately the rules are not set down and tabulated. The controlled variation of line, volume, shape, color, surface, and texture in the Piazza della Signoria are the solid equivalent of modulation in music. There is an exact analogy between music and architecture, and the rules for beauty in both are the same. Where a single house may be a melody, a whole town is like a symphony, as in Wells where the town squares ascend, movement by movement, to the climax of the cathedral. But in music there are rules for the ordering of harmony and counterpoint, for avoiding ugly sounds and producing a composition that pleases the ear, while in architecture the quality of rightness must be felt intuitively. In this it is more like poetry than music. If only there could be a canon of architectural composition that would help the architect to order his light and shadow, mass and void, plain surface and decoration, so that the total design should present the same succession of themes, of crescendos and climaxes, the alternation of calm and animated passages, the unfolding of a whole symphony by Beethoven or Brahms. In the absence of any established canons of composition, the architect must rely upon his own sensibility to produce town plans to which visual modulation gives constant variety and beauty within an overall unity of conception. Such designing by its example creates, or at least demonstrates, the as yet unwritten rules of visual harmony.

Yet modulation and variety are not elements of the design that can be stuck on to an otherwise dull plan to liven it up. If the variations in shape and size do not spring directly from the needs of the buildings—and therefore the needs of their inhabitants—then they will be just sham beautification and will in fact fail in their object of pleasing the eye.

In Gourna, by compelling myself to fit the houses, which varied in size according to the area of the original houses they were replacing, into a variety of irregular plots, and by being ready to vary the plan of each to suit the people who would live in it, I made sure that I should think carefully about the design of each one, avoid the trap of adding variety without purpose, and produce a village in which the playing modulations would have a demonstrable raison d'être. I gave myself the problem of arranging a large number of different dwellings on curiously shaped and angled sites; such a problem is creative and evokes an original and honest answer, while the problem of applying some beauty to a predetermined design can never produce more than a stale and insincere plan. My irregular plan made for variety and originality in design, for constant visual interest, and precluded the building of those boring ranks of identical dwellings that are often considered to be all that the poor deserve.

Public Service Buildings and Amenities

The Mosque

A mosque is basically an enclosure to shelter worshipers during their prayers. On Friday everyone must attend prayers in the mosque, where they hear a sermon that may range over a wide variety of moral, theological, or political topics. All prayers must be directed toward Mecca, so the architecture must provide for this; that is, orientation seldom accords with the directions of the streets in a town, and in many old mosques the transition from the street door and wall to the Mecca-orientated interior poses an interesting architectural problem, solved with a pleasing arrangement of passages and areas that serves too to make one forget that the street is just outside.

In the main prayer space the congregation assembles in long rows before the sheikh, rather than in columns as in Christian churches. (To encourage punctuality at prayers, those in the front row are said to acquire extra merit.) Each prayer is called for by the muezzin from the top of a minaret; in a large mosque the call may have to be relayed to the congregation from a stand in the center of the building. The worshipers must be clean before praying, and as few can easily bathe themselves at home, all mosques provide a place and water for washing.

The most striking difference between a mosque and a Christian church is that the mosque has no centerpiece like the altar, where architecture and ritual meet at a common focus, except for a niche (the kiblah) in one wall to indicate the direction of Mecca, and a pulpit nearby from which the sheikh may speak. The mosque serves the worshipers, secluding them from the outside world, reflecting back from its plain walls their thoughts and concentrating the attention upon God. For this reason there are no pictures or statues—at the most a few texts written up—and there is no ceremony. It is not thought necessary to approach God through intermediaries nor to interpret him by means of symbols.

The portrayal of lifelike figures closed to them, Arab artists turned all their skill and sensibility into perfecting their calligraphy; in the great mosques of Islam only the word of God may decorate the walls, yet this austerely intellectual intention is beautifully subserved by the grace of the letters themselves. The curves of written Arabic are compressed and constrained within a narrow stone frieze where the characters are interlaced with formal vegetation, so that the wall is ringed with an endlessly varied pattern, in tracing which the worshiper is led back all the time to the word of God.

74–76 To make a building that should have that sober and calm air that leads to quiet meditation and prayer, I had to consider how the light would fall upon its walls and be distributed in its rooms. I believe that wherever a tradition of building exists, there the religious architecture of the locality will have grown to represent its people's idea of the holy, and I think it right to respect and keep the local forms and character—as I kept the Upper Egyptian tradition of a bold, straight outside staircase to the minaret, which stood up like a high pulpit above the mosque.

From an open courtyard with a few trees in it there opened out on four sides iwans for the four sects in Gourna. Except for the western one, these iwans were covered spaces, roofed with a whole flock of little domes dominated by a very large dome covering the pulpit and the kiblah over the main iwan. The domes were supported on arches, so that the worshipers could arrange themselves in very long ranks across the whole width of the building. The fourth iwan, on the west side of the courtyard, opposite the main part, was roofed with groin vaults, and of trapezoidal plan. The north wall of the mosque was very long and extended, at an angle to the south wall, considerably beyond the main body of the building, to contain the ablution rooms, which jutted out to the northeast. Certain other structures grew out from the main complex: a minaret with a long, straight external staircase over the front entrance, a vaulted arcade that would serve as a madyafa, a room for the sheikh, a small room for private prayer and meditation, and a storeroom.

The worshiper had a choice of two ways in. If he was clean, he would enter on the south side. He would go through a high, arched doorway beneath the staircase, into a small paved forecourt, with a flower bed in the middle, from which he would pass into the main courtyard of the mosque. On his left he would see the vaulted iwan; he might then walk to his right across the courtyard and enter the main iwan under the large barrel vault, until he stood beneath the big dome, directly in front of the kiblah. Looking around him he would see, to right and left, ranks of square columns supporting arches on which rested shallow domes. Above his head the big dome (this, by the way, was of baked brick—the only dome in Gourna not of mud brick). Lit softly from four windows in the drum and by the diffused light from the courtyard, the iwans presented a subtle and lovely pattern of space and solid amid which the worshipers might find nothing to distract them from their prayer.

If the worshiper was not clean, he would enter at a door leading directly into the ablution rooms. Here he would find on his right a passage leading past the water closets to a double row of shower cubicles, where he could wash himself completely; in front he would see a hall for minor ablutions—the washing of the head, arms, and legs. This hall had (running round two sides), a sunken trough to carry off the water from a row of taps at about chest height round the wall. In front of each tap was a block for the person washing himself to sit on. This arrangement was adopted after experiment as the one that gave the greatest comfort while one washed one's head and feet.

After washing, the worshiper would go down a long corridor,

past a small chapel for private meditation and prayer, past the storeroom door, and turn left into the main prayer space. Or he could go on into an open courtyard planted with flowers, from which he could enter the main courtyard with its three tamarisk trees and walk across the thick carpet of needles into the main iwan.

The sheikh would enter the mosque by a small door in the north wall, opposite his own house and madyafa. He was provided with a little room in the northwest corner of the mosque as a study. The room was interesting because it was entirely irregular and needed an ingenious use of all the variations on vault, arch, and dome to cover it; it held no right angles, and no two dimensions were the same in it, while from its door there was a pleasing false perspective through a row of arches in the iwan that became progressively narrower toward the far end.

Another feature of note in the mosque was its madyafa. Since most people arriving in a strange village go straight to the mosque, where they will meet various villagers, exchange news, and arrange for their lodging, I thought it desirable to provide for this habit. Against the west wall, outside, I built a long passage with a barrel vault over it, open to the north to admit the cool breeze and with a door into the forecourt. Here were seats and two water jars, so that visitors might sit and gossip in comfort.

The Marketplace

In village life market day is as much a holiday as a day of business. It is especially the women's day, the one day in the week when they can leave the confinement of the house and enjoy the freedom of walking, dawdling, and gossiping as they please. A woman will take what she has to sell—a chicken, perhaps, or a basket of eggs, butter, 77 cheese, into the marketplace, where for once the monotony and restriction of her daily life is forgotten; she will turn her wares into money and spend the rest of a long, noisy, dusty, delicious day picking over the goods on sale, fingering cloth and oddments, and assessing the quality of spice, grain, beans, and greens before buying up her groceries for the week. Above all she is living in society and feeling part of the world. Here the ancient inhibitions of her society are, by ancient custom, relaxed, and she has permission to be a member of the crowd instead of a member of the family.

Her menfolk have another manner on market day. Not for them the vulgar haggling over vegetables down around the stalls. It is their privilege to conduct the sale of large and serious animals like cows, donkeys, and camels; they sit all day long in the café, gravely bargaining, offer and counter-offer made with the slow deliberation of moves in chess, while the day passes in civilized conversation and important silences.

As the mating instinct in man has been diluted and evened out to become a continuous drab irritation, instead of the periodic sexual explosion that it is with animals, so in the city the needs of trade are served by a steady, colorless rhythmless scurry of commerce, while in the village trade has rhythm and season like all the rest of peasant life. With all their inconvenience, these intermittent bursts of trade bring great rewards in making of commerce a festive communal activity, almost a ritual, much more personal and exciting than the smooth anonymous machine it has become in the city.

In the market all the transactions for the week are concluded on that one day; it is the heart of village economy that beats once a week, and that weekly pulse shows clearly the villager's economic health. To the market comes all the produce of the district—all crops, all beasts, all local manufactures. There are not enough customers to keep many shops in a village; at the most there may be a shop selling coffee, sugar, rice, oil, and matches—all of them necessities for which there is a daily demand—but no wise merchant would keep other articles, for he would never sell them and would soon go bankrupt. Only on market day can the villager find grain and vegetables, for in the country where every square inch of land is given to cash crops there are no kitchen gardens, and vegetables come from the market gardens near the city. Only then can the peasant buy new animals or the housewife her pins and needles. The peasant and his wife will find in the market, cloth, clothes, shoes, and cosmetics; all sorts of food; furnishings like rugs, carpets, and linen; pots, pans, and primus stoves; axes, spades, and baskets. Here in the market you can see at a glance—or almost!—how rich the village is. Not only that, but you can, too, examine the villagers' taste in household goods.

A walk through the stalls in the market will provide evidence of the peasants' changing sensibility. The goods that sell are no longer the most beautiful. How many local weaves have disappeared before the annihilating competition of brash factory prints, how the sober traditional wares have been ousted from the market by gaudy plastic goods! Homemade simplicity gives way before the overelaborate mass-produced trinkets of the city; whenever you find some beautiful village-made article, you are told that it's out of date and no longer made. What defense can the feeble peasant culture put up against the clamorous attack of Western industry?

For all the color and excitement that market day brings into the village week, in most villages the marketplace itself is squalidly commercial. The monopoly of marketplaces in Egypt is owned by a private company, and only on this company's grounds can markets get a licence. Usually a barren square of waste land is fenced with barbed wire, provided with a gate and a tax collector, and little or nothing else is done for the comfort of the people who come crowding and jostling in with their goods and their animals. The site is seldom shaded from the sun, nor does it have much in the way of permanent buildings or water.

78–86 I planned that the marketplace of Gourna should provide a more amenable background to the weekly market. The animals would be accommodated at permanent mangers, each set at the right height for camel, goat, or donkey, and all shaded by numerous trees laid out in a regular pattern. The stall holders would be provided with a row of shady vaults under which to spread their wares, and there would be a café for the men to sit in.

The marketplace, as I have said, was situated in the southeast corner of the village, convenient to the railway halt. To enter it from the railway side one would pass under a monumental gateway with two arches, and could then look straight down the very broad road to the other gate, on the village side, with its single arch and large pigeon tower on the left. On market day this roadway would become the pitch of the grain merchants, who would spread their heaps of golden corn under striped awnings all the way down it. Immediately to the right you would see the café, roofed with six domes, and, stretching along the northeast wall to the other gate, a row of fourteen deep vaults, in which were the stalls. Deep inside each of these vaults, on a low platform, the merchant would squat in the middle of his goods and bargain with the crowd of women before him.

On your left you would see a mass of trees, regularly spaced like an orchard to shade the maximum area, and beneath them the long mangers, each with a water point at the end, each with a number of animals tethered at it, and between these mangers men walking and examining the beasts, while an odd camel, donkey, or cow might be paraded up and down by its owner, on display. These animals, being for sale, would be charged a toll on entering the market; the others, which just brought their masters and goods to market, would be kept outside. I provided a donkey park, likewise planted with trees for shade and with mangers and water points, just outside the marketplace, by the railway.

The Theater

A peasant society is, in Egypt, still very different from urban society. In a village all sorts of arts still exist—pottery, weaving, and metalwork, for example—and into the texture of village life are worked many ceremonies and forms of recreation that are just as much a part of folk art as are the manufacturing arts.

At a wedding, for example, there is a band to provide music and a dancer, while the young men of the village come strutting in to show 87 their prowess at quarterstaff fighting and to challenge the champion of the badana. Quarterstaff is a sport that goes back to the time of the Pharaohs, and it is still widely practiced all over rural Egypt. Whenever two or three peasants get together in the fields, round a fire at night, perhaps, a couple of them will start sparring with their sticks. On more public occasions, as weddings, the fighting can become quite brisk, and the protagonists sometimes get hurt. Yet, dangerous or not, this fighting is a better entertainment for spectator and player than any that the town provides. The cinema and radio cannot give the audience that sense of community that a live show does. Only in a theater or watching a real game can the audience feel that it is a single spirit, reaching as one person to the fortunes of player or actor. That same audience, broken up into the isolation of its several houses, cannot be conscious of itself at all. Even in the darkness of a cinema, the story on the screen proceeds rigidly, never bending or adapting its speed or tone to the mood or number of the watchers.

Then why not provide Gourna with a permanent theater, where we could present the dances, songs, and sports of everyday life and preserve them, too, from the inevitable extinction that awaited them if they were left unsupported to face the competition of film and radio. In a theater they could find a pleasing background, an enthusiastic audience, and, above all, a permanent venue that would make possible more frequent shows than the occasional weddings of village life did.

I must not pretend that a theater is a customary feature in Egyptian villages; indeed, that in Gourna is the only one there is. Yet it is, to my mind, as necessary as a village hall or a school, and ours has proved its worth again and again with unforgettable performances that have caught the imagination not only of the villagers themselves but of tourists and visitors from other countries.

The theater was something between a Greek and an Elizabethan 88–90 one. It was an unroofed trapezoidal space, with the stage occupying the large side, rows of stepped seats lining the other three sides, and the arena or orchestra in the middle. The stage was a simple stone platform about 3 feet high and 35 feet wide, open to the sky and set flush with the proscenium wall. On it was a permanent set, providing two scenes, one an interior or courtyard, the other a street. The interior scene occupied most of the stage, and consisted of an entrance in the middle of the back wall, with a balcony over it, reached by a staircase on the spectator's left or from backstage by a door giving straight on to it. There were further side entrances, one to the spectator's left and others from behind a zigzag permanent screen on the spectator's right. This screen, pierced by two windows and a doorway set against the lines of perspective, suggested (to a pliable imagination) the street façade. The whole stage area except for the proscenium opening was enclosed by a wall some 25 feet high.

On each side of this stage area was a lobby, roofed with six domes, that served as an entrance. The considerable backstage space would be used for storage and as a dressing-room for the actors.

91 In front of the stage was an arena about 36 feet square, sand-floored, that might be used for performances or displays like quarterstaff fighting. It was reached by a flight of steps on each side of the stage.

The audience was accommodated on six rows of stone seats, banked as in a Greek theater, but around the three sides of the square arena. These seats would hold about five hundred spectators, while another two hundred could stand in the broad gallery running round the back of the seat banks. This gallery had a pergola over it, was walled by claustras on each side, and at the back had a plain wall with a projection room in it for film shows.

The performances were nothing like plays in the European 92 theater. There was no written script and no producer. A stage manager would decide the order of presentation, and contrive to get on and off the stage a succession of dancers, mimes, and bards, so as to tell a connected story.

Before a chattering audience packed on the stone benches and standing in the galleries behind, under a cool starry sky, the stage stands empty and dark. Quietly, from somewhere behind the stage, a solitary voice is heard singing. The talking dies down and the audience lean forward intently as the song comes nearer. There is no light yet, as the singer emerges and crosses the stage, a dark leisurely shadow, to settle himself down slowly and comfortably in a corner. He strikes a match and lights a fire ready laid there, and with his back to the audience goes on with his song. On the balcony above, a window opens, then a door, and a girl comes out to listen. She hangs a small lantern up beside the door, and saunters down the steps and over to the singer, who sings on, not noticing her. She steals past him, out through the door of the street façade. One or two friends of the singer come in and sit down round his fire, listening.

Then the men of the rival tribe begin drifting in, to gather on the other side of the stage, where they light a fire and bring their own singer. The two tribes begin to compete for the hand of the girl, in a formal exchange of taunts and challenges. Each poet in turn sings a verse about his rival, which is picked up and repeated in chorus by his companions, who then sit down in pretended indifference while the other poet composes a reply to cap the taunt.

Verse answers verse across the stage as the two singers compete in skill, chorus follows chorus, while the young men finger their staves, edgy and proud, fierce to battle for the girl. One by one and two by two they drop down to the arena, where a third fire is lit, and there, silhouetted against its flickering light, they strike the first sharp blows in the struggle. More men crowd round them, on foot and mounted on horses and donkeys, and as one fighter or another is defeated, another man takes his place.

As the contest gains in pace and excitement rises, so more fires are lit, until the whole theater is jumping and crackling in the blaze of half-a-dozen bonfires, and the fight is hugely shadowed on the walls as the young men prance and spring. Sticks clack and whistle through the air, and the cries of the actors are echoed back by the audience, every man of it on his feet and yelling his support at the top of his voice. Usually, in fact, the audience joins in, men jumping down from their seats to replace the fallen warrior.

But the fight is over; one man has fought his way to the top, overcome all challengers, and won the girl. He is carried triumphantly to the stage, while the mob disperses—some to the stage after him, some back to their seats in the audience. The wedding ceremony is prepared, with the victor enthroned in the middle of the stage. The musicians gather, there are dances and a wedding procession all by the gay firelight, until at last the party breaks up, and as the fires die down, one by one, the guests go off, singing away into the distance. One fire still burns, where the first singer sits, his tribe defeated and his back to the bridal couple. The thin notes of his ballad fill the theater as his fire burns lower and goes out. The only light now comes from one little lamp on the balcony.

The bride rises, leads the bridegroom up the steps, in through the door on to the balcony. She takes down the lamp and shuts the door. Alone in the darkness the singer gets up and wanders slowly off; his plaintive song is heard for a little while, growing fainter, till it fades away entirely. The show is over.

Schools

At about this time, the Egyptian government presented itself with a rare opportunity in architecture. A new school building program was launched to provide four thousand schools for Egypt, the majority to be in villages. With enthusiastic official backing, new ideas in architecture could be taken into the remotest corners of the country, buildings made that would immediately become part of the people's daily life and start an architectural renaissance to match the cultural renaissance that the new schools would initiate.

By starting so late, compared with other countries, Egypt was well placed to learn from the experience of all the other countries of the world in school building. These had much to teach her; in England, for example, all the schools built before 1939 had been found to fall short of the postwar standards laid down for new schools. In America years of study had produced the most extravagantly spacious and richly equipped schools. There was no lack of good advice on school building.

Yet the Ministry of Public Works began to erect a uniform type of school in all these different villages. I was shown a design for a type of school to be located in Alexandria and Nubia—one 650 miles south of the other, with a totally different climate and type of pupil.

There used to be a style of architecture called the *amiri,* introduced by the khedive or the amir for the palace and the government buildings of the land. Adopted by these alien rulers to mark themselves off from the natives they despised, at best never more than a dingy imitation of European magnificence, it became when transplanted into the mud villages of Upper Egypt, cut down in scale for economy and prominently sited to impress the peasants, as visually devastating as a dustbin on a flowerbed. The squat façade and regimented windows promise dusty, rectangular classrooms inside, the uncompromising city-souled stance declares the school twin brother to the police station, and its sheer ugliness ought to ensure that it is never permitted the remotest connection with education. Inside, it might as well be a post office as a school. I remember one such building where, under the full blaze of the Egyptian sun, the lighting in the classrooms had been so bungled that the electric light had to be on from eight in the morning till seven in the evening. The ministerial style has, in the name of economy and modernity, condemned our villages to schools without the beginnings of the internationally accepted minimum facilities.

The amiri style has fallen into deserved disrepute, but the spirit that inspired it still flourishes, and to-day a new amir style—a stale French-modern architecture—is spreading across Egypt as one generation of architects after another catches up with the fashion. Although the ministerial style is so irrelevant to the needs of country education, however, we should not uncritically embrace the standards and ideas of even the most enlightened foreign architects. Even among the most enlightened school architects, there is a very prevalent and fundamentally wrong way of approaching the problem of building a school. The architect considers the function of the building, observes the flow of pupils, the rhythm of the teaching day, the processes of transferring knowledge in the classroom; he works out the optimum temperatures and lighting intensities, and from the beginning he sees the school as a factory and devotes his skill to streamlining the ordering of children. True, they are handled as tenderly as pigs in a canning factory, conveyed from stage to stage of their educational experience with smooth, soundproof, air-conditioned, and hygienic efficiency, but the architect hasn't even begun to address himself to the task of school design.

Only when he has provided these mechanical prerequisites, which should be incorporated without question or argument in every school and accepted by the architect as a minimum standard, as natural to a school as a roof or a floor, only then can he start to consider the real problem of designing the building. He is rather like the pianist, who can only start to interpret the music he plays after he has mastered the technique of piano playing.

He must approach the design of his school as he does the design of a church or a mosque, for it is the same sort of building. In the school it is the children's souls that will grow, and the building must invite them to fly, not cramp them like a Chinese shoe. With a few fateful lines on his drawing board, the architect decrees the boundaries of imagination, the peace of mind, the human stature of generations to come. As long as his school shall stand, its walls and windows will speak to little children at their most unprotected age. He has the grave duty of creating in a building a source of love and encouragement for these children and must let nothing come before it.

If love goes into the work, it will always show. If the architect considers every detail lovingly, seeing the children living and learning within his walls, following them in their work and play, if he sees them as they really are, not as miniature grown-ups, he cannot help but give them a building that will be kind to them.

The average adult, with thirty years' growth of thick skin around him, can scarcely imagine the precarious bases on which a child's confidence rests. Yet the school architect must see the world through a child's eyes, not merely to understand a child's needs in size and space, but even more, to understand what will comfort and what will frighten a child.

From the moment of birth onwards the child experiences the daily sapping of that sense of absolute security—the biological security of the womb—that he once knew. More or less roughly, according to his mother's care, he learns to depend upon himself in his encounters with a hostile environment, but it takes him a long time.

Many full-grown men find that their hearts sink as they meet some adversary in their life, and they long to fly back to the safe retreat of their mother's arms. How much more overwhelming must a child's despair be on meeting the unfriendly world.

The architect must engage all his skill to make the classroom a room that will engender the confidence and sense of security that a good home does. If he does not, he is crippling the educator's best efforts at the outset. That is why the teachers and architects who try to cater for future changes in educational theory by designing classrooms with movable partition walls which can be shifted about to suit new standards are defeating their own ends. Shapeless classrooms that are forever changing their appearance, being cut up with screens and having their furniture rearranged, produce restless, nervous children. They are featureless classrooms, blank as an empty shop window or exhibition hall, and they cannot become familiar and friendly to the children who live in them, while the hesitation and uncertainty that inspired the design can only undermine the child's slowly maturing self-confidence.

I used the word "live" quite deliberately, for a school to which children come for a few hours a day, to be filled up with lessons and sent home, is a clumsy and cramping aid to education. The classroom should be a home to the children, where they can have a life of their own, and not just a place where they can be gathered together under the eye of a teacher. Consider, for example, the recommended area for a classroom. The growth characteristics of children have somewhere been studied, and it has been shown that a child between the ages of six and eight needs three square meters of floor space in a classroom. Further, one teacher is supposed to be able to handle thirty children; so an adequate classroom needs ninety square meters of floor space. But this means a room of 9 × 10 meters, which will look huge, like a garage, and will in no way seem friendly and trustworthy to the child.

Simple arithmetic will not provide the answers in designing really beautiful classrooms.

From my own schooldays, I preserve almost no memories of my primary school (Mohammed Aly School), which was designed and built by the Ministry of Public Works on the usual plan of a row of identical classrooms with a corridor in front of them. This was, if not actually ugly, certainly characterless and artistically neutral.

My secondary school—the Khediveya School—was quite different, and from it I preserve the most vivid and delightful memories of unexpected corners, odd-shaped open spaces, halls and classrooms of all shapes and sizes, and lovely gardens. The casual surprises of the architecture must have quickened the imagination and sensibility of many schoolboys, who doubtless absorbed their quota of instruction too. Yet the building was not designed as a school at all; it was an old palace.

There had been no school in old Gourna, and in the normal way the village would have had to wait its turn in the school-building program, to receive eventually a charmless building in the ministerial modern style.

93–99

I thought it would be a good idea to forestall this by building a school—or rather two schools, one for boys and one for girls—according to my own standards. This would perhaps induce the ministry to provide some teachers ahead of schedule, and could even become a model for later school building in the district. When the buildings were complete, the ministry was very pleased with them; they liked the style and even more they liked the cost. I had, of course, built them in mud brick, and when by the ministry's invitation I built another school at Fares, it worked out at about one-third the price of the usual design.

So that the classrooms be kept calm and free of dust, they were disposed around paved courtyards, rather as the iwans of the traditional mosque schools locked into the central courtyard of the mosque. A carefully planned layout—not just an accidental open space with a flower bed in it—is very valuable in organizing a number of separate blocks into a coherent composition. Quite often each block will be well designed, with its several rooms and corridors arranged pleasingly, but the blocks themselves will be scattered haphazardly and meaninglessly about the site. It will be left to the gardener to try to tie them together with lawns and flowers. Now if the architect treats the outdoor space between his buildings with the same respect as the indoor space enclosed by his rooms, and consciously uses the various blocks to give shape to this space, he will not waste any of the site. Every square foot, roofed or open, will contribute meaning to the whole. Why, these open spaces can be turned to quite practical uses: a particular juxtaposition of buildings may suggest a stage, and so a quadrangle becomes an auditorium, or it may prove possible to use a patio as an open-air assembly space or classroom. Again, a series of open spaces leading out from classroom to street, so that the child goes through cloister, patio, quadrangle, and playground, each with its particular character, will give him a pleasant succession of feelings on his way out of and into school.

As the children came into the school they would enter a small courtyard with an ornamental pond in the middle. The design of this was copied from a wall painting in the eighteenth-dynasty tomb of Rekhmire; it was to be a little square basin with a cluster of tall palms planted regularly round the edge, giving a charming suggestion of candles on a birthday cake and showing the water between their stems. Giving onto this courtyard was the assembly hall and the school offices, including the headmaster's room and a room for the visiting doctor.

The children would walk sedately through this courtyard, which would welcome them with its beauty, and pass under an archway into the main courtyard between the two rows of classrooms. This courtyard was paved, so as not to be dusty, and had the middle of it planted with trees.

There were four classrooms on each side, each roofed with a large shallow dome and around 400 square feet in area. Because of the need for a square shape for the dome to sit on, the extra space needed was added in the form of vaulted iwans on two sides of the square. This arrangement gave a sufficiently large classroom but one that was divided into three clear and distinct areas. In my opinion this is a very humane kind of classroom, because the boy does not feel lost in a vast unfriendly room, but is always sitting in a space to his own scale. Rooms like this are a happy consequence of working in so humble a material as mud brick, which imposes structural limitations that force us to build from the ground upward, bearing in mind all the time the problem of covering our building. We can't just lay a concrete slab over our walls to roof them; every brick makes some contribution to the roof and bears some responsibility for the final shape of the space that we are enclosing; the limits of its natural strength make us divide up the roof space into several human-sized elements.

At the far end of the classroom-courtyard was the school mosque. Inside, the most interesting feature proved to be the lighting. This was provided by four small windows set high up in the dome, so that an extremely pleasant and restful illumination was diffused evenly throughout the whole interior space. Calm lighting like this made the building serious in atmosphere and encouraged peaceful meditation. There was no dazzling blaze of light from an unshielded window, nor any distracting views of outside, but, like the big village mosque, this little one returned the worshiper's thoughts in upon himself and encouraged his meditation.

It has occurred to me since that this is the best way to light a classroom. In Egypt at least one cannot stand too much brightness, and classroom windows set at eye level, which admit the direct outside light—all the quivering glare reflected off the dusty streets and dazzling white walls—create big contrasts of lighting intensity, so that reading becomes positively uncomfortable. Yet to make a classroom lit just by high windows would be to make it too enclosed and austere—a classroom is not a mosque. It would be a good idea to provide a little privacy outside in the form of a small garden with low-growing flowers and grass, and to let the pupils see it through low windows set at floor level, in the Japanese way. This garden could be backed by a wall that did not reflect the light, so that each window would become a living picture, in restful low tones, to refresh the children during their lessons. This, combined with windows high up in the dome to provide gentle, even lighting, and perhaps with stained glass windows to amuse the children further, would make a lively, cheerful, yet calm classroom, and this is certainly what I would do if I had to design another school.

100–101 The classrooms were provided with a simple and very effective system of ventilation. There was above each room a square tower like a chimney with a large opening facing north. The cool north breeze would come in through the opening, high up and dust free, and would flow down over trays of wet charcoal, set like baffles in- 102–104 side the chimney. This device produced a drop in temperature of 10°C.

The Hammam

In a laudable desire to encourage cleanliness among the peasants, the government had provided public showers in a number of villages. Though the thought was good, in practice these showers were not used, and stand today, forlorn memorials to the clumsy, institution-minded public benefactors who installed them. The peasants did not use them because, in the first place, the government purse didn't stretch to the provision of hot water, and nobody can be blamed for not feeling enthusiastic about a cold shower. Then again, the attendants were government employees, who were too uninterested to do even their proper job of keeping the establishments clean, let alone try to make them attractive, while the slow operation of government routine frequently left the baths without soap.

A public bath housed in an uninviting building, tucked away in a back street or attached to the mosque latrines, its welcome as cold as its water, is never going to become the social institution it ought to be. Yet at one time the *hammam* was the center of the most fashionable society in every town in Egypt.

When Napoleon invaded Egypt, the hammam, or turkish bath, was a flourishing institution. It had come to complement the mosque, facilitating the customary Friday-morning "major" ablutions of the worshipers, and so important was it considered that to build a hammam was held to be a charitable deed of the highest order. Safgan el Saouri says that no *dirham* can be better spent by a believer than that which the hammam owner spends on improving his establishment. The hygienic virtues of the hammam are justly celebrated, and attested today by the popularity of turkish baths in many of the cities of Europe and America. Certainly, in those days anyone who felt an illness coming on would, to forestall it, go straight to the hammam for an invigorating steam bath, for illnesses were held to arise from lack of perspiration. The plentiful sweat induced by the steam is so patently good for you that taking a bath assumed a ritaul importance in life, and an illness was not considered to be completely past until the patient had taken his *ghosl el seha,* or bath of health, which confirmed his recovery.

Yet, more than this, the hammam was a gathering place where men could exchange news, gossip, conduct business and discuss political matters in an atmosphere of luxury. For the women even more, the hammam would provide an excuse to escape from the restriction of the house. When the hammam was in fashion, it played a most important part in the life of townswomen, who would put on their best clothes and most valuable jewels for their weekly visit. There they would choose brides for their sons and brothers, and arrange their marriages, while just before the wedding day itself the bride would be taken to the hammam to be combed, scented, and depilated, and made ready for the ceremony.

It should be emphasized that the hammam was used by everyone, rich and poor, even those who had private hammams in their own houses, because it was a public meeting place, and that in towns the hammam declined only when the rich moved to modern quarters unprovided with hammams. Then, when the only customers were the poor, the standard of service and cleanliness went down, and the hammam degenerated to its present squalid condition—a dirty relic in the slums of our big cities.

I thought that if the hammam could be reintroduced into the Egyptian village, it would at once prove more acceptable than the government's shower baths. It has an air and tradition of luxury, and under a private owner it would give more solicitous attention to its patrons than the showers did. Not only that, but it would be more inviting, because hot. A steam bath cleans the skin much better than a cold shower, and if one is massaged as well, the whole body is relaxed and toned up, so that the bath becomes a mental as well as physical refreshment, relieving nervous strain, anxiety, and worry.

If we were to reestablish the hammam, it would clearly be advisable not to change its general character, so that those people who were already acquainted with its benefits would continue to be attracted by it. When the prescriptive sociologist wishes to manipulate people into the patterns and activities he favors, it is by means of institutions like the hammam that he will be most successful. As nature gets her essential work done by making it pleasant, so that people and animals even fight to eat or to reproduce the species, so the wise sociologist or politician will use some irresistible lure rather than compulsion to achieve his purpose. The hammam, I hoped, would tempt people into yet another web of social integration and help to give everyone in the village a wide, varied, and strong collection of social contacts and at the same time an opportunity to delouse himself.

For a village the simplest way of equipping a hammam is to have a boiler whose steam is led to the steam room, and from which hot water can be piped for the bathers' individual ablutions. In the Gourna hammam the bather would come in, pay the *hammamgi* at a counter by the entrance, and be given towels and a dirty clothes bag. He would then go through to the *maslakh,* or undressing room, and take his clothes off in a cubicle there. He would hand in his clothes to be washed, and go into one of the bathing cubicles. Here he would mix hot and cold water from taps in a *korna,* or mixing bowl, and, sitting on a low stool, would pour the water over himself with the *tasset el hammam*—the traditional small bowl. When washed, he would pass into the steam room, stay there for a time, perhaps being massaged, then go out into a warm room, and thence to the counter where he would collect his clothes, now laundered. He would go into one of the dressing cubicles—separate from the undressing ones, to ensure that they were really clean—and when dressed would pass into the rest room to chat and perhaps smoke a narghile with his friends. This route ensured that, as far as possible, dirty or infested clothing would not come into contact with clean clothes, and the hot water system was cheap and practical for a village which could not afford hot showers.

The Brickyard

Gourna was to be built of mud bricks; making these is a craft, and involves several distinct operations. You don't just scoop up some mud and fashion each brick as you need it. The standard Gourna brick was of a set size and consistency, so as to be a dependable unit that could be incorporated in our planning. To make it you need ordinary earth from the site, sand from the desert, straw, and water. The earth and sand are mixed in the proportion of 1 : ⅓ by volume. This mixture, we found by experiment, gave good results, producing a brick that did not shrink excessively (pure earth shrinks up to 37 percent after it has dried) and was economical in straw. To one cubic meter of this we added 45 pounds of straw, and mixed it all with water. The mixture was then left to soak and ferment for at least forty-eight hours; the fermentation produces lactic acids that make the bricks stronger and less absorbent than more hastily made ones, while the straw so mixes with the earth that the brick acquires a highly desirable homogeneity of texture that an unfermented one does not have.

When the brick mixture is fermented, it is carried in baskets to the molding place where the brick maker takes a small hand mold. This mold is simply a rectangular frame with no top or bottom; the brick maker puts it on the ground, fills it with mud, and lifts it up. The molded brick stays behind on the ground, which has been strewn with sand and straw. This method means that the mixture must be very wet, so that the mold can slide off without one's having to press down on the mud at all. A wet mixture has several disadvantages: the bricks shrink too much, so that they sometimes crack or warp, and they pick up a lot of dirt underneath as they are drying, so that the mason has to waste time cleaning each one before he lays it. I designed a hand press that enabled us to make bricks under pressure with a much drier mixture, thus obviating these disadvantages. The freshly molded bricks are left in the sun to dry, being turned on edge after three days and taken off to the brick stacks after six days. There they remain for as long as possible (all summer, preferably) to dry out thoroughly before being used in building.

In building Gourna we would need millions of bricks. To produce them on this scale involved working out methods of ensuring that the output was kept high and that the quality was consistently good, as well as ways of controlling the cost of labor. Our brickyard was de-
105 signed to this end. Brick manufacture occupies a six-day cycle, and so each team was provided with six mixing troughs and six molding grounds. Earth was to be brought from the Fadleia Canal tippings by Decauville trucks, and sand from the desert by lorry. The troughs were to be filled in rotation, one per day, and left for two days; then the bricks would be made. Each molding ground was big enough to hold 3,000 bricks—the estimated daily output of a four-man team—and these bricks would be laid out in rows of 32 bricks each, thus making it easy to check the number made. The number 32 was arrived at by observing how many bricks a seated man can conveniently lay side by side. One man can lay 16, two men, 32. The team would move on the next day to the next molding ground, but the day after that someone would come back to put the bricks in the first one on edge, and on the sixth day the bricks would be carted off.

Working Day	Fill Trough	Mold Bricks	Turn Bricks	Remove Bricks
1	(1)	(5)	(3)	(6)
2	(2)	(6)	(4)	(1)
3	(3)	(1)	(5)	(2)
4	(4)	(2)	(6)	(3)
5	(5)	(3)	(1)	(4)
6	(6)	(4)	(2)	(5)
7	(1)	(5)	(3)	(6)
8	(2)	(6)	(4)	(1)
9	(3)	(1)	(5)	(2)
10	(4)	(2)	(6)	(3)
11	(5)	(3)	(1)	(4)
12	(6)	(4)	(2)	(5)

In fact we had five teams working; so we had five sets of troughs and molding grounds altogether.

Ideally, such a brickyard should be situated outside the area scheduled for building, so that it does not have to be moved when its site is needed. Furthermore, if it is outside the building area, it can be made permanent; it will always be useful to the village, which will always be building and repairing houses. It should, too, be situated between a canal to supply water, and a drain to take it away, and close to the supply of earth; if an artificial lake has been dug, then it will be close to the tippings from that.

In Gourna we were working on a restricted site and could not build a permanent brickyard.

The Peasant House

There is a difference in kind between a peasant's house and the house of a townsman. The peasant family's whole life depends upon one or two cows and an acre or so of soil. If the cow dies or the crop fails, the family must starve, for there is no insurance scheme to save him, no dole, no benevolent governmental soup kitchens.

The difference between a peasant's way of life and a townsman's is reflected in their houses. Whereas in the town a house is meant to accommodate just the people who live in it, in a village the houses must hold a large variety of bulky stores and the owner's cattle as well. In the town the kitchen is a small room with a stove in it, a basin, and a tap. In the country the service area spreads all over the house. Instead of a little cupboard hanging on the wall, with two or three tins and a loaf of bread in it, there are belongings and stores hanging from the roof, clothes strung across the corners on a bit of rope, grain piled up on the floor, and odd possessions stuffed into little holes made in the mud walls or balanced on mud ledges that serve as shelves. Instead of an electric power point or a small tin of kerosene, the house is crammed with fuel: faggots, maize and cotton stalks, dried dung, all heaped up against the walls or piled on the roof.

There are hens running in and out among the dust and babies, there are even cows inside the house itself, so that it looks more like a barn with some people putting up in it than a real family home. The peasant lives so close to want that he cannot afford to neglect even the most cumbersome economy. He will laboriously gather in fuel and bake his own bread because it saves him a farthing a week. He will live on sour cheese from thin skimmed milk because he has sold the butter for money. He will never taste a green vegetable because all his land is growing cash crops. He is in the grip of creeping famine; although the Nile will never fail and the crops are always assured, this in Egypt, where twenty-seven people live off every six acres of farmland, merely assures the peasant of the same inadequate nourishment as last year. To hold on to even his present miserable living standard he must treasure every last leaf and grain of salable crop and treat his cows as jealously and tenderly as his children—more so, in fact, for he will say that if a baby dies he can make plenty more free, but if a cow dies he must pay to replace it.

So we had to allow generous storage space and large cattlesheds in the houses for Gourna. We thought of various alternatives. The fuel that is generally stored on housetops in Egypt often causes the most devastating fires that spread and burn down whole villages, cattle, crops, and all. Therefore it seemed sensible to store these flammable materials safely in some big communal building, just as it seemed more hygienic to have common cowsheds far away from the houses. But the peasants would part with neither crops nor cattle. How could the women go running about the public streets all day to fetch fuel and to milk the cows? And besides, a cow needs constant attention and would be unhappy away from its family.

Then why not scatter the houses about the fields, so that each one could have space for all its needs? But this would not do, because an isolated, small, and poorly protected house is too tempting a lure for thieves, and also it would be more difficult to supply services to scattered houses than to a compact, small village.

I planned later another village in which the houses backed onto vegetable gardens where cabbages and fruit trees would grow and where the cows would walk up to their stalls in the houses along little paths beside these gardens. This would preserve an air of the country right through the village, and make it a small-scale garden city—a "vegetable garden village," in fact. But in Gourna we had to huddle the buildings together because the site was small, and we had to give each house its cattleshed and its storage space inside the restricted area allotted to it. For this reason, too, all the houses had to be two-story ones.

Housing the cattle, storing their fodder, dealing with the manure, finding room for fuel, odd crops, food, and personal effects—these were the problems which had confronted the peasants for many years. Their solutions were often clumsy, primitive, and very inconvenient, but we could learn from them. Sometimes we could take a positive hint, as from their way of grouping all the services around the courtyard. Sometimes we could see what not to do, like storing flammable crops and fodder on the rooftops of close-packed houses.

106–112

The household services—cooking, washing, and latrines—were grouped around the central courtyard, which had a loggia where the family could eat. Also on the ground floor were the guestroom and the cattlesheds. Upstairs were the bedrooms and the fuel storage bin. This was located convenient to the cooking fire and oven, but guarded carefully from the danger of fire by high sides and by being so situated that it was shielded from the next-door bin by the mass of the bedrooms.

The anthropologist, concerned with man, is apt to mark the stages in man's progress by the tools he uses, so that civilization proceeds from the stone age, through the bronze and iron ages, to the age of steam and electricity. The architect might well draw up a parallel scale, in which the graduations would be the domestic conveniences used by man—and woman. He would note the kitchen sink age, the plumbing age, the refrigerator age, and so on. He would also observe that most peasants are, domestically, well back in the stone age.

To equip his kitchen up to the most modern standards would cost the peasant more than he earns in a lifetime. A refrigerator or an electric stove would be as far beyond his means as an aeroplane; even such apparently humble appliances as a hardware sink or a porcelain washstand are far too dear for him. Quite apart from the fact that his village has no electricity or drainage, he cannot afford the plainest domestic necessities as sold in shops. If his house is to be made pleasanter to live in and easier to manage, then simple homemade appliances must be devised to do the same job as the costly, factory-made ones of the city.

The peasant lacks a few things without which he cannot improve his home much. The first is space; the second is an ability to arrange the separate units into a pleasing and efficient whole; the third is certain materials that are needed, if only in small quantities, to make improvements in his surroundings. With a little cement, a few pipes, a bag of gypsum, he could make himself an oven which would not smoke the rooms, a hygienic latrine and a system to give him running water. With a little imagination he could make himself a platform to raise his cooking fire out of the dust.

Cement and gypsum do not exist in the village, but pottery does. In Upper Egypt the villagers store their oil, milk, and water in unglazed pots that they make themselves. For water this is an excellent practice, as it gets cool, but for oil and milk it is not, for these substances when they seep through the pottery go bad in the middle of it. If only the villagers would glaze their pots, how much more sensible it would be. And if they had a good glaze that could be fired at a low temperature, we could use the village kiln to make glazed pottery for a lot of other purposes too. Glazed tiles, if they could be cheaply produced, would greatly lift the standard of comfort of the houses; we could tile parts of walls so that they would be easily washed; wherever people rubbed on them or water might splash them, tiles would make the housework lighter and the walls brighter. Around the sides of the built-in bed, at the back of seats, on the floor of the cooking platform, as lining for the cupboards instead of vermin-collecting mud, we should put our smooth, impermeable tiles. Tiles would introduce variety, too, so that the texture of the walls would alternate between bright, hard, colorful surfaces and the soft mat of whitewashed mud. Even the human body has its soft surface—the skin—and its hard surface—the nails; the tiles would be the nails of the mud brick house.

A flourishing tile industry would also encourage decorative art. In Rosetta and Damietta, where tiles were once produced, they were largely used to make decorative dadoes in the houses there. If our tiles became popular, we could have the children painting them and build up a school of painters in Gourna.

It should not be too difficult to start such an industry. The ancient Egyptians could make ceramics perfectly well; in the third-dynasty tomb of Zoser the walls are covered with blue tiles. The tombs in old Gourna are full of statuettes and scarabs in glazed pottery. The antique fakers today can still make imitation scarabs like the ancient ones, though they usually get the glaze by melting it off bits of ancient pottery, rather than making a fresh one from raw materials. So perfect are the imitations, and so beautifully modeled and engraved, that they fetch high prices even when known to be modern. One of the best craftsmen in this line was Sheikh Omar el Mata'ani, who could sell his scarabs for L.E. 2 each. I wanted him to help me form the school of glazed pottery and ceramics, but nothing would persuade him to part with his professional secrets. His reluctance, though perhaps prompted by an understandable fear of competition, was very frustrating to me. We should have to start a school where the craft of pottery could be taught scientifically, where we could carry out research into glazes that would run at the temperature of the local kilns, and we should try to design simple kilns that could achieve higher temperatures. Such a school would promote a village industry that with time and breakages would establish itself permanently and would evolve its own methods and patterns.

The Bedroom

The shapes of the rooms in the houses grew from the nature of the building material. Mud brick undergoes a change in its physical properties when it sets dry and hard and when it gets wet again.

There is a room plan that seems to lend itself particularly to mud brick architecture. A square, domed room with vaulted alcoves off it, reproducing the ka'a layout of an old Arab house with its high central hall, clear of furniture, perhaps with a small fountain in the middle, and the iwans leading off it, each with its built-in seats, its carpet spread across the middle of the floor, and its runners round the edge for people to walk on. Houses like these may be found in old Cairo. Their characteristic central hall—the dorka'a—derives from an open courtyard, and the whole plan is reminiscent of that of an old Iraqi house or the earlier houses of Fostat, with central courtyard and the iwans at the sides. I had used the basic plan in my pre-Gourna houses; I used it in the school, for the classrooms, and it came very naturally for private rooms in New Gourna too.

All the strength of a curved mud brick roof derives from its geometrical shape. To make so humble and weak a material span a room, one must be exceptionally careful in designing the vault and very generous with one's safety margin. Now, though a vault is fairly strong and convenient in many ways, it is not as strong as a dome. Where a mud brick barrel vault may span three meters, a dome will span five. Its spherical shape has all the virtues of an eggshell or of the modern concrete shells with their double curvature that are being used today to cover concert halls, hangars, and grandstands all over Europe and America.

The greatest enemy of mud brick is damp. The mud may get wet from rain, from dew, from capillary attraction out of the ground, or simply from the humidity in the air. To keep it dry, or otherwise circumvent the effects of damp, one may apply various remedies. Seepage from below must be prevented, and a damp-roof course is indispensable, while the bricks may be protected by waterproof plaster made of bitumen-stabilized earth. Once mud bricks are protected from damp, they will last forever. There are domed and vaulted buildings, quite unprotected, in Bagawat and Kharga Oasis, that have withstood for 1,600 years the winds and sandstorms of the desert, simply because they don't get wet.

But for the ordinary peasant, living in a damp place, these kinds of protection are too expensive or not to be found close at hand. Although Gourna has a very dry climate, I wanted it to be a true model village, whose buildings could be copied safely by any peasant with no technical help anywhere in Egypt. For that reason I chose a dome span of three meters and a vault span of two-and-a-half meters, increasing the thickness of the walls on each side of the iwans by twenty-five centimeters. This makes the structure extremely rigid, so that if it is protected only by an ordinary damp-proof course and a simple plaster it will stand any weather anywhere.

To roof such a room, we first build the vault over the iwan. We then use this vault as a centering for the arch that has to support the dome on the open side. With two rings of brick built onto it at the end, it is sufficiently reinforced to take the dome. Usually, because the courses of the vault incline toward the back wall, the walls carrying the vault have to project a little into the central square; so the top of the arch should be exactly in line with the walls, to give the dome a perfectly square shape to sit upon.

113 The room was to be used in this way: the vaulted alcove, or iwan, would contain a built-in bed, with room for keeping things underneath it, and a scorpion trough to baffle these insects if they tried to get into the bed. Opposite the bed alcove was another small vault over a cupboard, a neat replacement for the usual rope on which the peasant hangs his clothes and other effects. The central area would thus be kept clear of furniture and would give a sense of space and dignity to the room. This would be a great improvement on the usual peasant room, which is a small, dark, ill-ventilated place.

The peasant has no window, or, if he has, it is so badly fitted that there is a draught from it, and he blocks it up and makes a small hole up near the roof. But sleeping in the bed alcove of the new house, tucked away out of the line between door and window, he will be perfectly snug and untroubled by draughts.

Baking and Heating

The baking oven is in a corner courtyard. It is an ordinary mud oven, such as can be bought in the market. There is a custom by which a family when it is baking must allow the next-door neighbors to cook their bread in its oven. Thus families bake every third day and economize in fuel.

Since the winter can be quite cold in Egypt, the peasants use various ways of warming their houses. Often they have a baking oven inside the bedroom in addition to the one in the courtyard. This is a large structure, taking up a lot of room. Since it has no chimney, the smoke pours out of it, swirls round the room, and escapes through the door. The interior of the room, which has hardly any proper ventilation, gets black with soot, becoming insufferably dark and stuffy. Because of the baking oven's inefficiency as a heating unit, the whole family usually has to sleep on top of it (after it has gone out, naturally), and the cows are frequently brought in to share and add to the warmth.

Another popular method of heating, used particularly when there is no baking and the oven has not been lit, is the charcoal brazier. This, however, gives too little warmth and exhales poisonous carbon monoxide fumes. Neither baking oven nor brazier is at all efficient, and both are dangerous to health.

To find an effective and cheap method of heating, you must go somewhere where the climate can be really cold and the people are poor. I went for this purpose to Austria, where in the villages of the Tyrol I discovered an excellent heating and cooking device that has been used over the centuries by the peasants there. This is the *Kachelofen,* a stove with a very intricate system of partitioning in-
114–115
side that directs the hot gases of combustion backwards and forwards to allow more time for the heat to radiate into the room before they escape. It can be damped down after the fuel has burned down to a few glowing coals, by closing the fire door and the chimney, so that it will continue to give out a comfortable warmth all night, like a hot water bottle in a bed.

In Austria the kachelofen is made of very simple materials: inside, fireclay tiles, and outside, glazed decorative tiles, called *Kachel,* whose design and application has become a well-known folk art. A still simpler variety has thin walls of large flat pebbles from the bed of a river set in rich lime mortar.

For Egypt the kachelofen principle, realized in the cheapest of materials, seemed a most promising solution to our heating problems. I found an old woman who made the ordinary village baking
116
ovens out of mud and donkey droppings, and taught her to make kachelofens out of the same materials. She learned very quickly and could soon turn them out for the same price as the baking ovens, about thirty piasters. They would burn anything, even the household sweepings and kitchen refuse; I designed a type for the richer families, which worked with oil and water drops and burned like a furnace.

One type, incorporating a baking oven, was set inside the bedroom against the wall, with the oven door opening outside into the courtyard. Another type for heating only could be put anywhere. 117 The houses were designed with flues in the most suitable places, wherever kachelofens might be needed, so that when these stoves were bought they had only to be connected up.

Cooking

The peasant woman usually cooks over a fire built on the ground, stirring the food in a pan placed on two bricks that enclose the fire. In the summer she cooks in the courtyard, and in the winter inside the house. The fire is smoky, the food is near the ground and gets 118–119 dusty, and the large quantities of fuel kept close by sometimes catch fire and burn down the house or even the whole village. Continual use of an open fire indoors fills the house with the smell of cooking and blackens the walls with soot, a disadvantage aggravated by the fuel used—dried cotton stalks, cow stalks, and any sort of sticks or straw that can be collected from the fields. These substances give little heat, take up a great deal of room, and are excellent material for producing smoke without fire.

Our problem was chiefly one of tidying up the organization of the cooking system and getting rid of the smoke. The first thing to do was to make a permanent kitchen, where preparing and cooking food would be carried out summer and winter. For this I chose the family room or loggia, giving south onto the courtyard and from which the bedroom led off. I had already arranged to store fuel out of harm's way on the roof. Now I provided a large, ready-use fuel bin in the kitchen, to the right of the fire. Fuel could be stuffed into the top of it and pulled out through an opening at floor level. The fire itself was designed only after prolonged observation and careful analysis of a woman's movements while cooking.

Since Gourna is so hot, it was clearly important to retain the squatting position for the cook, as this has been shown to be far more comfortable than a standing position. The fire was enclosed in a permanent grate, with a firebrick grid for the pans, and had a large hood and flue over it to collect and lead off the fumes of cooking. In fact, the final result was exactly like the usual kitchen range of many European countries, but cut down to a height of some twelve inches. It is important to note, however, that for functional design it would not have done to take a short cut and, without analyzing the way the unit is used, simply to assume, since Egyptian women sit for their cooking, that a lower version of the European range was the answer to our problem. One might make all sorts of serious mistakes by adopting so lazy an attitude.

Immediately to the left of the fireplace was a sink, supplied from the roof tank through a pipe, and drained to a grease trap and the borehole in the courtyard.

Because in the summer it would be intolerable to light the kachelofen in the bedroom and bake in it, I also provided a second, summer oven outside the kitchen area. These kitchens proved workmanlike and popular. Even when the owners used primus stoves, they found it convenient to put them in the fireplace, under the hood, for which I was very glad; there is nothing more ugly, more perfectly dirty and slatternly, than a primus stove in the bedroom with a sooty greasy pan on it next to a colored counterpane that needs a wash (somehow the two things seem to reinforce each other's dirtiness), and to get the pan out of the bedroom was a good step toward a tidy, spacious house. The kitchen can be a beautiful room, especially when the utensils are locally made, but when these utensils get out of place, it becomes a center of ugliness that spoils all the rest of the house.

The Water Supply

Our main problem in providing a washplace, shower, laundry, and latrine was the supply and drainage of water. These units were grouped close together, so that waste water could be conveniently drained away, and they were supplied from large, glazed storage jars on the roof. The storage jars, which had to be refilled by hand from public pumps, may seem less desirable than a running water supply to each house. In fact, in spite of all the advantages of running water, it must be introduced with care and after carefully considering its effects on society. In India, where certain villages were supplied with pure water on tap in the houses, the girls still preferred to go down to the river and bring back heavy jars of dirty water on their heads. This was because fetching water was their only excuse for going out, and thus their only chance to be seen by the young men of their village. A girl who stayed in the kitchen, drawing water from the tap, would never get married.

In peasant society, whether in India or Egypt, we see again and again how the rigid and seemingly antiquated framework of tradition serves all sorts of unexpected practical purposes. If one useful item of traditional life is removed, then we have an obligation to replace it with some other item that will perform the same social function. If, for example, we take away the communal water point, then we must provide some other device to facilitate the contracting of engagements—and, indeed, to smooth the exchange of gossip. Such a device suggested itself to me in a revival of the hammam, or turkish bath, discussed earlier. As the practice becomes more firmly established among the village mothers of using the hammam for assessing the beauty and character of eligible girls and of arranging marriages, so gradually the daily parade of girls to the well may become less of an exciting, husband-catching expedition and more of a disagreeable chore. Thus, after about a generation, the village women might be ready to make use of water laid on in their houses. It is hard to imagine a village in Egypt without its black-robed women, erect as queens, each with her water jar (*ballas*) carried nonchalantly on her head, and it will be a pity to lose the sight. Who knows, too, but that stooping with a bucket to a tap in the yard may destroy the magnificent carriage for which our women are renowned.

For the time being we stuck to public pumps in Gourna. Each one or two neighborhoods had its hand pump, drawing water from deep down where it was free from harmful bacteria. The pump would be inside a small, domed room provided with seats round the wall where the women could sit and chat while waiting their turn.

120–121
In all villages and poor city quarters the wells and water points are surrounded by a vast morass caused by the overflow of the water. My pumprooms had their floors paved and sunk two steps below groundlevel to make sure that no water could escape and muddy the ground outside. The overflow was drained away through an underground trench, provided with an inspection chamber for keeping it clear of obstructions, and it went finally to feed fruit trees in the neighborhood square. Thus the two functions of the water point were well served; practically, there was plenty of clean water, and socially, drawing it became a pleasant, cool, and leisurely pastime.

Once the water was taken back to the house, the girl would carry it upstairs and empty in into the reservoir on the roof. Here there would be one or two large Ali-Baba jars embedded in the roof and connected with one another by galvanized iron pipes. They would be situated in the shade, but where they could receive a draught, to keep the water cool, and they would be glazed inside to prevent loss of water. An unglazed pot that allows the water to seep through to its outside surface and evaporate cools the water more, but the loss is not worth while, and it is as well not to have water constantly oozing out onto a mud roof. The pots would be placed directly above the bathroom and would have an outlet to a galvanized iron pipe in the bottom of one of them. If water was needed elsewhere the supply would lead from this pipe through similar pipes suspended from the ceiling across the middle of the rooms, so that if the pipes began to drip they would annoy the family, who would be forced to mend them, whereas a dripping pipe against a wall would probably be left to go on damaging the wall and plaster for months.

A possible improvement on this system might be to put an extra reservoir at ground level and to install a small hand pump to fill the roof pots, thus avoiding the need to carry water jars upstairs.

Normally the villagers store water in the courtyard in large unglazed jars called *zeer,* and dip water for use out of these with a thin mug or small pot (the *kooz*). They hold this little receptacle in one hand to pour the water over dish or baby held in the other hand. If they could be given a tap, both hands would be freed for the job of washing, which would make housework much easier.

Laundry

Most Egyptian women do their laundry in a canal or, if a little richer, in a large basin called a *tesht,* which forms an important part of the trousseau. In Gourna there was no canal; so the houses had to be provided with a laundry place inside. After making careful observations and measurements on people actually doing the laundry, and even trying the positions myself, I designed a simple arrangement of a shallow pit with brick walls and floor, plastered with cement, a circular stand in the center to carry the tesht, a seat conveniently close to the stand, and a trough in one corner. Thus the woman could sit down at the tub, as she was accustomed to do, and keep clothes soaking in the trough at the same time. She would get her water piped from the roof pots, and when she finished she would simply tip up the tesht and pour the water onto the floor of the pit, whence it would drain away through a hole in one corner into a borehole.

122–124

The same laundry pit could be used for washing the baby and as a bathroom. In fact, although I put the first ones in a corner of the courtyard, where women usually do the washing, in later designs I transferred the laundry pits to the bathroom proper; the bather could sit on the center stand and, in winter, mix his hot and cold water in the trough or, in summer, use a cold shower fixed above his head. The great advantage of these pits was that, like the one round the public pumps, they prevented the waste water from running all over the place or being tipped out into the courtyard or the street. While not upsetting the local laundering customs, they made the whole process neater and drier.

Latrines

Nearly every peasant in Egypt suffers from ancylostoma and one or more intestinal diseases, caught directly from infected persons' excreta. Because there are no proper latrines or drainage facilities, typhoid, bilharzia, dysentery, and ancylostoma are rampant. Besides killing slowly, they so debilitate the sufferer that he can neither work well nor enjoy himself. It is an urgent task to stamp them out, and the architect can do much toward this. If village houses can be provided with clean latrines, flushing systems, and sanitary drainage, the incidence of these scourges will be greatly reduced.

Many authorities have experimented to find cheap and hygienic latrines. Because it is very expensive to install European-type water closets, which need an ample supply of piped water and a capacious and elaborate sewage installation, the experimenters have tried sand closets and boreholes. The sand closet system consisted of two deep trenches, to be used in turn for six months each. There would be a seat over the one currently in use, and sand for the user to throw over his excreta. The one not in use would be covered, and when six months had gone by, the contents could be removed and used as manure. Unfortunately, it was found in practice that six months was not long enough to render the manure harmless; the ascaris worm was found to be alive and vigorous; so the manure was just as harmful as if it was fresh.

The other system tried was the borehole. A deep hole would be sunk in the courtyard of the house, and a seat placed over it. This, though practical, was rather inhuman, for there was no privacy to an open air latrine. It could have been placed in a closet in the house, but boreholes fill up in time and have to be moved, so that it is impossible to make a permanent indoor closet for one. Furthermore, it is troublesome to start boring holes inside the covered part of the house, and inconvenient to find a new place for the lavatory every six months or so.

For Gourna I decided that some sort of waterborne drainage was essential. Colonel Abdel-Aziz Saleh, one of the army engineers, has designed a system whereby the bowl could be economically flushed while the user washed himself, by providing a pipe with one tap controlling two outlets—the first a thin, trickling one for personal washing, and the second a larger flow for the bowl itself. This water could drain into a septic tank shared between a whole row of houses—about ten families—and should prove reasonably thrifty with water; I reckoned that one peasant house would use about one-tenth of the water that an average large town house would. Later it occurred to me that a common septic tank might become a source of neighborhood quarrels, since it would be neither privately nor publicly owned. For this reason I decided to provide an individual drainage system for each household. This consisted of a large inspection chamber, designed to work as a small septic tank, which drained into a borehole working as a percolating pit in the courtyard. Thus the closet could remain in one place, it would be kept clean, and, when the borehole filled up, a new one could easily be sunk somewhere else in the courtyard and the septic tank connected with it.

The Stable

The problem of providing stables for the peasants' cattle does not arise until the peasants begin to crowd into villages. On the isolated farm there is a certain amount of room for housing the cows and plenty of open space to cope with the inconveniences of the manure pit, but in a village of many hundreds of families, each with its two or three cows, the human beings are forced into unhealthy proximity to the cattle.

A cow eats fodder and produces droppings; these two activities determine the architect's job. He has to provide the animal with a manger accessible to the fodder store, and he has to provide some way of preserving the droppings for manure without inviting all the flies in Egypt to take up residence in its village.

The peasant overcomes the manure problem like this: every day he shovels fresh earth over the droppings on the stable floor, which thus slowly ascends toward the roof, and every so often he cuts out this mixture and carts it off to the fields. It is, however, a method wasteful of manure; many of the valuable constitutents evaporate or soak away. The best solution would have been the European manure pit, a watertight, covered tank into which all the animals' urine drains, and into which straw and all other sorts of vegetable refuse may be thrown to form a rich compost. This will only work, though, where there are plenty of cattle; two or three cows don't produce enough urine to run down to the pit successfully. I therefore decided on a combination of both—to retain the peasant system of covering the droppings with earth, but having them shoveled out into a covered, waterproof pit every day. From here the manure could be carted to the fields when required.

The stables, then, consisted of a row of stalls, each three meters wide and covered by a vault. Each stall would hold two beasts, and had a manger which could be filled from a corridor running along the back of the stalls to the fodder store. Across a small yard from the stalls was a long, very narrow pit, half a meter wide, also vaulted, where the manure was stored. The floor sloped from ground level, at one end, down to about a meter and a half at the other end, and, like the walls, was made of bricks and lined with cement.

The roof was the usual mud brick vault—in this case very simple to make because it was so narrow. How this technique changes the appearance of the peasant's yard! Instead of scraping together the timber and thatch for a few skimpy and untidy shelters, he could now be as lavish as he liked with covered space—sheds and stores for all the odd needs of a farm were his for the building, literally dirt cheap, and so clean and elegant as to transform the whole appearance of the village.

Combating Bilharzia

The Artificial Lake

The artificial lake which I planned to occupy one corner of the village site was one of the most important features of Gourna. Though it may seem frivolous to take up a lot of useful land with a lake, and improper for an architect to concern himself with breeding fish and ducks, yet there was such necessity behind my frivolity as would make your blood run cold.

The scourge of Egypt is a disease called bilharzia. Nearly every peasant in the country has bilharzia. Bilharzia kills, eats away a man's strength, poisons his life, his work, and his recreation. Bilharzia is the greatest single cause of those defects that pull down our peasantry: the apathy and lack of stamina that are as marked in the social life of the people as in their labor.

It is a doom that no peasant can escape. Water, which gives life to man and crop, gives man bilharzia too. Whenever he goes into the water of canal or pond or rice field, whenever children splash about in the puddles of a drained irrigation ditch, whenever a woman washes her clothes in the river, bilharzia strikes. How can the peasant keep away from water? If he is cured of bilharzia—long, expensive, and dangerous though the cure is—he must inevitably go back to the fatal canals again. Water is life—for rice, for maize, for cotton, for sugarcane, for man himself—and water is the home of bilharzia.

What is this disease? It is a parasite that gets into the body from infected water and settles particularly in the bladder, liver, and other organs, piercing them, sucking at them, till they become like a bleeding sponge. It multiplies enormously in the body, and soon produces lassitude, anemia, and bleeding; particularly virulent parasites kill you. It is transmitted through infected water: a person with bilharzia passes out the eggs of the parasites in his urine, and the larvae get into a kind of water snail in which they live comfortably until they kill it and swim out into the water of canal or pond. They live in the water until the warmth of a human limb attracts them. They burrow into the skin, shed their tails, and are carried up in the bloodstream to the lungs, whence they get into the liver and bladder and lay eggs which are passed out into the water again.

All the water of Egypt is infested with these cercaria, or bilharzia worms, and every peasant works and bathes in this infested water. To irrigate their fields the peasants use mostly the *tambour,* or Archimedes' screw, to operate which they must sit with their legs dangling in the water. Even the more primitive *shadûf*—a bucket and lever machine—splashes them with quite enough water to pass on the cercaria.

In the Delta, where rice is an important crop, the peasant spends most of his time paddling in the water, and it is notorious that bilharzia is more prevalent here than in Upper Egypt. Here, too, they use the perennial irrigation system, watering the land all the year round from canals instead of depending on the annual flood as in Upper Egypt. The water in these permanent irrigation ditches is the chief stronghold of the cercaria, enabling them to survive when the dry fields of Upper Egypt would kill them. A worker from the Delta —so say the contractors, who ought to know—will do only one-sixth of the work that an Upper Egyptian can.

Then, too, in the hot summer everyone bathes in the canals and ponds. Children especially paddle and splash about in every patch of water they can find, in ditches, puddles and stagnant ponds. Since it is practically certain that anyone who stands for ten minutes in an Egyptian canal will contract bilharzia, it is not surprising that the incidence of the disease is so high.

Of course, so terrible a disease has attracted much attention from doctors and hygienists. One man, Dr. Barlow, devoted his entire life to combating this disease. Dr. Barlow was an American who came to Egypt after many years in China. He proposed exterminating the parasite by the simple expedient of decontaminating the whole river Nile, from its source to its mouth together with all its tributaries and all lakes and other bodies of standing water in the country. So radical a scheme would have been extremely expensive, besides being by no means certain in its results; for if only two cercaria were to survive in the myriad canals and ditches of Egypt, they would, like the animals in the ark, restore their unpleasant species to its former predominance and infest the whole country again.

But although it might be impractical to decontaminate the whole river, we might decontaminate part of it and keep the part permanently safe. For the river flows through all those small canals that water our fields, and the peasants are very experienced in controlling the flow of water. What could be easier than leading off water through a side canal, which could be cut off from the main canal and made to feed an artificial lake and decontaminate the water successively in both? And why not enlarge this side canal into a small lake?

Thus the idea of the artificial lake was born. If the villagers could have somewhere to swim where there were no cercaria, the disease must start to retreat. If in addition they could be protected while working in the fields, bilharzia would eventually disappear completely.

126 But the artificial lake would also solve another problem. As a tidy builder I had naturally been exercised to think of some way of removing the hole left after we had dug out earth to make bricks. All over Egypt, in every village there are these pits left after brick making; they even have a name—*birka*—and they are a prime source of malaria, for mosquitoes breed in stagnant water. So notorious are the birkas as nests of disease that several politicians have accorded a prominent place in their programs to schemes for filling them up. Somehow, though, the birkas remain. Of course, filling a hole is rather an intractable problem; the reader is doubtless not so simple-minded as to suggest filling it with earth, for he will realize that the earth must come from another hole, which in its turn must be filled up—a remedy for unemployment, perhaps, but not for malaria. It might be possible to fill these birkas with sand brought from the desert, where holes don't matter, but then someone must pay for transporting the sand, which costs a lot.

The idea of turning our birka at Gourna into a lake came to me because on one of our family farms we had a birka just like all the others except that a small canal ran through it. Thus its water was always running, it was always clean, and we kept ducks and geese on it, so that it was both charming and useful. Clearly the answer to the problem of the birkas was not to fill them in but to widen them, deepen them, and connect them to the canals, so that their water could not stagnate. Even birkas far from canals could be dealt with: fill them in with earth dug from a suitable site alongside a canal.

When I showed my scheme to Dr. Mahmoud Mustafa Hilmi, the director of the Parasitology Section at the Ministry of Public Health, he approved of it and suggested certain improvements: first, in order to deny a foothold to the snails which harbor the cercaria we should line the sides of the lake with stones, so that the water weeds the snails eat could not grow; and second, to ensure that the water be thoroughly decontaminated, we should dig an "ante-pond" in the shape of a channel some two hundred meters long, upstream of the lake beside the main canal, and provided with lock gates at each end, so that water could be held in it and decontaminated before being admitted to the lake proper. Thus the water would be doubly decontaminated, once in the ante-pond and once in the lake itself.

Powdered copper sulphate would be dissolved in the water from a bag hung in the stream by the lock gate; this would serve to kill snails, worms, and larvae but would unfortunately not kill the free-swimming bilharzia cercaria. To deal with these it would be necessary to hold them for forty-eight hours in a snail-free ante-pond; then they would all die. As to the mosquitoes, we would have to change the top ten centimeters of water, which would be automatically done every time we let the decontaminated water of the ante-pond flow into the lake. The system of lock gates made it very easy to do this; the required amount of water could be let out of the downstream gate while the upstream gate was shut; then the downstream gate could be shut, and fresh, decontaminated water would be let in through the upstream gate.

An important point about the artificial lake is that it should not be much above the level of the drainage canal that serves the area, for if it is, its water will seep into the surrounding farmland and ruin it; if, on the other hand, the lake is at the level of the drainage canal, then it acts as a fine drain for the farmland, which is thereby much improved. Correctly, the water level in the lake should be ten centimeters above the level in the drainage canal, so that the top layer of water can be run off over a small weir, which also acts as a permanent overflow passage. The side canal would carry the water from the main canal down a gradient of one in two hundred meters and into the lake.

Since bilharzia is so widespread a disease, not only in Egypt but throughout the whole tropical world, it is clearly desirable that the provision of bilharzia-free lakes should be encouraged.*

The lake, like the other features of Gourna, was supposed to be a model for the rest of Egypt. I have already remarked upon the grimness of most villages, where every square meter of land is used for growing crops, and where no space and no thought is given to providing amenities for relaxation. We can indeed justify the lake on severely practical grounds, but I never intended it to be practical in the way a post office is. I would like every village to have its artificial lake set in the middle of a small village park.

This park, together with the lake, will provide something quite new in the Egyptian village—a place for relaxation and recreation, where spreading willows are reflected in the clean water, where paths wind between mango, guava, and tamarisk to come suddenly upon

* "Because of the intensities of its morbid symptoms, its socio-economic aspects and its very wide distribution throughout the world, bilharziasis is one of the most important helminthiases (diseases caused by worms in blood vessels). It is estimated that there are about 150,000,000 infested people in the world suffering from this disease, in the transmission of which certain snails act as intermediate hosts. The discovery of new molluscicides (cyclic phenol derivatives) to control snails and the results of their use in bilharziasis control give hope of more effective and less costly control measures." Report of the World Health Organization.

the flowering bohenia, acacia, and jacaranda—a place where, in four or five acres preserved from commercial farming, the people of the village can find a kinder aspect of nature than that presented to them in the cottonfields.

For this purpose we must compromise with the ideal park of lawns, flowerbeds, and trees—the European landscape park—which needs a whole staff of gardeners to maintain it. Our park must provide shade, peace, and beauty without needing any upkeep. It must therefore be as far removed as possible from the customary railway station garden or municipal park, with its shriveled grass, clipped and withered bushes, and iron railings, from the formal patterning of the miniature Versailles that so many provincial municipalities adopt and then neglect. The village park needs trees. It must have no artificially grown lawns, no flowerbeds, and no railings. It must be planned to accommodate and soothe the people, and it must be hard-wearing enough to stand up to enthusiastic use. It must be a park of trees, rocks, sand, and cacti. Its beauty and power to soothe must derive not from patterned flowerbeds but from the grouping of the trees, the winding of the paths, the placing of rocks, and the juxtaposition of color, tone, mass, and shape in pleasing combinations.

I suggest we take advantage of the park to provide the village with fruit. A tree that provides abundant fruit and shade too is the common mango. A big specimen will produce up to two thousand fruits a year, and it needs little attention. The more delicate foreign and hybrid varieties should not be used, for although they give better fruit, they need too much care and anyway are rather small and unshady. Color may be provided by flowering acacia, by bohenia, jacaranda, and poinciana regia, while tamarisks are tough yet shady trees which carpet the ground with fine needles, very restful to walk and sit on.

The factors governing the size of a lake are two: the volume of earth needed for brick making, and the minimum quantity of water that will remain relatively clean between changes when bathed in by such numbers of people and cattle as may be expected to use it. A single house needs between 100 and 150 cubic meters of earth, and on an average holds five people. Then a village of five thousand people, or a thousand houses, will need at least 10,000 cubic meters of earth. If our lake has a mean depth of 2 meters, its area will be 50,000 square meters, or about twelve acres.

This is much more than enough to satisfy the second condition; a lake of only four acres would accommodate all the bathers—human and animal—that would use it every day, and if its water were completely changed every fifteen days it would still remain freer of bacteria than the average town swimming bath. Since land is valuable and, as at Gourna, it may be impossible to dig a lake bigger than four acres, it is comforting to remember that the earth for building need not necessarily come from the lake, nor indeed from any source farther to seek than the old houses themselves.

Although Egypt needs rebuilding, the materials for this are already there on the site; every village has in its existing houses much of the earth needed to make the new ones we must build. The average village will not need more supplementary earth than can be dug out of a five-acre lake.

A five-acre lake and a five-acre park may indeed seem to some people an unwarrantable extravagance. In a land where most landlords are too greedy to plant a tree to shade their houses because it might rob them of half a bushel of cotton a year, with what horror would they contemplate the wanton sacrifice of ten acres of productive land. Yet some landlords have been less careful of their acres: Ismail Pasha had in the gardens of his palace at Giza an ornamental lake covering ten acres at least, all for his own amusement. Surely it is not much to ask for five thousand people one half of what the pasha enjoyed by himself? And I do not ask it for their amusement, but for their very lives. The rent of ten acres is L.E. 200 per year. Is this too much to spend on a village of five thousand people when their lives depend upon it?

The Prophet tells us to bring up our children to learn riding and swimming. We cannot give horses to all the villages in Egypt, but we can and must give them lakes, and thus obey half the injunction at least. I have seen at the Meadi Sports Club how the physique of the children improves, how they come weak, thin, and feeble and are transformed by swimming into graceful and sturdy athletes. This transformation is available to the poorest peasant child in the land if we give them lakes. At present they swim indeed, but they pay a horrible toll to the bilharzia worm.

In all countries faced with big rural rebuilding problems, the authorities—no, let us not be vague, the prime minister—should attack the problem like this: at every village where the people are rotting in bad houses and riddled with bilharzia, a site should be selected for the lake. Engineers skilled in the new science of soil mechanics must examine the ground. When the best place has been chosen with regard to the quality of the soil and the proximity of a canal, the lake should be excavated at once. The government should provide machinery to dig out the earth as quickly as possible, and pile it up ready for the brick makers.

One country at least did not reject the idea of the artificial lake.

When the Doxiadis Associates were planning for the government of Iraq, that government adopted the idea and decreed that every village in the country should have an artificial lake.

In fact, the government should also provide, as a necessary complement to the lake, a properly equipped permanent brickyard, with presses, molds, and mixing troughs outside the building area proper, so that the builders may be assured of an uninterrupted flow of bricks and the villagers may acquire a permanent amenity. Once the earth is there, people will build, but the initiative in providing the earth must be taken by the government, which is also in a position to furnish heavy machinery and which can fulfill the role of shock troops perhaps better than that of architects and builders.

Further, if the soil analysis shows that the earth needs more sand added to make it suitable for bricks, then the government must cart the sand. These two operations—excavating the earth and adding sand to bring it to a suitable consistency—are the ones that generally defeat the peasant before he starts building. If they are solved for him he will be greatly encouraged. Thus, if the government applies its resources to lake digging, it will make a major contribution to new housing and to eliminating bilharzia.

Protective Clothes

The lake—a bilharzia-free bathing place—would not by itself stop the parasite getting into people, because, as was said before, all irrigation operations involve standing in the infested canals and ditches, and all peasants must water their land. So weapon number 2 against bilharzia must be some sort of protective clothing.

The Japanese succeeded in greatly reducing bilharzia by issuing rubber boots to their farm workers. Rubber is too dear for Egypt, but something else might do instead. After some thought, it occurred to me that if we lengthened a pair of ordinary peasant trousers to enclose the foot completely, and if we impregnated the trousers up to the height of the thigh with linseed oil, they might well resist water and the cercaria. I had a local tailor make me a sample pair of such trousers, of the same cotton cloth as the laborers' shorts, and these I soaked in boiled linseed oil and hung out to dry. I meant them to be worn with a rubber sole (cheaply made out of an old car-tire) tied on underneath, and I found them completely waterproof. I sent them to Cairo, to Dr. Mahmoud Mustapha Hilmi of the Ministry of Public Health. He said that they gave 100 percent protection against the cercaria, and that wearing them he would be quite prepared to wade through the pond where they bred the cercaria in his laboratory. Even a tightly woven cloth, untreated, he said, would give 60 percent protection.

An Educational Campaign

So here was our second essential weapon, the second prong of our attack on bilharzia, perfectly effective and cheap enough for everyone in the country to afford. The next problem was how to mount the attack, how to bring our weapons into action. The people must be persuaded to wear the trousers, to use the disinfected lakes. For this they must be made to see the cercaria in the water, made to see its progress through the body. An all-out propaganda campaign, using every trick and device of mass communications, must be instituted to make the peasants save themselves. Not a few tattered posters hanging in the railway station, inaccurately drawn and impossible to understand. Show the people the bilharzia worm alive and wriggling. Give them film shows, bring in microscopes that project the magnified slide on the wall. Let them fish a bucket of water out of the river, let them prepare the slides themselves, let the whole village see a great worm, three feet long, swimming across the wall of the village hall. Attack the children too. If they can't follow the film, reduce the matter to a fairy story. I wrote a play for them, the horrid tale of Bill Harzia, and dressed myself up as a (fairly) terrifying demon, in a goggle-eyed gas mask and a white sheet, all puffed up by an inner tube round my shoulders.

The play begins with a worried father sitting on his doorstep waiting for his wife to have a baby. A nurse comes out and congratulates him on the birth of a son, and one by one all the village children steal up to the door to ask after the new baby. There is a lively celebration, the *sebva,* on the seventh day after the birth, at which everyone dances and sweets are distributed, but at the height of the party there suddenly appears at the end of the cradle—Bill Harzia, the demon. He is visible only to the child, who not unnaturally starts to cry, so that after making threatening gestures Bill Harzia withdraws.

Now the child, Mahgub, is ten years old. The father is ill; he grows weak and anemic and at last he is seen to be dying. As he dies—of bilharzia—he makes his wife promise not to let their son go into the water. Yet how can the boy avoid the water? Without his father, the family gets poorer. Mahgub must find work. Where? His mother tells him never to go in the water, but the only work available is on the tambour of the shadûf. He goes from farmer to farmer, imploring them to give him work away from the canals, but there is none. And always as he walks, the demon walks behind him, creeps behind trees, and lurks ready to pounce on him as soon as he touches water.

At last he is so hungry, and his mother too, that in desperation he decides to break his promise to his mother, saying nothing to her, and to work in the water. So he goes to turn the tambour. As soon as his feet go into the water, Bill Harzia springs demoniacally to the canal side, produces a large jam jar, and begins to sprinkle cercaria all round the boy.

Gradually the boy changes. His face turns bright yellow and he becomes feeble and ill. He tries to play with his companions, but his strength fails, and he is taken indoors to lie down. Once more the children creep up to the door, with anxious faces, to learn how he is. He gets worse and worse, and his mother, who knows by now that he must have gone into the water, watches him dying of bilharzia like his father.

At this sad juncture, two strangers enter the village. They are, in fact, none other than Drs. Barlow and Abdul-Azim, easily recognizable in white coats and large spectacles. Clasping their bags, they begin to question the villagers. Is there anyone sick in the village? But yes, Mahgub is sick. What does he look like? He is all yellow. What else, does he bleed? Yes, and he is very weak. They run to the house, producing stethoscopes and microscopes from their bags, and examine Mahgub. Ah yes! We thought as much. This is the work of Bill Harzia. He is a demon, and Dr. Barlow has been hunting him all the way from China. Now listen! We shall cure Mahgub (they bring out an enormous syringe and inject some gallons of medicine into Mahgub), but what we want is the demon. We must catch him and kill him. The doctors gather all the children and hold a council of war, discussing ways and means of killing Bill Harzia. One brave young boy—a special friend of Mahgub—jumps up and offers to be a decoy. He will go into the water, catch the disease, and lure the demon to his destruction. Dr. Barlow laughs and says there is no need to catch the disease. Look! He rummages in his bag and produces, amid gasps of admiration, a large pair of trousers. These, he explains, are very special trousers. They have been soaked in linseed oil, and if the boy wears them he may safely go into the water and the demon will be unable to do a thing. The boy puts them on and steps into the water. Bill Harzia appears but falls back in baffled rage at the sight of the trousers, and the valiant doctors are able to shoot him, whereupon he expires with a loud hiss as he lets the air out of his inner tube.

Bill Harzia is dead, but still not quite harmless. Once again the doctors gather the children and warn them very seriously against going into the water unless they are wearing oiled trousers, and especially against swimming. Unfortunately this demon has poisoned all the water, so that it will still give them the illness if they swim in it. They must wait until a new beautiful lake has been dug, broad and clean, with trees around it and an island in it—a lake like the pasha's lake in Cairo—where there will be no danger and everyone may swim all day.

Gourna, a Pilot Project

Gourna was for me at once an experiment and an example. The village would, I hoped, show the way to rebuilding the whole Egyptian countryside. Once it was seen how cheap good housing can be, I hoped that there would be a great movement of do-it-yourself building among our peasants. In order to give the fullest information to future do-it-yourself builders, I wanted us to make this village from the earth up, to make every smallest detail ourselves, find out how to do it and how much it cost. We had to make our own bricks, our own mortar, dig out our own earth, quarry and fire our own lime, excavate for ourselves, lay our own plumbing, and do all our own carting. In fact, we were taking over all the jobs that in most such schemes of public works are usually delegated to private contractors—a liberty, incidentally, that only the Department of Antiquities could have allowed us, for as it deals with delicate ancient monuments it is permitted, alone among government departments, to engage its own workmen and supervise work directly through its own foremen and experts.

I hoped that by taking a close interest in every detail of the labor and the purchase of materials I should be able to produce a detailed cost analysis of the completed village. I should know where every penny had been spent, and I could say confidently that such and such a village, of so many houses and of so many public buildings, would cost just so much in money and would take just so much labor. My findings could be applied to any future project, and at long last we should bridge that mysterious gulf—which swallows so many millions of pounds—between the plans of national planning authorities and the visible buildings that result from those plans.

Although in Gourna we should have to pay our laborers, we should still be able to apply our system of planning and control to a village whose inhabitants gave their work free. We should still be able to budget for a village built by contractors, for we could add a profit percentage to the bare cost of materials and labor, and pay the contractor that. I particularly hoped that my findings would give definite and useful data to the people who administer schemes of "aided self-help" to peasant communities.

Also I hoped that we might patiently replant the techniques that had once flourished in the district but of which it was now denuded: the techniques of vaulted-roof construction that had retreated south towards the Sudan and which today maintained a precarious life in Nubia under the constant threat of extinction. Once gone, the knowledge of building these roofs would disappear forever, beyond recovery. Once cut the chain of succession by which father teaches son, master teaches apprentice, no amount of antiquarian research in the world can restore the knowledge. It might be possible slowly to restore these skills to the land that had once nourished them, if our experiment at Gourna succeeded and attracted the notice of architects and the general public in Egypt.

Gourna might have shown the way to a realistic national rehousing policy, a building plan that would have provided the millions of houses that Egypt needs at a price she could afford. Such plans have from time to time been mooted, based on the orthodox materials, methods, and building systems used in current practice, but no such plan has ever got beyond the first discussion in committee. The reason is always the same: too little money. Inevitably, so it seems, somewhere between the planning stage and the building, the cost swells and puffs itself up to such a size that the accountants take fright and the scheme is dropped. Patiently, the planners make another plan; the result is the same: it always costs much more than any government can afford.

Why should this be? There is one basic reason: no architect normally designs for peasants in the villages. No peasant can ever dream of employing an architect, and no architect ever dreams of working with the miserable resources of the peasant. The architect designs for the rich man, and thinks in terms of what the rich man can pay for. Most of the architect's work is in the town, and so he takes into account the resources of the town; he assumes the existence of the experienced building contractors and the sophisticated materials that are always used in town building, and he assumes, naturally, that his client can pay for them. The architect thinks automatically of concrete and contractors, wherever he is asked to build, and he never envisages any alternative to the system of private urban building.

All planning authorities are, of course, wholly dependent upon their architects for technical advice on building. Thus all planning authorities acquire, perhaps without realizing it, the architects' preconceptions of rural housing, and get a picture into their minds of how houses ought to be. They see them built of concrete, and built by ordinary commercial building firms.

The high cost of rural housing schemes results not only from the expensive materials used; it results also from the system by which the execution of the work is placed in the hands of private builders.

It should already be clear that there exists a perfectly adequate and very cheap building material in mud brick; I hope to show that there also exists a method of organizing the work—on any scale and in any location—that can save us all the heavy expense associated with building contractors. Just as the peasants' material—mud brick—is made available to us only if we adopt the peasants' building technique, so too we can build as cheaply as the peasant does only if we base our organization of the work on the peasants' practices.

It is only recently that governments have taken an interest in the miserable and rapidly worsening conditions in which most peasants live. In the same way, although people have been building houses for themselves for thousands of years, it is only very recently that they have begun to consult architects about the design of their houses. Earlier, a house was the sole creation of the builder (if he was a peasant in the country).

The architect is an expensive luxury; so he is found only where there is money. Because he works for fairly prosperous clients, the architect is not always concerned to cut down the cost of his buildings. This cost is determined by the building contractor who executes the work. The professional contractor, like the architect, tends to be expensive; so he too is found only where there is money. Now moneyed men in Egypt like to live in towns; further, only a fair-sized town can provide a sufficient flow of work to keep architect and contractor in business. Thus the people professionally concerned with building—the only people, in fact, who have any experience in large-scale building—live in the towns and have experience in building only under the peculiar conditions prevailing in towns. The architect always designs in the expectation that his design will be executed by a building contractor, and the contractor always assumes the existence of smaller firms to which he can subcontract the work, and of an adequate supply of materials and labor.

When a government or other authority wishes to build, it obtains technical advice from architects. Architects design and prepare estimates with the idea that the work will be executed through the customary agency of the commercial building contractor. For a project in a town—a hospital, perhaps, or a block of offices—the cost of building done in this way is acceptable to the authority. But when the authority comes to consider large-scale building in the country, particularly the rehousing of great numbers of peasant families, then at once the enormous cost of the project condemns it as impracticable. Thus, though many ambitious schemes of rural redevelopment have been mooted, none has ever survived the first committee meeting at which its probable cost was revealed.

The contract system must bear the blame for this high cost. The principal contractor farms out the work to subcontractors, who are severally responsible for such items as the masonry, the carpentry, the sanitary installations, the plastering, and so on. The subcontractor in his turn will put the work into the hands of a jobbing builder, who will actually engage laborers and supervise them on the job. There are several middlemen, each of whom takes his profit and helps to put the price of the job up. Materials too, when bought ready-made from commercial suppliers, tend to be dear.

There are two further disadvantages in having big rehousing projects executed by a private contractor. The first is that the primary contractor is almost as remote from the work as is the planning authority, so that he cannot exercise any detailed control over the building. The chain of responsibility, through jobbing builder, subcontractor, primary contractor to the planning authority is so alternated that no precise check can be kept on the cost of individual items. Neither is the contractor in close contact with the labor market, so that work may be held up or become unreasonably costly because there are no workers to do it.

The second disadvantage is that when a project is sufficiently big, it can disturb the labor and materials markets so much that the prices of these commodities are forced up well above their ordinary level. Thus very large building schemes do not secure any economy, and, instead of being cheaper, houses are actually dearer by the dozen. This is because no architect knows the real cost of building; he knows only the prices usually quoted by contractors. Not even the contractors know the cost; they are all at the mercy of the economics of the trade and cannot quote with any confidence for projects unfamiliarly large.

Why then do the planning authorities stick to the contract system? Simply because they rely upon their architects for technical advice, and the architects have no experience of any other method of executing work. It is very seldom that an alternative to the private contractor is considered when rural housing schemes are being discussed.

One alternative, though, has gained some favor recently. This is the system known as "aided self-help," and rehousing schemes based upon this method of securing labor have been enthusiastically fostered by United Nations agencies and others. Briefly the principle is this: the government, or the United Nations, or some other benevolent authority, provides the peasants in some depressed countryside with equipment and materials to build their own houses. The peasants give their work free, and, with the help of the machines and materials they have been given, they improve their own condition.

The trouble with this system is that the "self-help" lasts just as long as the "aid" does. The peasants learn how to work a cement mixer or how to fit up a prefabricated roof, but as soon as the free materials stop arriving, the peasants are as badly off as ever—except, of course, for the buildings they already have. The point is that they cannot employ the skills they have learned because they cannot afford the materials.

A further danger is that they may even lose the crafts they already possess, which enable them to make use of their own native materials. This may happen either by the traditional craftman's deliberate rejection of his old methods, out of mistaken admiration for the imagined superiority of the alien methods, or, more ironically, by the alien method's driving the traditional craftsman out of his job, taking away his work, and chasing him into some other employment. Then when the brief period of artificial construction is over and the expensive machinery breaks down and the supply of foreign materials dries up, there is nobody left to build in the old way. "Aided self-help," in fact, merely succeeds in giving the local craftsmen an illusory feeling of progress and superiority while tempting them into that most frustrating of blind alleys, a sophisticated trade that will inevitably be shut to them a short time later. Either they become zealous advocates of the new methods, more royalist than the king, and despise their old skills, or they are driven away to become farm workers. In either case their craft is destroyed.

It sometimes seems as if people in large, clean offices or large, clean universities in nice, progressive countries are offended by the existence of poverty and squalor among millions in the unfortunate countries. They cannot have this eyesore—or mindsore—existing; it's like an unwholesome beggar at their gate, and they want to get rid of it as fast as possible. How does the rich man dispose of the beggar? He sends out half-a-crown to buy himself peace of mind—or, more effectively, he builds a workhouse and legislates the beggar inside. The workhouse solution is perhaps discredited in the parish, but in international affairs it is still canvassed, in the shape—so I sometimes think—of "aided self-help." "Send out a million prefabricated houses." "Give them twenty shiploads of cement." "Give him sixpence to go away." "What a dreadful smell—give them some drains." "Well, at least they'll be better off in barracks than in those frightful hovels they've got now."

They won't. There is more beauty, and more self-respect, in the shanties put up by the refugees round Gaza than in any of the dreary model settlements erected by benevolent foreign bodies, while in Nubia each peasant lives in his own airy palace like a lord. If only "aided self-help" was really that! If only the aiders would see what the peasant at his best can do, and would direct their aid to helping him realize his own creative abilities, the plight of Egypt's peasant might not only be alleviated but made the occasion for an architecture that would win the admiration of the world.

The two most frequently suggested systems of executing large-scale plans—the contract system and the system of "aided self-help" —cannot cope with a problem the size of Egypt's. In the same way certain other solutions—for example the use of the army or of volunteer bands of students, or even of forced labor—will not work. If the peasant has his village built for him, as a kind of charity, then he will not gain the skill and experience that he would if he built it himself, and when the army, or whatever it is, has gone home, and the buildings in the course of time begin to deteriorate, the villager will not be able to repair them. It is exactly as if a man who wanted a garden went to a shop and got a dozen horticultural experts to come and make him a garden one weekend. It would be very nice for a week, but the man would lack the skill, and even perhaps the impulse, to keep it in good order—it would probably be too big or too exotic for him to manage anyway—and before long his garden would become a wilderness; if, on the other hand, he had made it with his own hands in his own time, he would understand every bit of it and be well able to keep it attractive.

If the system of "aided self-help" is to be successful, the following conditions must be satisfied:
(1) The materials given to the peasants must be cheap; cheap enough for the peasants to buy or for the government to give away free. (2) The materials given should be such as the peasants will be able to obtain for themselves without governmental help when the scheme comes to an end. That means, in practice, that they must be common local materials. (3) The materials should not need skilled labor to handle them, beyond what the peasants themselves can afford to engage: no more than, say, a village mason or carpenter. The materials should be such that most of the work can be done by unsupervised labor.

In brief, "aided self-help" must aid peasants to build in local, virtually costless materials, using skills which they themselves already have or can easily acquire. Above all, materials such as steel or concrete—or even, often, timber, which nearly always have to be imported—should be regarded with the utmost suspicion when it is proposed to hand them out to help peasants build their houses. Only when the country itself is producing these materials cheaply enough, and the inhabitants are earning enough money to buy them, are they permissible in national rehousing schemes.

Another system has been used in some places, though not widely in Egypt. This is the "nucleus" system, in which the planning authority designs one or two standard houses and builds *a small part* of each house, leaving the occupier to build the rest himself. The government-built bit is the nucleus, and the occupier's contribution forms the rest of the organism. Unfortunately, since the nucleus is usually built of concrete or baked brick, the peasant cannot afford to carry on in the same material, and sticks on accretions in mud brick. Thus there is no continuity or consonance between the two parts of the buildings, and the government's contribution scarcely deserves the name of "nucleus." Like other forms of "aid from above," the nucleus system does not stimulate local crafts or prepare the peasants to build for themselves.

Not until the technicians—the architects and engineers—who are charged with the responsibility of rehousing a peasant population acknowledge that a vigorous and self-perpetuating tradition of building can only arise from the enthusiasm of the peasants themselves, and that such enthusiasm can only spring up if the peasants see that they really can build good houses themselves for next to nothing—not until then will any national housing scheme in any underdeveloped country stand a chance of success.

If you want a flower, you don't try to make it with bits of paper and glue, but you devote your labor and intelligence instead to preparing the ground, then you put a seed in and let it grow. In the same way, to make use of the natural desire of the villager to build, we must apply ourselves to preparing the ground by creating an atmosphere or social climate in which building will flourish, and we must not waste our energy on the construction of buildings which, however smart or striking they may be, will be as sterile and unproductive as artificial flowers. Indeed, the seeds are already there in the ground, germinated and ready to push up to the surface; the plant has adapted itself over long centuries to the land, and will flower abundantly. We need only give it a little encouragement, a little weeding, a little hoeing, perhaps a sprinkling from the watering can. The least assistance from science, the smallest encouragement from the government will, if intelligently given, be enough to bring about a rebirth of peasant initiative in building that will be infinitely more powerful than any ready-made government building program can be.

The Cooperative System

We already know that the materials exist and are cheap; we already know the technique of using them; what can the peasants themselves teach us about organizing the work? How do the villages in those places still untouched by the commercial building contractor arrange their building activities?

They cooperate. When a new house is to be built in a village, everyone is expected to lend a hand. Many people help in the work, and the house is soon finished. None of these helpful neighbors is paid. The only return expected by a man who puts in a day building a fellow villager's house is that the fellow villager will do the same for him one day. Building thus becomes a communal activity, like harvesting, like dealing with a fire, like a wedding or a funeral. The villagers in Nubia seem to work together to help each other as naturally and with as little direction or supervision as ants or bees.

The cooperative system, however, can only work in this traditional way when it is dealing with traditional problems and when the society is truly traditional itself. A dozen new houses a year do not put a great strain upon the labor resources of a village. There is still time to attend to the fields and to all the other affairs of life. Similarly, when a man lives on what he grows, and money is a rare commodity, when he has not been tempted with the knowledge of what money can buy, he is quite willing to give up his time to building a house or two. No one has ever told him "time is money." But when a whole new village is to be built, then building takes up a disproportionate amount of the community's time; and when a man works for a wage, he is unwilling to work for nothing.

Nonetheless, if a system of cooperative building can be made to work, it will have enormous advantages over any system employing professional builders. First and foremost, a village built by its own inhabitants will be a living organism, capable of growth and of continuing life, whereas a village built by hired professionals will be a dead thing that starts to fall to pieces the day after the builders leave. Second, a cooperatively built village will be much cheaper than one built by hired labor—in fact, it will be the only kind of village cheap enough for a country like Egypt to afford in large numbers.

If the traditional cooperative system can be made to work under nontraditional conditions, then it can clearly be expanded and applied to a mass housing program.

The basic motive in the voluntary donation of time and labor in the cooperative system is the desire to receive similar help oneself. "Do as you would be done by," in fact. Every neighbor, by helping build a house, establishes a right to receive help himself, opens an account in a kind of labor bank. If this principle is recognized and if the exact amount of work to a man's credit can be calculated and recorded, the cooperative system will begin to appeal to even the most commercially minded peasant.

Obviously, anyone would like a new house if it is bigger, cleaner, and more beautiful than his existing one. Anyone would be ready to build such a house for himself if shown how. The snag is that a house is essentially a communal production: one man cannot build one house, but a hundred men can easily build a hundred houses. "All right," says the peasant, "I want a house, so let's build it—but why should I build a house for Ahmed?" Only if the peasant's own contribution to the house can be accurately and impartially measured, and recorded as a loan to society, which society will repay in the shape of a house, can the suspicious peasant be persuaded to join in a scheme of communal cooperative building.

In order to measure the work lent to the community by any individual villager, and to state this loan in terms of the building owed to him by the community, it is necessary to know in the minutest detail two things: one, how many hours' useful work any given worker has done, and, two, how many man-hours of work have gone into any component of a house. The first of these pieces of information can be had by a careful system of ordering work and checking progress. The second we found during the course of the work at Gourna; we analyzed the cost of each piece of work and established a standard piece which could be stated in terms of money or of man-hours—for each stage of the work on every kind of building.

In-Service Training

If a village is to be built by its own future inhabitants, then we must give them the necessary skills. However much enthusiasm the cooperative system may engender, it will do little good if the people don't know how to lay bricks. The number of fairly skilled workers needed to build a village is too great to admit of hiring outsiders, for this would put the cost up much too high.

Usually, when people talk of training they think of schools, and it seems natural to establish technical schools to train the peasants in the necessary building crafts. I must emphasize strongly that technical schools are not the answer to our need for skilled workers. They inevitably teach far too elaborate a course, when we need men who can perform perhaps half a dozen operations in masonry; they tend to become academic and to induce prejudices in the students' minds against practices not found in the textbooks; they give the graduate a diploma, which makes him feel so grand and important that he despises manual work and prefers to become a clerk in a government office; they are very expensive and would add considerably to the cost of a building program; and, finally, they would produce a large number of elaborately trained craftsmen who, when their own village was finished, would find no work to do and would be lost to the trade and to farming.

No, we need a method of teaching the peasant the elements of practical building so that he can contribute usefully to the building of his village, but we don't want to turn him from a productive farmer into a highly skilled but unemployable mason. He must acquire a handy ability to put up walls and stores on his own land; he will be in a position to help his neighbor with a bit of building and to keep his own house intact and trim, but he will always consider himself to be a farm worker, not a builder. There is indeed a place for the technical school course; we need highly skilled professional craftsmen who will be a permanent acquisition for the country, and they may properly be trained in a technical school, but the mass of semiskilled workers need a different training procedure.

I suggest that these workers be trained on the job. It would be difficult to train a large number of apprentices on small jobs such as private houses. That is why it is necessary, if a village is to be built by the cooperative system, to start with the public buildings, which provide plenty of opportunity for training the villagers in building crafts that they can later apply to their own dwellings.

Furthermore, if the public buildings are built in the same way, by the same methods of construction as the private houses, the village will be assured of architectural harmony and will be spared the sight of a group of buildings proclaiming their officialism and self-assumed superiority in their alien architecture—a separateness that too often is more than a surface appearance and that comes out too in the attitude of the people to the officials.

By training the villagers on the public buildings, which will be erected first as the core of the village, we can make use of the architects and master craftsmen engaged by the building authority, and they can pass on their skills to the people. Then, even if the authority cannot afford to build many private houses, the skills will have been implanted, the village center will be there, and the inhabitants will be able to go on for themselves.

Some building operations are very easy to learn: squaring a room, for example. Others are more difficult. Building a vault is a very skilled job, and in Nubia it is reckoned that an apprentice needs three years to learn how to draw the correct curve freehand. It is possible, of course, to give the inexperienced builder a templet of the correct curve, so that his job becomes one requiring care rather than knowledge. To speed up the training of apprentices we did this in Gourna, and it worked quite well, but our master mason, Abdul-Aziz, was furious with me. He said that he had his fingers banged whenever he made a mistake, and now we were giving away the secret to these lads who hadn't worked for it. I have come to the conclusion that Abdul-Aziz was right; his attitude was that of the medieval masons, the *compagnons* of the French guilds, who jealously guarded the secrets that enabled them to build the complicated arches of the Gothic cathedrals in which every thrust and stress is minutely calculated. The masons would give tracings of each arch by the master mason, and could never depart from them. Both in medieval Europe and in Gourna or Nubia a mason would have to have matured in his craft for a certain time before becoming ready to receive the highest secrets of it. There is no real short cut to craftsmanship, any more than to other forms of knowledge. It is easy to apply a formula in engineering, for example, but unless you understand how it is derived you may run into difficulties.

The maturing of skill is an experience of considerable spiritual value to the craftsman, and a man who acquires the solid mastery of any skill grows too in self-respect and moral stature. In fact the transformation brought about in the personalities of the peasants when they build their own village is of greater value than the transformation in their material condition. Each craftsman individually gains in understanding and dignity, while the village collectively acquires a sense of society, of interdependence and brotherhood that only such cooperative achievement can give. Because of the spiritual value of constructive skill, I have often preferred what may seem to be the hard way in building. For example, there seem to be many advantages in rammed earth over mud brick—notably that the brick making operations are cut out and that no skill, only brute force, is needed to make walls. Yet I have always considered bricklaying to be a far more ennobling activity than pounding away for hours at a mass of earth in a wooden form. Even practically there are advantages in developing skills; a mason who relies on templets to get his curves right could not safely put a vault over walls that are not parallel.

I have already explained that a cooperative building system can only work if a man's work can be recorded as a loan to society and repaid in the form of a building. Now clearly the work of a skilled mason should be assessed more highly than that of an untrained laborer. Again, if the community allows its masons to spend their valuable time instructing trainees, someone should pay for this time. Therefore a scheme of in-service training should provide for the trainees to pay for their training by giving their newly acquired skill to the community at a lower rate than the normal. I worked out the following scheme for in-service training, which was applied in Gourna:

The helpers—the young men and boys who do the unskilled work—are invited to watch the masons at work so that they can get an idea of the kind of work done. The training course is advertised both verbally and in writing, with a detailed explanation of the stages of 128 training, the skills to be taught, and the rate of pay appropriate to each stage. Those among the helpers who seem keen to learn and who show any aptitude at all are placed on the first rung of a ladder leading to their final qualification as mason. There are five stages of training:

A. Trainee: daily wage, 8 PT (the same as an unskilled boy-laborer).
B. Apprentice: daily wage, 12 PT.
C. Assistant mason: daily wage, 18 PT.
D. Mason: daily wage, 25 PT.
E. Master mason (*moallem*): daily wage, 35–40 PT.

Those accepted into class *A*—trainees—will be taught to square a layout for a rectangular unit, to lay bricks for walls 1, 1½, and 2 bricks thick, to lay bricks for intersecting walls, and to lay bricks for corners and jambs. All these walls will be built dry, using no mortar.

After two weeks' training the learner will be tested to see if he can lay 200 bricks an hour accurately. If he passes, he will then work on the actual buildings in progress, helping two master masons by handing them the materials they need. He will also watch their work with more understanding, having been trained, and will learn from watching them. He must stay for two weeks on this job, at the same wage as a laborer (8 PT).

Then the trainee proceeds to stage *B* and goes back to the class to be taught more of his trade. He will lay bricks for the same walls as before, but this time he will use mortar. He will build ½-brick partitions of red brick with earth mortar. He will learn to build square columns 1, 1½, and 2 bricks thick, and pilasters 1 and 1½ bricks wide on walls of various thicknesses. If in the two weeks of lessons he masters these operations, he will go back to the main job for two weeks, where he will assist two master masons by filling the core of the walls they build. This is useful work, but does not demand the skill of a qualified mason, for the helper does not have the responsibility of aligning and leveling the walls. While he is doing this the trainee is paid 12 PT—more than a humble laborer, because he has now graduated to the rank of apprentice. The value of his work we may say roughly is a quarter of that of the two master masons, or 20 PT per day. The 8 PT difference between his wage and the value of his work may be taken as a repayment to the community for his training.

After doing this work satisfactorily for 2 weeks, he returns to the class at stage *C*. Here he learns to build segmental arches 1½ bricks deep on walls 2 bricks thick, with spans 0.9 and 1.2 meters (for windows and doors) and pointed arches 2 and 2½ meters' span. If he passes his test, this time at the end of one week only, he becomes an assistant mason and goes to work on the job for one week at a wage of 18 PT. We may consider now that his work is worth that of a master mason (50 PT per day), and so we gain 22 PT per day from him.

His next course of lessons lasts two weeks, when he is taught to build vaults without centering over a span of 1½ and 2½ and 3 meters and to build a Byzantine dome (on pendentives) of 3 meters' span. In order to graduate from this stage, he must be able to build a vault 1½ meters' span at a rate of 1 meter linear per hour (152 bricks P.M.L.), a 2-meter vault at 60 centimeters per hour (204 bricks P.M.L.), a 2½-meter vault at 30 centimeters per hour (272 bricks P.M.L.), and a 3-meter vault at 20 centimeters per hour (340 bricks P.M.L.). The dome, consisting of 1,400 bricks, has to be built in two days by two trainees. As masons work in pairs, these norms are doubled for a pair of trainees. On graduating from this stage, the trainee receives the title of mason; if he does not pass the qualifying test, he is returned to the job for at least one month as an assistant mason, after which he may be readmitted to the course, if he chooses to come back, only on the understanding that he will not be paid.

The graduate mason, who may now earn 25 PT per day, is free to take work as and when he likes on the job. After this stage of training, whether the trainee passes or fails his test, his future career, the work he does, or the additional training he takes, is left entirely to him. In this way only the keenest want to take the next stage of training.

This is to give the trainee his final qualification as master mason. He must build domes on squinches, 3 meters and 4 meters in diameter, and a vault on walls which are not parallel, with the large end 3 meters' span, keeping the apex horizontal all the way along. This is a very tricky business, for the springing must be gradually raised as he proceeds. Then he must build a staircase supported by vaults. This course lasts for two weeks, and on passing, the trainee must then work for one week on the job with the stone masons, learning to handle stone. At last he is given a certificate showing what he can do, which declares him to be a fully qualified master mason.

The whole training of a master mason takes seventeen weeks and costs about 800 PT, or L.E. 8. The time is ample, for trainees who pick the work up quickly will learn faster, and the investment of

L.E. 8 will be fully repaid even before the trainee finally graduates, while if we consider that for his first month as a master-mason he is paid 10 PT per day less than the usual rate, or 15 PT per day less if he remains at the grade of mason, we find that we make an overall profit on each successful trainee. As the average graduate will work for some months before he is good enough to deserve full pay, he will pay back quite enough to cover the salary of the instructor.

Such a training system is a practical and popular way of producing the skilled workmen we need. It commends itself even to contractors, should the government wish to make use of them, for the contractor's biggest worry is how to find the labor he needs in remote places. I have approached several big contractors to find out if they would be willing to use masons trained like this, and they all welcomed the idea enthusiastically. It would indeed save them money, for to induce a mason who lives in a town to go out to some distant village the contractor has to pay him double the usual rate. Nevertheless, a project would be still cheaper if the government loaned equipment to the small local builders instead of engaging big contractors, for it will anyway be the small builders who do the actual work, so that if they are given the chance of using the equipment that in the normal way they could not afford, the big contractor's profit can be knocked off the bill, local enterprise and prosperity encouraged, and the training of local craftsmen more easily put in hand. A striking proof of the practicability of this practice appeared in the building of the school at Fares, for which no contractor had so much as submitted a tender, although the contract had been offered for three successive years.

We bought L.E. 200-worth of equipment and lent it to the small local builders, with the result that the school cost only one-third as much as normal ones in more accessible places. The Fares school has ten classrooms, a specially designed large library and a large, multipurpose room backing an open-air stage for theatricals, and cost 6,000 L.E., while another school of the same type, in the town of Aswan, the capital of the province, having only nine classrooms and ordinary room used as library, cost L.E. 16,000.

The master mason, after graduation works at least one month for 30 PT. A graduate who reaches the grade of mason and is working on the job without going on to training for master mason will be paying back 360 PT per month instead of 240 PT. A master mason who shows high skill in building during the first month after graduation while working on the job will have his daily wage raised to 35 PT. If he continues to show progress in his technique during the next month after this rise, he will finally be given the full wage of 40 PT (see appendix II).

Gourna Not an End in Itself

For me Gourna was not an end in itself but a first tentative step on the road to the complete regeneration of the Egyptian countryside through rebuilding its villages. In Gourna a completely new concept of rural housing was tried out and proved practicable. The first part of this book presents a program for applying this concept in a nationwide village rebuilding campaign.

It may be objected that rural housing is not the most urgent problem facing Egypt; that one would do better to devote one's attention to providing work or food or some other more basic need. No one can deny that Egypt's most urgent task is to improve the life of her people. By far the bigger part of the population is to be found in the villages; that is to say, most Egyptians are peasants, who live very miserably. It is therefore by its success in raising the standard of living of these peasants that any government and any political doctrine in Egypt will be judged.

Are better houses then, the first essential in raising this standard of living? Perhaps not, but is food? The standard of living is not determined solely by the amount of food people eat nor the age at which they die. The U.N. Economic and Social Council has suggested a number of "components and indicators for the measurement of levels of living," among which figure such items as "recreation," "human freedom," and "conditions of work." Health and food consumption are indeed taken into account, and so is housing. The standard of living is determined by many factors, and housing is by no means a negligible one. It is also the one that I, as an architect, can give advice on.

Even when housing conditions are admitted as an element in the "level of living," too often the quality of housing is assessed according to the provision of a mere room and sanitation. Yet it has been shown time and again that a room, or two rooms, and a toilet do not necessarily raise the level of living. Overcrowded rooms, rooms overrun with chickens and other animals, do not contribute to a feeling of contentment and security. If housing is to be a factor in the standard of living, then it must be housing that provides space and beauty as well as lavatories. Unfortunately, because housing seems to rank after nutrition as a factor in keeping people alive, planners often seem to think that the barest minimum is all they can afford, rather as some people think that their responsibility is finished once they have provided a soup kitchen to feed the unemployed.

The soup kitchen is not enough, nor is the minimum house. Any family needs a house adequately large, private, and peaceful, with room for animals and other such indispensable accessories to its life.

Some people in authority say that it is impossible to give the peasant this. They point out the difficulty of paying for good houses. The average income of an Egyptian peasant is L.E. 4 a year. How can the peasants ever pay for any sort of a house, let alone a big one? Even with government loans, most of them cannot afford the starkest utility designs presented to them. Money—say these people, and they are right—does not exist in the country. Houses cost money, and the bigger they are, the more they cost. We cannot afford anyway to give houses to all the peasants; so in order to house as many as possible, the houses we do give must be of the lowest acceptable quality. The soup kitchen attitude at its worst.

These people have been frightened by a figure—L.E. 4 a year. Because they conceive of houses as things that come out of factories, that are the products, directly or indirectly, of big industry and big business, they cannot conceive how any house can be bought for L.E. 4 a year. And indeed, so long as their thinking remains bound by the monetary system, imprisoned in the edifice of contract, subcontract, tender, and quotation, they will never see any way of providing the people with houses fit to live in. Every solution so far suggested for Egypt's rural housing problem starts with the assumption that a concrete house is better than a mud house—that the first step in improving peasant houses is to "improve" the materials, not the design. Such "improved" materials are invariably ones made by big industry: steel, cement, etc. Of course these cost money, and the more you have in a house—the bigger the house is, in fact—the more you have to spend. Quite rightly, our planners come to the conclusion that we cannot afford to give spacious concrete houses to the peasants. Not only spacious ones; we cannot afford to give even the smallest concrete houses to all the peasants who need them—a fact that is frequently glossed over.

No, any solution that involves paying for industrially produced building materials and commercial building contractors is doomed to certain failure. We haven't enough money. If houses are to be built at all, in sufficient quantity, they must be built without money. We must go right outside the framework of the monetary system, bypass the factories, and ignore the contractors.

How is this to be done? How can we rebuild four thousand villages without using money?

129 The answer is to be found in this photograph. It shows a room in a peasant house in Nubia. This house, like several hundred others in the villages round Aswan, was built without the expenditure of one piaster. No building contractor came within ten miles of it. It contains no concrete, no steel, no materials at all except what were produced on the spot. It took about a week to erect—the whole

house of which it is part was built in three weeks. These are its practical virtues. For its aesthetic qualities, the photograph speaks clearly enough. Sufficient to ask where, in any mass housing project sponsored by any national or international authority in the world, you will find such mastery over space, such assured handling of proportion, such harmony, dignity, and peace. For those who have eyes to see, this room is the answer to Egypt's housing "problem."

What aspects of the problem does it solve? First, that of money. It is built entirely of mud and costs nothing. Second, that of space. With the money problem solved, there is no limit to the size of the house; ten rooms are as cheap as one. Third, that of hygiene. Space means health, both physical and mental, while the material, mud, does not harbor insects as thatch and wood do. Fourth, that of beauty. The demands of the structure alone are almost sufficient to ensure pleasing lines, while the fact that it is a costless method gives the designer perfect freedom to produce spatial beauty without feeling the construction of a tight budget.

And how does this room manage to solve a problem that has baffled all the architects and planners in Egypt? What have the Nubian peasants got that our architects haven't? First, they have a technique—that of vaulting in mud brick. This liberates them from expense, enables them to build a whole house, roof and all, without spending money. Second, they have a custom of cooperation in their daily lives, so that when a house is to be built, all the neighbors come and help, and there is no question of hiring and paying laborers.

The moral to be drawn from this photograph is twofold: build houses out of mud brick, and use the freely donated services of their future inhabitants to build them.

It may reasonably be inquired, at this stage, what the Gourna experiment has to add, if this photograph shows so much? Well, the Nubians have been building like this for six thousand years, and nobody has taken the hint yet. Architects whose experience is confined to city building need some convincing when asked to design in mud. When large-scale building is called for—whole villages, by the hundred—they want to know whether the Nubian methods can be adapted to such schemes without losing their advantages of costlessness and beauty. They may also want to know whether the mud brick house can incorporate the sanitary fittings and other amenities that modern civilization demands and whether it will prove to be as strong as a house made of more respectable materials.

I do not claim that Gourna has conclusively answered every one of these questions. The major ones, regarding modern amenities and durability, are indeed answered quite satisfactorily, and we showed that peasant techniques and materials can be employed in large-scale architect-designed building schemes. To the crucial question of cost, Gourna only suggests an answer. For Gourna was a very special case. We were not rebuilding an existing village, with the glad cooperation of the villagers, but building on a new site a receptacle for a population that was to be moved against its will from its accustomed home.

To be really cheap, rural building must be done by the peasants in voluntary cooperation, and not by paid laborers. I had worked out a method of incorporating the villagers' traditional cooperative building customs into a large-scale project such as building a complete village, but because of the Gournis' objections to being moved, I was unable to make use of this method. I had to hire laborers and pay them. Nevertheless, it was quite easy to subtract the cost of this labor from the total in order to arrive at an estimate of the cost of a similar scheme using free cooperative labor. After Gourna I very much wanted a chance to try out the system of voluntary cooperation in some large building project.

A Stillborn Experiment, Mit-el-Nasara: *Iblis in Relentless Pursuit*

The chance came when, in 1954, a large part of the village of Mit-el-Nasara was burned down. Two hundred families were left homeless, living in tents and very distressed, and the government wished to rehouse them as soon as possible.

Each family was to be offered L.E. 200, of which L.E. 100 was an outright gift from the Ministry of Works and L.E. 100 a loan from the Ministry of Municipal and Rural Affairs. It soon became apparent that this sum would not be enough for a family to build itself a new house through the usual medium of private contractors, and so I was invited by the Minister of Social Affairs to act as consultant on a committee that was to provide these new houses.

I found that the homeless families were expecting the government to provide them with new houses like a fairy godmother. The prevailing attitude appeared to be: "Well, if they can give us L.E. 200, why not L.E. 400 or L.E. 1,000?" I thought that L.E. 200 might indeed be enough to cover the cost of such materials as timber and pipes that could not be made locally as well as the skilled labor and technical assistance, provided that the villagers themselves would contribute the unskilled labor and would lend their animals to help carry materials.

We soon understood that we could not possibly keep account of the labor contributed by and the building owed to each of the two hundred families, and that if we tried to deal with each family separately, we should never be able to ensure a regular flow of laborers;

people would always be going off to the market or out to the fields and we should spend more time organizing than building. It would also be impossible to recruit people indiscriminately, or by any sort of roster, for they were not to be paid, and so such a method would be kind of forced labor. For these reasons we decided to divide the population into about twenty family groups, and to ask each group to choose a representative—an elder—with whom we could negotiate. The family group would be made responsible for finding its quota of labor at the right time; the houses would be made over to the family group; and the contract would be signed with the family group, as represented by the elder. Each of these groups would comprise some twenty families and could produce at least thirty laborers; it could arrange things so that a poor family gave less than the others and it could keep up the supply of laborers while allowing individual families some latitude in their obligations.

Community Development at Grassroots Level

Having decided this, it was necessary to explain the proposals to the villagers. At first they were hostile to the idea of mud brick, but when it was explained to them that there was no other way of getting a house for the money, and that with this system they could have a large and beautiful house, they accepted. By this time we had made our estimates, based on the information we had obtained in Gourna, and calculated that we could rehouse the village for L.E. 84 per house, thus putting L.E. 16 in the villagers' pockets and enabling them to do without the L.E. 100 loan.

These estimates took the form of a complete work program. A plan of the village indicated where each family group was to have its houses, and a schedule showed what part of the work was to be provided by the unskilled labor of the peasants, what by the skilled labor hired by the government, and what part of the labor was to be expended on training. Each party contracted to supply a given quantity of labor, and any family group defaulting on this obligation would lose all right to government assistance.

Once the proposals had been explained and the villagers had agreed to the idea of spending their money on architects and craftsmen rather than on concrete, we had to show them the kind of houses they would get.

We arranged for five of the "elders," together with five masons from the village, to travel to Gourna, where they would be entertained by the Gournis and shown the buildings there. At the same time we prepared plans of a number of sample houses and, using these plans, made detailed estimates of the amount and kind (professional or cooperative) of labor each would involve. We chose the site for the new sector, but we waited before planning the layout until we should have had time to investigate the social structure among the families, to size the groups, to appoint the elders, and to discuss the distribution of families in the neighborhood units. All this had to be done before we could start designing individual houses.

We were prepared to consider the size and reasonable wishes of a family when designing its house—we had no objection to the family paying extra for an extra-large building or for luxurious fittings, for example—but we had to make it clear that our main concern was to house the distressed and not to satisfy the capricious demands of those who could afford a private architect.

There is in every village a traditional and very reasonable tendency to look upon "the government" as a kind of heathen god, to be feared, propitiated, prayed to, and from which unexpected blessings may descend, but it seldom occurs to the villager that the government is something you may cooperate with, something with which you may even conclude a reasonable agreement on tackling a problem. We had to persuade the villagers of Mit-el-Nasara that the government's powers were not divine and limitless, but that on the contrary they were represented very precisely by the L.E. 200 already offered, and that all the government was now offering was good advice on how to spend the money to the best effect. The cost of everything—architects, engineers, machines, masons and clerks—had to come out of that money. If the villagers availed themselves of our expertise, then they could have good houses very cheaply, but only if they contributed the unskilled labor and much of the transport themselves, for nothing.

In the event, the villagers readily understood the proposals and were enthusiastic about them. They were very miserable in their tents and, unlike the Gournis, had nothing to lose by accepting our scheme. Unfortunately, just as at Gourna, the government lived up to its reputation as a heathen god by abruptly handing over the responsibility for every building in the country from the various ministries to the Ministry of Rural and Municipal Affairs, which was not sympathetic toward the methods I had evolved and at once gave the job to its own architects to be done in the orthodox and expensive concrete way. The Mit-el-Nasara project was thus never completed in the way I had envisaged. Nevertheless, from the villagers' encouraging response to our explanations, I think we may draw the fairly optimistic conclusion that cooperative building would work in most cases of village resettlement in Egypt.

I was particularly encouraged to see how the villagers, as soon as they learned that sand from the bed of the river would be needed for brick making, and this sand would have to be dug in the few weeks before the river rose, took all their donkeys and camels and themselves dug and carried all the sand we needed, without waiting for contracts or agreements or elders or for any of our paper organization to make accounts of their work.

One interesting technical discovery emerged from the Mit-el-Nasara project, and that was how to make bricks quickly. Because of the acute distress of the villagers we had to build the village as quickly as possible, and so I was ready to use any means of saving time. Dr. Ytzhar, a soil mechanics consultant to the Baum-Marpin Company, came to help us, and he suggested speeding up brick manufacture by mixing the dry constituents—earth and sand—in a mechanical cement mixer with a carefully controlled quantity of steam. The steam would penetrate the lumps of earth much better than water could, and would envelop each particle in a film of water, thus achieving instant and complete amalgamation of earth and water in exactly the right proportions without the need to make excessively wet mud and then leave it for days to dry.

We found that this steam-wetted mixture, if made into bricks in a mechanical press under the same pressure as a Winget machine produces—eight atmospheres—could be used in building immediately. We had samples of the local earth analyzed in the laboratories of the Engineering Department of Cairo University, where it was found that a quantity of sand had to be added to improve the granular graduation, and when this was done the bricks would take a compression of forty kilograms per square centimeter. These sample bricks were made with improvised equipment in the workshops of the Baum-Marpin Company, who showed interest in our findings and were prepared to lend us considerable help in producing the bricks for the village.

It should be stressed here, though, that this use of machinery was proposed only because of the villagers' urgent need for houses. In an ordinary village, where the people already have houses of a sort and can take their time over building new ones, there is no need whatsoever for machine-made bricks. A strength of forty kilograms per square centimeter is quite superfluous and, since such bricks are denser and more conductive than sun-dried ones, may even prove positively disadvantageous. Certainly they cost more.

There is an unfortunate tendency among many architects and engineers, when they tackle low-cost housing, to introduce expensive complications that are not really needed at all. Many of the experiments on the stabilization of earth with cement and bitumen for use in building seem to me to be misdirected. An ordinary mud brick, dried in the sun, is perfectly adequate for building an ordinary house, and can in Egypt be made for next to nothing. It needs no more protection than a coat of waterproof plaster, and, if stabilizing materials are to be used, they would be more economically employed in this protective plaster rather than throughout the whole thickness of the wall.

The engineer has a different outlook from the villager; he thinks that the stronger a component is, the better it must be. He tries to bring the mud brick up to the standard of concrete, but in doing so he turns it into an industrial product instead of a peasant product. He makes a brick that is unnecessarily strong and beyond the resources of the peasant to make or buy. Really low-cost housing must not need nonexistent resources; mud brick houses are today made all over Egypt without the help of machines and engineers, and we must resist the temptation to improve on something that is already satisfactory.

National Program for Rural Reconstruction

The Gourna project was started to meet a unique situation and was not primarily part of any scheme for rural development, but any future village rehousing projects—except for isolated emergencies caused by flood and fire—will be undertaken in order to improve rural living conditions.

It is probably true to say that every village in Egypt needs rebuilding, if merely to ensure that its inhabitants have houses that come up to a minimum standard of habitability.

However, these are matters of national policy that are properly the concern of the nation and its governors—I merely wish to record the opinion that a rehousing scheme can work only as part of a wider, national redevelopment scheme.

If such a huge program of rebuilding is ever to be undertaken, it cannot be simply an architectural operation. If every village in the country is to be rebuilt, a general program must be developed for the total development of the whole countryside. Such a program would involve reconsidering the whole question of population and land balance, to determine the optimum division of the population between country and town and the optimum distribution of the rural population over the countryside. The aim should be to achieve the total exploitation of the total resources of the country, and their fair distribution among the total population, for Egypt cannot afford to let any source of potential wealth lie untapped, nor to leave any section of her people underprivileged.

Such a program should proceed by carefully planned stages, or else there will be much distress. Training must precede building, and the effects of every change allowed for. Just as in an irrigation scheme you have to prepare your drainage system before you bring water, so in socioeconomic planning you have to be prepared to deal with sudden surpluses of population and labor. Mechanized agriculture, for example, will create unemployment unless there are jobs waiting to absorb the redundant farm laborers.

In the same way the industrialization of crafts can produce so much unemployment that any increased production is quite outweighed by the resulting social misery. In planning the modernization of a country, every effect of any measures proposed must be calculated with mathematical precision; the vague optimism of politicians is no longer a sufficient guide to the serious planner.

The population of Egypt has reached thirty million while there are only six million acres of arable land. The situation can be put in more homely terms if we imagine a family of twenty-five trying to live off six acres of farmland—clearly an almost hopeless task if the whole family is to be adequately fed, clothed, and housed and the children educated.

The link between too many mouths and a falling standard of living is immediately seen in a family, but in the nation the chain of cause and effect is not immediately clear; overpopulation declares itself in disease, unemployment, and crime, and it is tempting to explain away these phenomena as having other causes. All our planning can only make the best of a fundamentally intolerable situation. This is indeed a noble task, but the root cause of Egypt's poverty is overpopulation. Overpopulation has two basic remedies: population reduction and increased production. The population may be reduced either by measures of birth control or by emigration, thus easing pressure on resources.

Agricultural resources are already almost fully exploited in Egypt. The most optimistic estimates foresee an increase in arable land, as a result of the High Dam and the New Valley project, of two million acres. So even if the population stays at the present level we shall have twenty-five people living off eight acres—still too many.

However, resources may be used more effectively. There is room for considerably greater exploitation of mineral resources, for example, which implies industrialization. The standard of the arts of production may be raised, thus increasing productivity, while production may be directed to exportable goods, which will bring in a greater return in basic necessities like food than would the direct production of food itself.

The state has in its power the promotion of birth control and productivity, but emigration and even export depend upon whether other countries want Egyptian settlers and goods, and so are not entirely amenable to planning but are rather the domain of international politics.

It is here, in predicting the complex chain of cause and effect that is linked to any major economic act, that we need all the skill of the statistician. It is exactly in the comprehensive long-range forecasting of total situations that statistics can be useful to us, and not in the designing of individual houses.

Raising the standard of living puts the same strain on a country's resources as does an increase in population. Egypt is already overpopulated, and the population is growing fast. Her natural resources are fixed in quantity; so it must seem that any attempt to raise the standard of living in the sphere of housing must add to the gravity of the situation or have an adverse effect upon the other vital needs or investment in industry.

Building is often held to be consuming a nonproductive investment, but this is a very dubious view. Apart from the question of the final end of production, which some would say is to increase the welfare of the people, there is the fact that investment in building leaves a country with a building industry—with plant, skilled workers, and experience. Furthermore the improvement in the health and happiness of the population is certain to be reflected in an improvement in production generally, so that investment in housing is at least comparable with investment in new machine tools and other capital goods.

The only resources that can be rapidly exploited without great investment are the human resources. In the making of goods for domestic comfort—and this includes houses—cooperative craft production is at least as effective as industrial production, and needs no expenditure of foreign exchange. Releasing the productive potential of the Egyptian people would be an economic advance comparable to striking a major oil field, while the social benefit would be immeasurably greater: this is what is meant by "ekistical" efficiency.

Thus the whole program will move at a speed determined by the slowest developing element in it. These elements are (a) the kind and amount of *natural* resources, i.e., mineral, agricultural, hydraulic, etc.; (b) the human resources, i.e., the number of workers and their degrees of skill in various jobs, such as agriculture, fishery, mining, industry, crafts; (c) the standard of living of the people, which depends on the revenue and the way it is spent. That some individuals prefer to spend money on objects of indulgence such as more wives or television sets instead of necessities like wholesome food and good housing should not deflect the planner from offering them what he thinks best for them. The people should, ideally, choose wisely, but the authorities should make that choice easy and even restrict opportunities for unwise choice.

The program will thus move in a series of stages, the first of which will be the development of human resources, i.e., the coordinated training of the population in the skills that are really needed. This stage will be so phased that the right quantity of the right skill is available at the right time. It is important that the emphasis in this training phase should be on immediately useful skills, so that trained workers are ready to carry out the next phase. All kinds of abstract training, academic study, and pure science, though of course indispensable, are not to be regarded as the only kind of knowledge needed in an education planned as part of such a program. Existing schools, universities not only in Egypt but all over the world, amply cater for academic studies of all kinds. The gap to be filled by the training program of the first phase of the general development plan is in the practical education of the great mass of people in the front line of reconstruction. It is at the level of the town and village council and the family itself that initiative and energy are needed to tackle the problem of raising our standard of living. Too often general plans and policies do not percolate down to these levels but stay up in the region of high policies and high finance, where the units are millions, well above the heads of the people who deal in milliemes.

Just as physical planning should come down to the level of the brick and the straw, so socioeconomic planning should consider the family and the individual among the poorest whom we want our services to reach. Unfortunately, however poor the individual in an underdeveloped country may be, his government usually has a few million pounds to bestow upon plans and projects for rural development, and these millions—foreign aid, perhaps, or internal revenues—attract swarms of experts and organizations whose sole object is to make money. The charm of spending other people's money is that a lot of it sticks to the spender, and the postwar years are dotted with the wrecks of projects irresponsibly undertaken by planning bodies and business organizations that are little better than opportunists. You make grandiose plans, sell them to some gullible government (which thus gets credit for being go-ahead and dynamic), import your organization at a suitably impressive fee, and by the time the government has tumbled to the fact that the project isn't going quite as promised, you've made your money and don't care. There is not much money in mud brick or any other local building material, and not much advertisement in detailed local inquiry into the way the "untouchables" live. Thus we cannot expect businessmen to be very interested in cooperative building. But since such a rebuilding program would occupy very many years, during which time the demographic and economic picture would change considerably, any proposals to encourage population shifting should be made only after every aspect of human settlements in Egypt has been thoroughly investigated and after a careful prediction of future trends has been made. Such an investigation must take into account the needs of the people in services, and their probable future needs as the country develops. It would be a survey involving sociologists, social ethnographers, and economists as much as demographers, and it would give a picture of the population as the living organism it is, bringing to bear on the descriptive sciences of many kinds, human as well as mechanical. In short, it would be an ekistic survey.

Without such a survey, no really far-reaching plans can be laid. To plan without knowledge of the facts, without a prognosis of the future pattern, is to invite sure disaster. Money spent on an ekistic survey is never wasted. Even though, after the facts are known, we find that we cannot afford to do very much for the peasants, still we shall have the indispensable foundation for whatever we do decide to do. For every step taken—especially by an official authority—every building erected, even every brick laid is a decision taken about the future condition of Egypt. Such a decision must be either right or wrong, must, if it does not help the country toward a good and workable solution to her problems, push her further into the confusion and expense involved in bad and unworkable solutions. Only with the information furnished by a comprehensive scientific survey of the countryside in the whole country can we be sure that our targets in a rebuilding program are the right ones, and only thus, too, can we be sure that any given decision helps us to achieve those targets.

For example, in regional planning it is necessary to decide which settlements shall be market towns, which large villages, and which small villages, and to distribute these types of settlements in their correct proportion evenly over the region. That is to say, we have to make a plan of the ideal distribution of settlements over the region, superimpose it on the plan of the existing settlements, and see what changes are desirable. Where in any one case no very radical move is indicated, it is probably better not to shift the site of a village at all. There are two attitudes among Egyptian architects toward this aspect of rural planning: one would have a clean break made with the old village, and build a new one in each case well removed from the old, while the other would have the original village rebuilt *in situ* and bit by bit. I favor the latter, provided the public amenities and utilities are installed from the outset, and for this reason: when a settlement is rebuilt, it is good that it be done with the greatest economy and without, even temporarily, splitting the village into widely separated parts, a new and an old. If the new village is built some way from the old, on a completely new site, there will be for some time a hamlet being noisily and messily built, and another hamlet being progressively abandoned and rotting away. If, on the other hand, the new village is started close to the old, and preferably to the east so as to take advantage of the natural westward spread of habitation,* then new buildings will gradually replace old ones on the same site, according to the remodeled plan, so that the whole renovation process will be more intimately part of the villagers' daily life and the village will never be cut in half.

A settlement consisting only of farmers is not enough to constitute an organic community. A fair standard of living demands the existence of well-mixed occupational groups which can supply the appropriate services to maintain the standard.

A planned distribution of population would involve recommending a particular balance of occupations for every settlement. In building a new village or replanning an old one, then, it would be necessary to decide how many of each kind of workman the village needs—the number of carpenters, the number of weavers and barbers and teachers. But such calculation can only be done on a regional basis, because many occupations will be comparatively rare: a doctor, for example, may serve ten villages or more. In agricultural villages in England according to the 1931 census an average of only 41 percent of the working population was actually engaged in agriculture, the remaining 59 percent being distributed among various trades, professions, and services. In Iraq, on the other hand, over 90 percent of the working population in agricultural villages is working on the land. It is certain that the standard of living is linked closely to the diversity of employment in a village; the number of teachers, doctors, and shopkeepers in a community is probably one of the best guides to its real prosperity and stability, just as the number of plumbers, for example, suggests the state of sanitation. Unfortunately the planner will not find much information to help him in working out the desirable ratios of occupations in a rural settlement. Surveys have been made from time to time by the U.N. and other institutions, such as the International Labour Organization, on existing settlements, and one may analyze national demographic statistics from many countries, but the conditions in one country give no indication of those in another, nor do these studies help in determining the minimum diversification of employment necessary to an acceptable standard of living.

* Human settlements are observed to spread toward the west and north, in the absence of natural obstacles to check growth in these two directions.

Nevertheless, this lack of facts is no reason for not now starting to investigate a matter so vital to the planner. The most urgent need today is to begin research on the minimum basic need (in terms of the U.N. list of "components") of the basic population unit.

If the national rural building program is to be completed in a reasonable time, an adequate number of architects, engineers, administrators, and unskilled workmen will have to be engaged upon it, whatever the system of work and organization may be. In our proposed cooperative system, the skilled labor will be gradually trained while we are building the public service buildings, as previously explained.

The soil mechanics engineers will need to be equipped and prepared to investigate the suitability of soil for various purposes: making earth bricks, stabilized-earth bricks, baked bricks, water-repellent plasters, and earth concrete, besides examining the bearing power of the soil for foundations and the related problems of subsoil water, etc. They will be supported by a central research laboratory for a general investigation of the properties of earth as a building material. Because of the impending increase in the use of earth for building, we might well concentrate on it more of our research resources, which hitherto have been largely devoted to cement and concrete.

Besides the central laboratory, there will be a number of mobile laboratories, mounted on lorries, for investigation on the spot. Each of these lorries will have to serve a fairly large area, so that about ten lorries altogether, each in the charge of one soil mechanics engineer, should suffice.

A certain number of clerks and accountants will be required. As we are changing from the contract system of work to the completely new cooperative one, a new system of accounting will be needed. It must apply both to the construction of the public service buildings, to be undertaken by the government with paid labor, and to the private houses, which will be built by cooperative labor. Such an accounting system is already devised (see appendix III); so the accountants will not be called upon to create any system themselves but will simply apply one already there. They will, incidentally, be fewer than under the contract system, for the system of control will not, as usually hitherto, be duplicated between government and contractor.

Of course, accounting will be necessary for building the private houses only in those villages where the tradition of cooperative labor no longer exists. In traditional societies such as that of Kharga Oasis there is no need at all for accounting, for the people will take part in the building naturally, without balancing what they put in against what they get out. Indeed, the communal adventure of building a village by cooperative work should raise the morale, the self-respect, of the society, and give it a sense of common purpose that will be of immense spiritual benefit to its members.

The architects, each of whom will be in charge of a succession of village projects, will have to be specially trained beforehand. Unfortunately the training provided in our architectural schools today does not even begin to help the architect who tackles rural problems. This training, based on that offered in European schools, is aimed at the needs of the town, the building of office blocks, flats, banks, garages, cinemas and other large edifices, but completely ignores the needs of the countryside. In a European architectural school such one-sidedness may be excusable, for in countries like Britain 80 percent of the population live in towns, only 5 percent work on the land, and by far the greater part of the nation's wealth comes from urban industry and commerce. But in Egypt, where 90 percent of the population live on the land and 90 percent of the wealth comes from the land, to pay no attention whatsoever to the needs of the countryside is surely rather irresponsible in an architectural school. Yet just because of this academic indifference, there is an altogether too light-hearted attitude to the very grave business of remodeling our villages.

To remedy these defects by transforming all our university curricula would be quite impossible, at least in a short time. For one thing, a completely new teaching staff would be necessary. Therefore, in order to produce enough architects with an understanding of these rural problems, we should have to establish a postgraduate training course for them. Such a course should last two years and should include, besides a study of the overall condition of the Egyptian countryside,—the demographic, sociological, and economic facts—the peasant methods of construction and materials, and the principles of town and village planning. When the student is perfectly familiar with all these matters, he must familiarize himself likewise with all that has been done in Egyptian architecture, with the whole history of the native style in Egypt.

Just as the medieval cathedral mason in France was not allowed to put one stone on another until he had completed a pilgrimage to all the great ecclesiastical buildings of France, so our rural architects should make a pilgrimage to the places where the great tradition of Egyptian building is best exemplified—to Giza, Beit Khallaf, Thebes, Hermopolis, and Kharga—and they should visit and examine the places where the tradition is still living like Aswan and the many tombs of sheikhs scattered up and down the country, where a serious, unfanciful, and dignified building of peasant materials can be seen, where there is a sense of occasion in architecture somewhat more than in the ordinary peasant building, yet uncorrupted by alien materials and art.

This immensely rich museum of Egyptian culture should be studied seriously. The student is not to visit these sites perfunctorily, like a rushed tourist, but he must examine every example intelligently, making measured drawings of it, and applying all his critical capacity to the work. Such a study of standing works of architecture, linked with a profound understanding of all aspects of peasant building, of the materials, the method of construction, and the principle of design, should effect a revolution in the student's attitude to architecture. First he will gain immeasurably from a study in three dimensions and full size and texture of the building types he will be designing. So much of the work done in architectural schools today is entirely abstract—mere playing with plans on paper—that many qualified architects will design buildings in a style that is more true to the paper than to real life. So completely has the school course become dissociated from real buildings that the architect almost ceases to think in terms of solid materials—he draws plans in his office, hands them over to the contractor, and never sees the finished building. The very plan of the curriculum devotes separate lessons to the aesthetic and engineering aspects of architecture, and pays no attention at all to the relationship of a building to its environment, so that we find it a common practice among architects to distort the facts of nature—the shapes of hills, of trees, of human beings, even of mechanical things like cars—in order to make their renderings suit the style of their buildings when the design ought to suit the environment.

But if our two-year course on rural architecture starts from the real buildings, works back from them to architects' plans, and all the time keeps before the students the shape, size, color, texture, and feel of the buildings that make up our great tradition, then surely some part of this tradition will emerge in the design of these students.

Each village must have an architect to supervise its building, at least until enough builders are up to safeguarding the general layout, and until the village builders are used to erecting the house types. Even after he has moved to another village, the architect must keep an eye on the first one through periodical visits until its rebuilding is completed.

We will assume that there are 4,000 villages in Egypt, to be rebuilt over forty years. Then we must rebuild at the rate of 100 villages per year. The number of architects to be employed will then depend upon how long each one stays at each village.

Our average village of 5,000 inhabitants should be able to provide at least fifty masons. If it takes three masons one month to build a house, then fifty masons can build about 1,000 in six years. However, the architect should be able to leave the village after three years, returning only now and then to advise the villagers. Thus, after the second year of the program, when there would be from 300 to 400 villages under construction at any one time, it would be necessary to have 300 architects working on the program.

In order that these 300 architects be able to work confidently, they must be given a special training in "ekistics." But the architects must also be able to give all their attention and enthusiasm to their work, and for this they must be well paid; the work itself is thoroughly worth while, being nothing less than the creation of the national environment, perhaps for centuries to come; but however worth while the work, no architect can keep his mind on it if he is struggling to maintain a decent standard of life. I suggest that a scale of pay be established, calculated like most architects' fees as a percentage of the cost of the building.

Under the cooperative system the actual cost of each house is negligible, but if a village were built by building contractors, it is impossible that any house cost less than L.E. 500. Let the architect, then, take 1 percent of the cost of the house. That would be L.E. 5. If he works on a village for three years and builds 1,000 houses, he will earn L.E. 5,000 in three years or L.E. 1,550 in one year. However, this is a lot to pay a young architect. Furthermore, it is desirable that the salary scale should allow for recognition of seniority by showing steep periodical increments, in order to keep the services of these highly specialized experts, the like of whom would not exist anywhere else on earth. Therefore the salary scale might start at L.E. 900 a year and go up by the equivalent of L.E. 50 a year to L.E. 2,400. The job is worth it. Neither is this an excessive salary, for the annual bill for architectural services would be about L.E. 500,000.

The sum of L.E. 500,000 should not be considered large. Remember that it is a percentage of the total expenditure on building, and about the lowest percentage that architects would draw anywhere in the world. One percent of the cost of building is absurdly little to pay for an architect-designed house. In Switzerland, by law, you must spend 2 percent of the cost simply on artistic embellishment of the house, while it is customary for an architect in private practice to take as his fee 10 percent of the cost of any building worth less than L.E. 1,000.

It should be borne in mind that this 1 percent or L.E. 500,000, would provide that element of creative work that is essential if a low-cost housing program is to be really successful. Furthermore, an adequate salary would free the architect from financial worry and enable him to concentrate on his real work. Too often a government architect begins to grow resentful of his employer because other architects in private practice get so much more money than he does. If the government architect regards the government as mean, then he adopts the attitude: "Why bother? Give them what they pay for." This whole disillusioned and unenthusiastic approach can be transformed if the employer is generous. Generosity begets generosity; a well-paid architect feels that it is his duty to give all his energy to his work; instead of being bitter and cynical about government service, he is grateful that he has been relieved of material worries, that the way has been cleared for him to work as a real artist and the opportunity given him to develop his skill and sensibility to the utmost.

A further benefit would accrue from this comparatively modest outlay. We should have a team of architects working at the very highest level of their art, working as a team, continuously advising, criticizing, and revitalizing one another's work, a body of artists freed from commercial pressure and enabled to devote their whole lives to the refinement of their performance. Three hundred such architects would be a national treasure indeed.

At Deir el Medina, there was just such a group of architects, painters, and sculptors working together and living in an "artists' village" together, generation after generation during the whole period of the Middle Kingdom, who were responsible for the greatest works of art in Ancient Egypt—art that is subtle and varied, yet traditional; truly collective art at its finest.

Could not these three hundred architects that we need even live together for a time in a village like Deir el Medina? Our rural rebuilding plan will assuredly need a center to coordinate the work, and a center of research and training too. Why not combine the research and coordinating center and the training school for rural architecture, or more largely "ruralism," into a single Village of Rural Arts? We already have a project for a City of Fine Arts, on which L.E. 1,000,000 will be spent. I suggest, then, that a village be built—the first village under the rural rebuilding program—to be just such a center of rural studies. It should be in close contact with ministries and with other scientific and artistic bodies, yet it should be a real village and preferably close to an existing village which is within the plan. It should be conceived and built according to the principles already laid down, and it should be built by the architects themselves as a practical application of their course in rural architecture. It should eventually contain libraries, classrooms, laboratories, lecture and assembly halls, but also practicing workshops where the peasant craftsmen would develop their crafts—pottery, weaving, carpentry, building, plastering, etc.

There would be masons from Aswan living there, makers of stained glass windows from Cairo and mat and basket weavers from Sharkeya, together with the architects. Each would have a house where he would live with his family, and teach his trade to apprentices, and all would be members of the community. There would be rooms too for visitors, craftsmen, and others, and for foreign architects and artists interested in our activities.

As a nation—and even quite a poor one—may invest in a national orchestra, which is a permanent credit to the nation, so it may very well invest in a national team of architects. Even if the country contains three thousand fiddlers playing on street corners, they are not worth nearly so much, artistically, as one permanent orchestra with a hundred musicians, which can cultivate a tradition and devote all its time to improving the standard of its performances. In the same way three thousand architects working each by himself for private clients, through private contractors, cannot be compared with three hundred architects working together consciously to create a national tradition in building.

The building program for the country would involve first of all a national survey of resources and needs, and an overall plan, within which detailed plans would be made for each locality. Thus the planners would work on two levels, in the "high command"—a central policy-making body—and in the field, implementing the decisions. Needless to say, there would be no rigid exclusiveness between the two levels and no feeling that one level is superior to the other; on the contrary, professional personnel would be freely interchanged between the headquarters and the field, and all would have the responsibility of sharing in planning decisions.

From the outset some estimate is needed of the proportions of different professions needed for the whole planning body. So far we can make only two points: that the weight of the work be taken by architects, so they preponderate, and that they have adequate support from other specialists. Provisionally, we might suggest that our complete team be made up as follows:

1. Architects, planners	300
2. Soil mechanics engineers	10
3. Structural engineers	5
4. Economists	15
5. Social ethnographers	15
6. Geographers	6
7. Administrators	15

While the architects will be on the job continuously throughout the whole period of reconstruction—forty years so that there will always be 300 architects in the team—some of the other workers, such as geographers and economists, will deal with work of a once-for-all nature, so that the experts may be reduced in number as time goes on. But we should plan from the start for an ekistic team, with at least these sciences represented and in approximately these proportions.

When the regional or national survey and plan is completed, the time will come for beginning the actual building program. A village will be selected and the investigation team will visit it.

The first steps in the program will always be to organize the recruiting of labor and to prepare the building material. Under the system of voluntary cooperation, labor can be recruited only after the population has been analyzed and divided into family groups or badanas. This division of the population will be left entirely to the villagers themselves. The families will group themselves naturally, anyway, and there must be no pressure on any family to enter any particular group for reasons of administrative tidiness or to facilitate design. It does not matter in the slightest if some badanas consist of twenty families while others consist only of five or six. Neither is there any reason to confine any one group to related families; we have made use of the natural tendency of family groups to live in the same neighborhood, but families quite unrelated may quite well choose to live together. The Arabic proverb says, "Choose the neighbor before the house."

As previously explained, each family group will be represented by a spokesman—an elder of sheikh—who will conclude all agreements with the planning authority on behalf of the members of his group, and who will be the permanent intermediary between the planning authority and the people in his group. The member families will be asked to sign a statement agreeing to their inclusion in the badana.

Each family will next be asked to state its requirements in rooms, stabling, and area. When we know how much building each badana wants, we can calculate how much labor—so much per day—will be drawn up, making due allowance for periods such as harvest time when there will be no labor to spare from the fields. When it is quite clear to the badana what its responsibilities are, a contract will be signed by the authority and the spokesman, agreeing for a certain amount of labor to provide a certain number and size of houses.

After these data have been collected, a plan for the village will be prepared, showing its present condition and its future development. On this plan the location and boundaries of every family neighborhood will be shown; the area of the plot given to the badana will be the sum of the areas of the individual houses plus a certain percentage of this area for the neighborhood square and the internal streets. Each spokesman will sign his acceptance of the location of his family neighborhood according to a legal authorization accredited to him by the members of the group.

The boundary of each family neighborhood will be determined on this initial plan, but internal arrangement, the siting of the individual houses, the shape of the square, etc., will await the detailed design for that badana when its turn comes in the course of building (for design work will continue step by step with actual construction until the village is finished). Thus, although the course of the main roads, the sites of the public buildings and the main open spaces will be defined from the beginning, at least within the family neighborhood, we shall not know until much later exactly what land is to be private (house sites) and what to belong to the public (the neighborhood square).

Such indefiniteness is quite essential if we are to extend the benefits of deliberate individual design to every house in the village. To do this, the architect needs time; if the layout of each house has to be marked on a plan before any construction begins anywhere in the village, the architect will be forced into mass design, into multiplying a single design many times, and his presence as a creative artist will not be necessary once this first plan is drawn.

The chief building material will be earth, which will come from the excavation of the artificial lake. Therefore, while the villagers are divided up into family groups and acquainted with the building proposals and the organization of labor, this lake must be dug, and at the same time its surrounding park must be planned and planted.

The site of the lake is determined by several factors. First, the earth must be suitable for brick making. Therefore test drillings will be made at the most desirable location, and the earth analyzed by the soil mechanics engineer, who will say if it is suitable for bricks and whether any quantity of sand should be mixed with it. If the earth at the best location for the lake proves unsuitable for brick making, then some other place must be used for an earth quarry; the lake may still be sited in the best place to give recreation to the village, while the earth dug from it can be used to fill up the earth quarry. Second, the lake should be sited so as to take advantage of the villagers' habits. If they have some place (*morda*) where they regularly go to swim, it should become part of the lake so that they may use the same paths as before.

The other factors determining the siting of the lake are these: the position of canals to feed it, the direction of the prevailing winds (the cool northwest ones) and of the occasional hot dusty ones (from the southeast), and the position of the brickyard. As the lake will be in the middle of a parklike area, the trees of which will cool and clean the wind, it is best to site it to the southeast of the houses, so as to intercept the hot southeast winds. The brickyard, near which the excavated earth must be deposited, should be fairly close to the lake, to minimize carrying difficulties, but at the same time far from the houses and downwind of them because of the nasty smell from the kilns. (Kilns for lime burning and brick firing will be situated in the brickyard.) Therefore, the ideal site for the brickyard is south to southeast of the lake and the park, the trees of which will screen it from the village.

Digging the lake and dumping the earth near the brickyard is clearly a job for the Ministry of Public Works. A few machines and a Decauville railway can finish the job in a few weeks, much more quickly than the peasants could with their simple hand tools. It is very important to dig the lake quickly, in order to save the time of the engineers of the Public Works Department who must supervise what is in fact quite a complicated engineering operation, and of the fish-breeding specialists and horticulturists from the Ministry of Agriculture who will supervise the construction of the fishery and the landscaping and plantation of the park. If the lake is dug by hand over a long period, water will seep into it before it is finished, and if it becomes waterlogged before the system of feeder canals and lock gates is ready, the water will stagnate and mosquitoes will breed. Moreover, we must ensure that we have all the earth we shall need for the whole village before we start building, so that there will be no holdup through lack of building materials.

3 Fugue
Architect, Peasant, and Bureaucrat

I should have liked to end my book here, with the practical advice of the last section, and to include in it only the constructive and hopeful material of the first part of the book. All I have to say to other architects and to the general public has been said.

But the Gourna experiment failed. The village was never finished, and is not to this day a flourishing village community. It would not be fair to the reader to let him suppose that the principles explained earlier will automatically succeed in practice. At the same time, I should not be fair to myself and my country if I let the principles stand condemned because this one attempt to apply them failed. It is not just Gourna that is held up, but all real hope of bringing a decent standard of life to the Egyptian peasant.

Because Gourna was never finished, the whole theory of mud brick construction and the attitude to rural housing implied by the use of nonindustrial materials and traditional skills was condemned as cranky and impracticable. Not only was nothing done to complete Gourna but no attempt was made to find other practicable ways of getting peasant houses built. While building at Gourna was underway, and ever since the work stopped, it has been represented by ministerial architects as, at the politest, an interesting failure, a sentimental excursion along a byroad that could never lead to success. The slanders have been whispered in the corridors of ministries and appeared even as late as 1961 in a foreign paper.* Therefore, I must answer these charges before proceeding further.

It is easy to say vaguely that peasant obscurantism and bureaucratic hostility prevented me from completing Gourna, but it will be more convincing to let the history of the project speak for itself. What follows is not in any sense a diary recording the progress of work on Gourna. It is an attempt to make the reader understand why that work stopped, and so I have picked out as examples some of the most striking obstacles and intrigues. Again, I should not like to be put down as fainthearted for succumbing to these misfortunes; these,

* The Daily Telegraph, 20 October 1964.

I emphasize, are only the great trees in the forest, emerging from a tangled and thorny undergrowth of petty obstruction, conspiracy, inefficiency, and delay that contributed more to my final demoralization than did the big obstacles. Indeed, so numerous and irritating were these little daily pinpricks that I wanted to bring them to the notice of my superiors; yet I obviously could not send in an official report whenever, for example, the men's wages failed to turn up on time, as was always happening, and they went on strike, or when the stores sent me twenty kilograms of nails without heads, because I had not specified heads in my indent. I did suggest, however, to Shafik Ghorbal, the Undersecretary, that I compile a dossier of minor irritations and send it in periodically for him to read; he didn't welcome the suggestion.

As a result of these obstacles, work at Gourna proceeded very erratically. Whenever we received the money and materials to build, we built furiously and houses grew like desert flowers after rain. And whenever we were seen to be building, or so it seemed, there came a drought of supplies and work withered and stopped. In the first three seasons we worked for eleven and a half months out of thirty. After the fourth season almost all construction stopped, and the only work done consisted in counting up the stores. But to begin at the beginning.

First Season: *1945–46*

The design work started in August 1945 when Kamel Boulos Hanna Bey handed over the land. At the same time I wrote to my old friend Hadji Boghdadi Ahmed Aly, asking him to gather our company of masons. These were the men with whom I had been going from village to village, like a band of strolling troubadours, building farms and resthouses for the big landowners. I asked Boghdadi Aly to recruit as many new masons as he could, too. Our gipsy life was over, no more would we unpack our tools in some remote farm or suspicious village, with the local builders looking on hostilely. We had a whole village to build, and our client was the government; I could promise the men plenty of work and sure pay, and I would at last get a chance to teach new apprentices the secrets of the trade, something previously denied me because the local masons in villages where we had built had always, and rightly, been jealous of our intrusion, which took away their living, and had therefore refused to learn; indeed, the Aswani masons too were secretive and did not want to share their skill.

By October of the same year, when work began on the site, I had completed the plan of the village, designs of most of the public buildings, and designs of a single experimental row of houses attached to the khan. This row included houses of various shapes and sizes from which the Gournis could get an idea of the possibilities of the new accommodation being offered them and so be able to consult with me more helpfully when I came to design the houses for particular families. I intended these experimental houses to be attached to the khan as dwellings for such officials as the Ministry of Industry might send to run it.

During the time between our acquisition of the site and our starting to build I worked mostly in Cairo. One day, when I was in the offices of the Department of Antiquities, someone remarked that the assistants who had been appointed to help me were there in the building. Would I like to meet them? I was very pleased to hear this and asked to be introduced to them at once. We walked along to a room where there were six young men standing in a row. We greeted each other, and I proceeded to make the acquaintance of each one individually.

I approached the first. "What is your name?" "Michel." "I am delighted to meet you. Are you an architect?" "No, I have a diploma in carpentry." "Oh. And you?" "Amin Isa, specialized in decoration." "Oh. And what about you?" "Ahmed Abdullah." "Now you must be an architect." "No. I am a specialist in wall painting." "Really. And you?" "Mohammed Abu el-Nasr." "Very pleased to meet you. I suppose you are a sculptor or something?" "No. I specialized in weaving." "Thank you. And you?" "Azer." "Also a weaver?" "No, I didn't specialize in anything." "Then what are your qualifications?" "Well, I've got the elementary school certificate and I can read and write."

After I had gathered my wits, I reflected that it was not really so important that I had no supervisors to help me. The important thing was building, and that would be done by the Aswani masons. They would work without supervision and could, indeed, teach a thing or two even to qualified architects.

After this the department appointed an assistant director to help me. He was an architect, graduated from the School of Fine Arts in 1933. I was very pleased to think that I should have another architect to help me; one hand cannot clap by itself, as the proverb has it, and I should get along far more confidently with a little professional assistance.

When I met my assistant, though, I was somewhat taken aback by his immediately assuring me, in the most confiding tones, on the matter of our personal comfort in Gourna. He was, he said, an excellent cook, and I could trust him to secure all the provision we might require in Upper Egypt. He went on to detail the quantities of rice and clarified butter we might be expected to consume, the ways to get eggs, and how to ensure that chickens were fit to eat. I must say that the question of what I was to eat had not occurred to me before, and considering that we were just across the river from Luxor, teeming with the most resplendent grocers' shops, his anxieties seemed a little uncalled for.

But we were still in Cairo, and I was burning to start building on the site. My enthusiasm for the project and the tight time schedule impelled me to the feeling that every minute was precious, that every second lost meant a brick not laid, so I sat the poor young architect down, plunged him immediately into a jungle of figures and lists, and hurried him into helping me compile a catalogue of all the equipment and materials we should need.

The administration had given me a new book of railway warrants; so in my hurry to start building, I sent off my assistant with instructions to go first to the Physical Department of the Ministry of Public Works and get the theodolites, Cook's level, measuring tapes, etc., and then go to the site and prepare the foundations of the mosque. I thought it proper to begin with this building as the spiritual center of the village and thus most fitting for a ceremonial foundation stone laying, and also because the orientation of a mosque is predetermined—in this case, I have been careful to ascertain, it was 121° 10′ from N. My assistant had already been with me to see the site and was perfectly acquainted with my plans; so off he went full of confidence.

I, in the meantime, intended to stay in Cairo and arrange for the delivery of the first essential materials and equipment. Since all our buildings were to have stone foundations, we needed lorries to carry the stone; then to make our bricks we, like Moses, needed straw.

I equipped myself with a railway warrant and took the train for Luxor. At seven next morning it arrived, and I got off with all my suitcases, trunks, rolls and rolls of plans, instruments, gramophone, records, bits, pieces, odds and ends—for I was going to stay in Gourna for a long time—and I found a great crowd assembled to meet me. This crowd—to become a feature of all my arrivals and departures at Luxor station—was composed of all sorts of people who had some connection with the work or who hoped to be engaged, and with it I set off like a sultan for Gourna. There in the old village we had been given a rest house, which I wanted to have a rest in. It proved to be a square, oppressive, Teutonic building, apparently transplanted from Tewfikieh Street in Cairo, and it had once belonged to the German Archaeological School. I never liked it, because of its windowsills at chin level and its garish floor tiles, but while I had to live in it I selected a comparatively inoffensive room on the roof with a good view.

Once rested, I got on a donkey and rode down to the site. As I approached, I could see the most encouraging signs of activity where the mosque was to be. I came up to where my assistant was standing, and saw that indeed the foundations were all beautifully marked out in lime. I was especially pleased because my assistant had been a pupil in my surveying class at the College of Fine Arts; so I patted him on the back and asked him, in pedagogic pride, "And how did you lay it out so nicely?" "Oh," he said, "I just drew the plan on the ground." "Yes, but how did you do the orientation?" "Orientation? Well, I thought it would be best parallel to the road." "But the orientation—the angle—Mecca—didn't you use your theodolite?" "Theodolite?" "The instruments from the Ministry of Public Works!" "Oh, yes, those. Well, you said we must do something at once. You know, impress the administration, make a show. Don't worry, it looks good."

And he went on and on, in his disagreeable screechy voice, pouring out a stream of suggestions alternately nonsensical and immoral, until I found myself thinking for the first time in my life that the ear is not quite a perfect organ—you can't shut it like the eye. I promised myself that I should get rid of this assistant at the first opportunity, and turned to the real work waiting for me.

The chief merit of the whole Gourna project was its low cost. At every stage I had to keep the other expenses down to a level comparable with that of the mud bricks. This meant a careful phasing of the operations so that no laborers or masons were kept idle on the site waiting for materials; the straw must be ready for the brickmakers, the bricks and stones ready for the masons, in sufficient quantities at the right time; otherwise we should pay out too much in unproductive wages.

We had to build about nine hundred houses—apart from public buildings—within three years. It is possible to work for only ten months in the year in Upper Egypt, because during July and August the temperature goes up to 45°C in the shade and 80°C in the sun (113°F and 160°F). In thirty working months, then, we should have to build nine hundred houses, or thirty per month or one per day.

I made estimates of the materials and labor needed to construct, respectively, a small house and a large house. I then found the mean of the two estimates, and could thus predict what quantity of materials we should need per day, and what men and equipment would be necessary to maintain such a supply.

We asked for two lorries, hoping to get another four in the following year's budget; in this way we could spread the expenses of the heavy equipment over more than one season.

I was determined to get as much work done as possible on the production of building materials. I knew that the Aswani masons, once started, would cause houses to spring up like mushrooms if they only had the bricks.

As the chief materials—brick and stone—were to be made and quarried by us, my first concern was to take on enough labor to get production moving. There were to be two main classes of workers: skilled and unskilled. In charge of the skilled workers, who would be mostly the masons and quarrymen from Aswan, I placed Hadji Boghdadi Aly. Boghdadi had come down to Gourna, as he explained, just to give me a hand; he said he was too old to work, but would like to do what he could to help me get the new project going, for old times' sake. Furthermore, he had brought me his son, also a mason, who had been to the crafts school and obtained a diploma in carpentry.

Over the unskilled laborers, who would all be recruited locally, I put Ahmed Abdul Rasoul. He had been presented to me as one of the notables of Gourna, a man of an influential family (son of the eminent sheikh Mohammed Abdul Rasoul) and well accustomed to engaging labor for the Department of Antiquities.

The bricks, as will be remembered, were to be made of earth from the canal tippings until we got the artificial lake dug, of sand from the desert, and of straw which I was trying to buy. To provide water for mixing the mud I had bought four hand pumps in Cairo; to install and maintain these we needed a plumber, and Abdul Rasoul brought me his cousin, Sheikh Ibrahim Hassan, a huge man of enormous strength and very gentle temperament, who soon had them working. I decided to engage twenty-five four-man teams of brick makers, and Abdul Rasoul produced them with the greatest alacrity, offering indeed to find me fifty or a hundred teams if I should need them. These twenty-five teams would produce about 75,000 bricks per day, and we should be able to accumulate a good stack of bricks before the time when our masons should be ready to start building. These brick makers did not in fact come from Gourna but from other nearby villages, for in general trades seem to cluster in particular places, so that you can find, for example, a hundred brick makers in one village but none in the next. This was in a way a pity, for it was our policy to engage all labor, but particularly skilled labor, from Gourna itself. Unfortunately we found very little there: only four quarrymen and two masons in seven thousand inhabitants.

Stone for the foundations of the village would have to be quarried, but there were only two possible places nearby. One was to the north of the Valley of the Kings, next to the ancient quarries of Queen Hatshepsut, and the other far in the opposite direction, to the south of the Valley of the Queens. The first had hard limestone, suitable for foundations, while the second had soft limestone good only for making lime. It was not very easy to quarry stone from either, as the limestone strata alternated with thick strata of agglomerated aggregate that resembled concrete and took a long time to clear. Our difficulties were increased by the bad workmanship of earlier quarrymen from Gourna, who had blasted away all the easily accessible stone low down on the hillside, leaving the upper part overhanging in a very dangerous manner. A good quarryman cuts away a hill in a series of steps.

Of course, the department was not going to let us loose in such an important area of antiquities to blow up and cart off whatever we fancied; so a committee was formed, comprising the chief inspector of antiquities in Luxor, the curator of the Necropolis of Thebes, the head warden of the Necropolis, my assistant, and myself. We marked out the area allotted to us (later I put a small plaque in our quarry, as the ancients did, carrying the date and the purpose of the quarrying, but this displeased the chief inspector, who thought it irreverent and had it taken away although it was in my concession).

To work this quarry I intended to bring quarrymen from Aswan, where there is an unbroken tradition of quarrying going back to the eighteenth dynasty, when the granite obelisks were cut. However, there was no point in bringing the Aswani until we had explosives, for which it proved necessary to get permission from the Ministry of War.

My raw materials (except straw) and my labor were now assured; so it only remained to bring them together. Since there could as yet be no sign of the lorries, I began to review the local transport resources. These were of two kinds—camels and donkeys—and they were both expensive and inefficient, but it would be still more expensive and less efficient to have stone piling up in the quarries and masons waiting for it on the site; we could not afford delays, and so I asked Abdul Rasoul to see about hiring some animals.

Our first building was to be a drawing office. Hitherto we had had a tent on the site, which was otherwise quite bare, and in the tent we could neither spread ourselves while working nor lock up our instruments at night. I thought we might build the corner house of the experimental row by the khan. Although we had no stone for foundations, we could run up a temporary building, set on baked bricks, which would give us somewhere to establish ourselves on the site. Afterwards it could even be pulled down and rebuilt more substantially.

To build this I asked Boghdadi to send for four masons immediately and to ask another twelve to be ready to come. I also asked him for sixteen quarrymen, and turned my attention to the other and more faulty parts of the machine. My brick masons had made large inroads on the straw I had bought, and the straw the administration was supposed to be ordering for me could not be expected yet, but there were no signs of the rest of requisites, the lorries and railway, neither had any answer come to my letters to the administration inquiring about the state of the proceedings. This silence was not comfortable, and so I waited till the four masons had come and started building the first house, then took the train for Cairo to see what was happening. I could also take the opportunity of complaining about my assistant whom I could not possibly rely on.

I went to Osman Rustum, whom I discovered getting ready to leave Cairo. He had been appointed Town Director of Jaffa; he was the only person in the administration who understood and encouraged my plans, and he was being sent away. Anyway, I told him how my assistant had laid out the mosque carefully orientated toward the Winter Palace Hotel in Luxor instead of Mecca, how I would have to recheck everything I gave him to do, and how he was more concerned to impress our superiors than to do a good job; and I asked for a replacement for him. Then I inquired about my straw, only to find that nothing at all had been published, and that there was no prospect of getting it for at least another forty days.

In the matter of my assistant, Osman Rustum said he would do what he could to help me, and took me to the Director-General of Antiquities, the Abbé Drioton, who agreed that I must have a better assistant. But who? None of the department's architects in Cairo wanted to leave; most of them, in fact, openly regarded Luxor as a place of exile and I didn't want an assistant who considered himself my prisoner. At last I remembered a student of mine, Salah Said, who had seemed interested in the kind of building I was doing. I approached him and asked if he would like to come to Gourna. He said he would, although his parents disapproved very strongly, and so my assistant was relieved of his post and Salah Said put in his place.

Needless to say, my former assistant at once began an involved campaign against me, and this was at first directed toward my new assistant; various people began to whisper to him warnings against the Machiavellian intrigues that beset the life of an employee in the Department of Antiquities, and of the fiendish cunning of the

Gournis themselves. He was naturally upset, but said nothing to me.

After doing what I could to hurry up the delivery of my lorries and straw, I collected from the Physical Department the instruments that my assistant had forgotten, and went back to Gourna with Salah Said. We found that the first house was well advanced and that good quantities of bricks and stone were waiting; so I sent for the other twelve masons who were ready in Aswan in order to press on with the rest of the row. They came, and in no time at all we had used up all our straw. Since I could not keep the brick makers and masons waiting on the civil servants, I decided to buy straw from an account operated by the Inspectorate at Luxor for the purchase of little items. Against this account we were not allowed to put any item worth more than L.E. 5, so I was forced to buy my straw in handfuls, more or less: L.E. 5-worth every two or three days.

The job of appointing workmen—hitherto admirably handled by Rasoul—was one that many people were envious of. One day I got a letter from the curator of the Necropolis, telling me that some of the workmen I had were known tomb robbers and that therefore they should be dismissed. The letter went on to say that the curator had jurisdiction over the department's affairs in this district, and so he alone had the right to appoint workmen, which right he proposed to assume at once. I understood that this assertion was made at the instigation of his guards, who wanted a hand in the engaging of labor, and that he himself did not really covet the work. So I wrote back, pointing out that one of the benefits expected from our project was that it would divert people from tomb robbing, so that we ought to welcome as many tomb robbers as possible. I also offered to make him recruiter-in-chief if he would give me a written promise to produce the labor I needed in sufficient quantity and at the right time, so that the masons would not be held up. He at once renounced his claim.

There was more trouble over the quarrying of sand—not a particularly rare mineral in Egypt, but when my workmen went to dig some, the inhabitants of the nearest hamlet came out and stopped them, saying that the workmen were strangers and had no right to dig sand there. Again, it was because the villagers thought they ought to have been given the job themselves.

A Crafty Gourni

One day a Gourni came to see me. He was an enormous man with hands as big as tennis rackets, and he stood in the doorway twisting them together in embarrassment as he looked down on the floor and mumbled a shy introduction. He was Sheikh Mahmoud, and he had come to tell me how highly he regarded me. He had long held that I was a very good man, an architect of renown, an honest and active administrator, and that I was worth any half-dozen other employees of the department. I blushed modestly, and waited to see what he wanted. He went on to warn me against the serpentine conspiracies that would enwrap me, he gave me a deal of free information about the wicked intentions of everybody I had met in Gourna, and expanded upon the fates of several hapless civil servants who had earned their places in Egyptian folklore by falling victim to departmental intrigue. He concluded, amid a second shower of compliments, by saying that he would regard it as the greatest honor ever to befall his house if I would condescend to take coffee with him the next day. Somewhat weak from his eloquence, and wanting, too, to get to know the Gournis better, I accepted.

The next day, at ten o'clock, I went up to his house, where he received me with still more stately compliments, which would have been very welcome coming from, say, the new director who had replaced Rustum, a typical important government official with whom I did not feel at ease. Mahmoud invited me inside. I went in, my mind full of stories of the grand and primitive hospitality of the peasant, very sensible of my luck in being so invited to share this man's coffee, and somewhat nervous lest I somehow offend against the rigorous code of manners obtaining among these poor yet noble people. He presented his wife—a startling familiarity this, among members of his sect—and she seized my hands and forcibly kissed them, to my great embarrassment. He made me sit down, and while he was delivering a further instalment of his compliments and cautionary tales, his wife came out with an old cigarette tin full of semi-precious stones—agates and such—and scarabs. This she pressed into my hands, while he ordered me to choose whatever I liked. "It is I who should be giving you presents," I said; "This is not at all right." And I refused, and he insisted, but I did not take one; so he put away the box and reminded me, rather sharply, that even the Prophet had accepted presents.

Then he led the conversation back to the notable officials he had known—Professor this and Dr. that—and explained that they had all known and trusted him, that, in fact, he was the only man they had trusted. At last it came out. Could he be a foreman? He was highly respected in the village and could guarantee to engage only honest, hardworking men. He touched once more, in the most delicate way, upon my well-known discernment and justice, shook his head sadly over the story of yet another high official who, after closing his ears to all disinterested advice, had been plotted against and ignominiously dismissed from the service. Then he stood up, seized my hand, gazed earnestly down at me, and swore by all the most holy oaths of our religion that I must have a cup of coffee. Indeed, I felt I must, for I had now been there an hour and a half. Time passed, Mahmoud chatted on, from time to time dropping substantial hints about the job he was after, until, around midday, in came his wife with a large tray. My spirits revived, I could already taste the coffee as it soothed me and woke me up, and then the tray was put down where I could see it. On it sat the greasiest, yellowest, dirtiest, and most repulsive example of peasant cookery I have yet to see.

It was a pie, a huge, soggy pie, which gave me food poisoning just to look at it. Through my mind went all the stories I had heard of peasant pride, how touchy they were, how terribly susceptible to insult. I thought of the bedouin, who kills his last camel to make a feast for the casual passerby. I thought of my standing among the Gournis; and I decided. I stood up and swore by all the most holy oaths in our religion that I had come to drink coffee, not to be poisoned, that I would not touch a crumb of his nasty pie, and that unless I got some coffee I would leave.

He did not seem greatly offended; so we sat down and waited a bit more. After a quarter of an hour or so, the coffee arrived. I took the cup gratefully and was about to drink from it when I saw that it was black with dirt, its chipped and greasy rim had clearly never seen cloth or water, and I just could not put it to my lips. By this time I was quite hardened to trampling on the feelings of the peasant, and the sheikh must have been getting used to the rudeness of the city; I put the coffee down, thanked my host politely, and left, revolving plans for a hygiene center where the Gourni women could attend cookery classes.

In order to distribute work in the fairest possible manner, I thought I might ask the sheikh of each hamlet to give me a list of all the people in his hamlet who would make suitable laborers, so that I could appoint so many workmen from each hamlet, in proportion to its population. I wrote to the sheikhs explaining my idea, but not one answered. (I discovered later that they were reluctant to commit to paper anything that might afterward be interpreted as implying approval of the transfer of Gourna to the new site.) At last I got them all together in the house of Sheikh Mohammed, who was the son of the venerable Sheikh el Tayeb. At our meeting the sheikhs told me that they had already given full authority to Abdul Rasoul and to Sheikh Mahmoud—my friend of the pie—to recruit workmen on their behalf. Thus I was landed with Mahmoud after all; he had doubtless exerted his diplomacy to better effect upon his brother sheikhs.

I thought it better to make a firm and physical division between the respective spheres of influence of Rasoul and Mahmoud. Rasoul had already proved himself a good and trustworthy foreman and was familiar with the work on the site; so I left him in charge of all unskilled labor there—the brick makers and the men carrying materials about. Sheikh Mahmoud I packed off to the quarries to recruit and manage the unskilled workmen there, where he couldn't interfere with me very much.

There was one disadvantage in making Rasoul a foreman; he certainly produced the labor but he was far too enthusiastic. If he had had his way, the whole village, men, women and children, would have been on our payroll. Once we brought in a plumber to change a washer on one of the pumps, and at the end of the month I found him still working for us. It became practically impossible to keep track of all the workmen taken on and to check with the work being done; poor Salah Said did nothing else all day but wrestle with paysheets and receipts. Finally I sat down and after a fortnight's concentrated effort produced a masterly system of accounting that enabled us to see just who was being paid, what for, and whether he had done it. According to this system, fully explained in appendix I, no laborer could be paid unless he had been allowed for in an estimate made before a given piece of work was done. The estimates were made according to certain norms that we had fixed for different kinds of work.

This system also enabled us to see at a glance the state of our materials and funds and to disentangle from our bulk accounting the particular cost of any individual building. Indeed, I can now quote you to the nearest shilling for each separate component in a house, as if I were selling ready-made domes, walls, and vaults from a store; I can tot up the prices and tell you how much your finished house will cost.

Having thus arranged the control of labor, I set about engaging more masons for the real work of building. I brought twelve more from Aswan and found some in Luxor, so that before long we had forty masons all building houses as fast as they could. We concentrated on the neighborhood of the khan, and very soon the first street began to grow recognizable. I was very excited to see my village taking shape under my eyes, and very impatient with all the delays we experienced. We dug the foundations of the mosque (correctly orientated, this time) and I would have started on it, too, but we were still depending on camels for our stone, and to lay the mosque foundations would have taken more stone than we could possibly have provided, even if we had stopped all other work, for it was a very big building. I was waiting for the two lorries, which I had ordered as soon as we knew we had the site, in August 1945. At last, on 20 December 1945, one lorry came, the other one having been acquired by the department but allotted to some archaeologist with more friends that I had. A simple computation showed that with this one lorry we should take thirteen years to bring to the site the stone needed just for the foundations. I pointed this out to the department in a letter, and also reminded them that I had not been given the quarry equipment I had asked for.

Needless to say, there was still no sign of the straw, and this soon grew into my biggest problem. I was forced to cut down the number of brick making teams from twenty-five to eight, and consequently to lay off a number of the masons, retaining only the Aswanis, whom I could not very well send back to their homes so far away. These men were already in trouble enough because of the long delays before their wages came through; many of them had to wait, and work, for three months before seeing any pay at all. The Gournis fastened on these unlucky men with delight and lent them food and money at exorbitant interest, so that few of the Aswanis got anything at all out of their work at Gourna.

The Straw that Broke the Camel's Back

To keep things moving, I continued buying straw in tiny quantities from the account kept at Luxor for our petty requirements. This account could only hold L.E. 20, so our L.E. 5 straw purchases, repeated every two or three days, constantly exhausted it. I should not have used the account in this way, it is true, but to have stopped work altogether, the only alternative, would have been far more expensive.

At about this time I chanced to hear from a friend the very useful phrase: "I render you responsible for wasting the government's money." I wrote to the administration telling them of the slowing down of our work and accusing them of wasting the government's money by procrastinating over the straw requisition. This apparently touched them in a tender spot, for they contrived a clever scheme for getting rid of the whole Gourna project for good.

They did indeed accelerate the business of procuring tenders for the supply of straw and of adjudicating these tenders, but very ingeniously they charged the official whom they sent down to conduct the proceedings of adjudication with the additional duty of finding some excuse to close down the whole project.

After some days of industrious snooping, this person reported to his masters two grave irregularities in our proceedings. We had turned the local petty account to wicked purposes in spending it all on straw, and also most of our staff were not qualified for their positions. This second accusation, though justified, came oddly from the very officials who had forced these unqualified assistants on me. Nonetheless, their plot prospered, and in no time at all it had been decided to stop work on Gourna immediately and to transfer all responsibility as soon as possible to some other ministry. This decision was embodied in a big report that went all round the department collecting signatures and rubber stamps. At last it arrived on the desk of the Undersecretary, Shafek Ghorbal, who, to his great credit, was not appalled by the massed autographs of his department and refused to sign it.

This unexpected refusal quite overthrew the plotters, who instantly found themselves tangled up in their own nets. The unqualified employees were dismissed and soon learned that it was the administration that had dismissed them. They were most indignant against their former sponsors and spread a great deal of malicious gossip, to which I did not listen; I was very happy to have got rid of them and was in no way interested in justifying them and thus perhaps getting them back.

The conspirators had been so confident of success that they had stopped all further purchases of materials, so that by the time we had the purchasing system in action again the financial year ended. To make use of what remained in our budget, I bought water pipes for the whole project—10,000 meters; in spite of this we returned L.E. 6,000 of our allotment to the Exchequer. We had worked a total of three and a half months out of the ten, and built one small street.

A Plot to Break the Dike

Just before I went off on leave for the summer of 1946, I heard a most disquieting rumor. Some of the Gournis, it was said, were plotting to destroy the growing village by breaking the dikes that held out the river water during the annual flood. As I have explained, many of the Gournis were not at all pleased at the prospect of leaving their profitable hovels among the tombs and having to work for their living. It would be only too easy for them, one dark night when the river was in full flood, to creep down and dig through the dikes that protected the hosha.

I immediately took precautions; I bought many bundles of reeds to help fill in any breaches that might be made; I arranged for a constant patrol of twelve watchmen to guard the west dike (this was a private one belonging to Kamel Boulos; the other three all belonged to the Government and were well-guarded); I made the mayor of Gourna sign a statement saying that he made himself responsible for the safety of the new village; and I notified the administration and the local police major both of the threat and of the measures I had taken against it. The Nile flood that year was an unusually high one, but no one attempted to let it into New Gourna.

Second Season: *1946–47*

Straw Again

Although we had now secured permission on principle to purchase materials and equipment, we had to start again from the beginning by inviting tenders for the supply of straw. Thus it was not until 15 October 1946 that we had the straw on the site and could begin work. We had permission to buy three more lorries, too, but they did not appear till much later; nor did our new and properly qualified assistants, who had been appointed from the district of Kena. All this time the new director of the Engineering Section who replaced Rustum was most obstructive. I wrote again and again to him on urgent matters connected with Gourna—mostly on the non-appearance of the lorries and the assistants—and he did not answer one of my letters.

In spite of these annoyances work started very well, and we built most of the marketplace, finished the khan, and redug the foundations of the mosque. In November 1946 I was informed that of the L.E. 15,000 allowed me for that season I had L.E. 6,831 left. We had already bought most of our materials, and as our monthly wage-bill came to about L.E. 1,000, I reckoned that we should be able to work for another seven months, until the end of June 1947. Then, on 29 December 1946, I had a letter from the accounts department saying that we had only L.E. 1,403 left (although I had bought nothing since November and had paid no more than one month's wages) and warning me that if I contracted debts for wages above this amount, the department would not meet them. As it happened, I had already spent more than that by the time the letter reached me, and anyway I could not just go out and tell everyone to down tools and go home. I wrote back crossly, saying that we were not playing a nursery game, to start and stop work every few weeks, and that we had a number of buildings half finished that could not be abandoned in that state. However, we could not go on working without money; so in January 1947 work came to a standstill again, to be resumed in September.

The Pump

During this second season I came across a peculiarly nasty example of an official using his position to blackmail a defenseless peasant. We had found that the hand-operated pumps we had been using to supply water to the site could not supply enough; I therefore asked the administration for an engine-driven pump unit. They wrote back telling me that the engine and pump would cost L.E. 140 and the pipes L.E. 460, making a total of L.E. 600. Since this was more than we could really afford, I looked around for some way of economizing. When it became known that I wanted pipes, Ibrahim Hassan mentioned to me that he had about twenty meters of piping on his land and that he no longer needed it. He offered to sell me the lot and to install it on the site for L.E. 45. I at once communicated this offer to the administration, and as usual they didn't reply. I wrote a second time, and got a letter back from Mechanical Engineering saying that the price was very, very, very low—implying that the pipes couldn't be much good.

Two months went by, during which the administration, when it replied to my letters at all, told me that the request had to be seen and approved by the Finance Secretary; they did not send it on to him though, and I was still without my pump, which was already accounted for among the purchasings which had engulfed the budget of this year, and would be put on the next year's budget if not purchased and installed during the running work season. I was already alarmed at the way money was being squandered by the bureaucrats—in the matter of the three lorries that we had ordered, for example, we were told we must have privately built bodies for them at L.E. 200 a piece when there were ex-military bodies being sold at L.E. 15 a piece—so I wrote a letter pointing out that I was trying to save L.E. 415 of our budget, and repeated my threat that I would hold the administration responsible for wasting the government's money. This threat caused them to pass on the requisition to the Finance Secretary; just after this I was in the offices of the department when an employee there murmured to me that I would be wise to get the pipes for L.E. 45; as I had said L.E. 45, I didn't understand him at the time, and thought he was trying to be rude.

I went back to Gourna and noticed that Ibrahim Hassan, who always used to make a point of coming to meet me at the station, was ominously absent. When he didn't show up all day, I sent someone to find him. The messenger said he was in Luxor; so next day I sent again, instructing the messenger not to come back without him. When at last Ibrahim was brought to see me, he told me that he had withdrawn his offer, which was very, very low, that the job of sinking the pipes alone would cost more than L.E. 45, and that the cost of the pipes themselves would be L.E. 700. I was very cross with him, but my reproaches failed to move him, and eventually I decided to get him to explain his conduct in public.

I asked several of his relatives to join my own assistants and the people who had actually heard him make his offer, so that we could form a sort of "tribal court" before which Ibrahim could explain himself. He refused to say any more than that he couldn't carry out his offer, and just stood there, mulish and uncomfortable. At last I remarked bitterly that you can put a price to most things, but a man is beyond price until he puts a price on himself by withdrawing his word of honor. Now I knew Ibrahim's price. It was L.E. 700. I could write it on a label and stick it on his back. Then I turned to a friend of mine who was watching the proceedings, the photographer Dimitri Papadimou, and said in English, "I wish I had been dealing with my neighbor (Sheikh Aly). At least I know that he is a man who respects his own word of honor." I knew that they could all understand English, and that my remark would have greater effect as being apparently not intended for them. At this Sheikh Aly jumped to his feet and shouted to Ibrahim: "We can't have a man in the family who breaks his word. I swear to you now that we shall shoot you." Poor Ibrahim then broke down and cried.

At last he said that he would tell us the whole truth. The mechanical engineer of the department had come up from Cairo together with the head of the stores section, and Ibrahim had been summoned to the curator's office to meet them. There, in the presence of a clerk from the Inspectorate, they had asked him how many acres of land he had. Ibrahim told them five. "Then you will lose all five if you do this job for L.E. 45. The proper price for pipes is L.E. 700. Fathy has swindled you, and anyway he is not authorized to sign for the job; I am. If you don't go back and tell him the price is L.E. 700, we'll ruin you and your whole family."

After this confession I told Ibrahim that he should have come to me at once. I explained that his original price was a fair one, as the current cost of pipes was 90 piasters a meter, making about L.E. 18 for the whole lot, which left L.E. 27 for sinking them.

Thus comforted, he agreed to the original price and in front of all the witnesses signed an agreement to that effect, still crying. Dimitri remarked that he was crying out of one eye for shame and out of the other for the L.E. 700.

After such startling proof of the deliberate malice of certain people in the department I permitted myself one act of low cunning in order to show them up. I sent a letter to the director-general, but in it I said nothing of Ibrahim's final agreement, so that no one would know that the job was to be done for L.E. 45 after all. I simply asked how these people had dared to contact a supplier and try to make him break his agreement. I had a very curious reply, stating that as the mechnical engineer had contacted Ibrahim before the administration had received approval for my request from the financial secretary, there was no irregularity. It went on to say that I was now committed to finishing the work for no more than L.E. 45.

This letter was odd in that it was signed by the director-general himself and no one else. There was not even a typist's initial on it. Yet it was in Arabic, and the director-general—M. Drioton—could not read Arabic (although he signed his name in Arabic, but he drew his signature).

Nevertheless, I wrote a letter back asking for an official inquiry into this action of the mechanical engineer, the head of the Stores Section, and the clerk of the Inspectorate. I also mentioned that the work in question had been done for the L.E. 45 originally stipulated, thus showing that the plot had failed. To this letter I had no reply.

Later on, after the Palace had shown interest in Gourna, I sent in a report of this particular intrigue, and at once got a cable from the Undersecretary saying that my accusations were exceedingly serious and that he was coming personally to investigate.

He came and then sent a department lawyer. As I was telling this lawyer the story, he kept jumping up in indignation, scarcely able to believe his ears. "But do you have proof in writing?" he said. As a result of his inquiries we found that the mechanical engineer had been round all the dealers in building materials in Luxor, warning them not to let me have even an inch of piping. The man had obviously been determined to use this business to wreck the whole project. I also heard that the engineer had been fined eight days' salary.

The Cholera

The cholera epidemic broke out in 1947 in the village of Korein and it spread all over Lower Egypt very rapidly because the government, being taken by surprise, didn't have the means to fight it.

Although Gourna is in Upper Egypt, I thought it wise to take precautions against a possible outbreak there. In Old Gourna there were millions of flies, which patronized the same open wells from which the villagers got their drinking water, and since there were no latrines, one case of cholera would have brought about a bigger disaster than the gambia malaria epidemic which wiped out a third of the population in 1943–44.

The first thing to do was to analyze the well water, not so much to find what was in it as to force the authorities to do something about it. The result of the analysis was—number of bacteria: incalculable; lactic fermentation: 80 percent (when the maximum permissible is 20 percent). So the only solution was to sink several pipes to fetch the water from very deep down and to stop the people from using the open wells. There were no pumps on the market because the government had bought them all up for the epidemic districts. Then I thought of using the pumps which brought the water for brick making, but as this would involve taking them away from the site and back to the old village, I had to have permission from the Department of Antiquities. So I immediately went to Cairo and met the director-general, M. Drioton. I persuaded him that the clean water was to benefit the archaeologists and his department's employees, whose rest houses were luckily scattered all over old Gourna, and I did not mention that our pumps would also supply the villagers. He agreed in principle, but passed me on to the director of the Inspectorate, who had to authorize the move.

On meeting this gentleman I was pained to receive a categorical refusal even to consider my request. It was, he said, the business of the Ministry of Public Health, and no concern of his. I put it to him that the Ministry of Public Health had twenty million people to provide for and that the department was responsible for the health of its employees working in remote villages and exposed to infection. All he said was: "They can go to hell."

I answered: "If, which God forbid, one man should die when I had the means to save him and refused to, then I should consider myself a murderer." I left him, determined to go ahead without his sympathy, and arrived home with my resolve unshaken. I would take the first train back to Luxor, go straight to the site, uproot the pumps, and plant them defiantly in Old Gourna. Humanity commanded me to take the law into my own hands. I opened the paper and found that the government had decided to isolate Upper Egypt and had closed all roads and the railway.

I had to stay in Cairo until the epidemic had seeped through to Upper Egypt, when I was considerately permitted to follow it. I took the first train out of Cairo in a very uneasy frame of mind, for the first appearance in Upper Egypt had been at Ballas, only twenty miles from Gourna. Ballas is the pottery of Egypt—indeed, the word *ballas* means the large water pot that Egyptian women carry on their heads—and the disease had been brought there by the boatmen who carry the pots up and down Egypt.

Having got off the train in Luxor, I crossed the river to the left bank, where my driver, *osta* Mahmoud Ramadan, usually waited for me. He wasn't there, and they told me he was not feeling well. So far, I was told, there had been no case of cholera in Gourna, which was a great relief, so I went along to see osta Mahmoud. I found him in bed having just come round after being three days unconscious. To my astonishment I found that he had had all the symptoms of cholera—vomiting, diarrhea, and fever—and yet it had never occurred to any one to call a doctor until Mr. Stoppelaere heard of his illness and, suspecting the worst, brought one at once. When I inquired why my secretary Mr. Gad hadn't done anything to help Mahmoud, he explained that he hadn't applied in writing, according to the regulations. I remembered the motto of the department: "Let them go to hell."

Mahmoud, on recovering, went back to his truck, but apparently thought that I must have a specially soft spot for him since I had been so angry with the secretary. I had always favored him because he was the only driver who could maintain his truck properly, so, making the most of this, he came the next day and asked me to give his son a job as a workman. As his son was only nine, I explained that he would have to wait until he was a bit older, which caused Mahmoud to go off in a huff.

Half an hour later he came back and reported that the brake pipe in his lorry had broken. I said: "Well, go and mend it," as he usually did, but he drew himself up and said: "I am not a mechanic, sir." Et tu, Brute. He was a government official; why should he be any different from the rest? The incidence moved me to poetry:

> Each one a worthless, colored, cheap glass bead.
> All held together on one thread of greed.

The first day back, I had the pumps taken up and brought to Old Gourna, where we installed them at strategic points about the village. Having provided the means of getting pure water, the next thing was to persuade the villagers to take advantage of it, or rather to dissuade them from using the open wells.

At this time I learned that the hospital had just been provided with a doctor. Gourna had a little hospital, which had a doctor only when important officials were about to visit the antiquities. A doctor would then be sent from Luxor and some villagers hired to act as patients.

Because of the cholera, all doctors had been mobilized by the government, and one was sent to Gourna. His name was Hussein Abu Senna; he had just graduated and was a very pleasant and conscientious young man. To him I went to place myself and all my men at his disposal to fight the epidemic. Together we looked up the instructions that had been issued to doctors during the 1903 epidemic, for we had nothing else to hand. We had no serum, little disinfectant, and would have to rely upon our own resources. The instructions recommended quicklime, which we could produce ourselves in our own kilns.

Cholera is transmitted orally. Provided you do not swallow the germ, you cannot catch the disease. Therefore all our precautions amounted to making sure that there was no possibility of a germ getting into anyone's mouth. First, we had to make everyone understand the importance of observing all the precautions most strictly. There must be no gap, no omission at all, in our prophylactic measures! We had to be as rigorous as a surgeon in an operating room. All water was to be boiled, whether for drinking or washing. Nothing that could have germs on it was to be eaten. For example, the routine on coming home from the market was this: enter the house, put the bag with the vegetables straight away into boiling water, taking care not to put it down on anything first, wash hands in lysol, wipe the door handle with lysol like a burglar removing his fingerprints, and you were ready.

We had to get the villagers to realize that any stranger might bring the disease into the village, and that therefore visitors were to be discouraged. Even the traditional laws of hospitality would have to be suspended, and any visitor would have to be reported to the authorities. This came hard to a people who have always made it a point of honor to hide "wanted" men from the government, and even to conceal sick people from anyone who might want to take them away to hospital.

The doctor and I thought it only wise to have the assistance of Sheikh Mohammed el Tayeb. He was the son of Sheikh el Tayeb, an extremely old holy man who was deeply venerated by all the villagers. Sheikh Mohammed would succeed his father and was himself also very influential. He was the imam of the village mosque and would be able to explain our measures to the peasants in his Friday sermons. We accordingly invited him to our anti-cholera "committee." He proved most valuable to us, being quick to understand the situation and to grasp the medical details involved.

Since about three hundred of the villagers were working for us, we decided to open our health campaign on them. We gathered them together and spoke to them, trying to make them understand the reason for our precautions. To help them appreciate what a microbe is, we "magnified" them and described them as ants which would scurry about on all contaminated articles, and which could be left behind on anything a contaminated article touched. These ants lived on our hands, in water, on vegetables, were as persistent as and more elusive than real ants and were infallibly lethal. This picture was peculiarly effective, and what had been an abstract and incomprehensible theory assumed a horrible reality. My secretary, Gad Effendi, visibly blanched to think of thousands of invisible and deadly ants crawling over his skin, and remembering his treatment of *osta* Mahmoud I was very pleased to see that he had now begun to realize that some things might be more important than applications in writing.

Cholera had by now broken out in Luxor and Gamoula West, a village seven miles from Gourna on the same bank. It was Gad Effendi who brought me the news, and he was weak with fright. The situation was now very serious, and we called a council of the mayor and the sheikhs of the five hamlets and enrolled them in our committee. We met every day, exhorting the sheikhs to carry the campaign right into the people's houses, to watch out everywhere for gaps in our defenses, and to be more severe on cases of carelessness. We were all thoroughly frightened by this time, and when I noticed Gad Effendi licking his finger to flick over the paysheets which he collected from the workmen every morning, and reminded him of the ants doubtless lurking upon the paper, I took no pleasure at all in his terror.

Then at last supplies of serum began to come through, sent from India and other countries, and, as we began to innoculate the villagers, panic died down.

Gourna was saved, but the experience had shown me again how easy it is for indifference, stupidity, and negligence to be excused as resignation to fate.

One last picture from the epidemic: I was waiting, under the bamboo shelter, to cross over to Luxor by ferry. As there was quite a crowd waiting there too, I decided to take advantage of the occasion by starting a discussion on hygiene and microbes. Again I proudly introduced my ants. An old and venerable, white-bearded sheikh objected that one's fate was determined and written: *maktoub,* and that no mortal endeavors could change it.

"Your eminence, maktoub is perfectly clear in the case of somebody who jumps off a housetop or over a precipice; yet God himself said, 'With your own hands don't put yourself in the way of destruction,' and to swallow germs is just like jumping off a precipice."

The sheikh answered: "One can see the mountain or the house because they are standing there, but microbes are unseen."

"Though the microbe is not seen by the naked eye, yet it can be seen moving about under the microscope."

"Anyway, I believe only in what I see with my eyes."

"But, your eminence, most of our sheikhs are weak-sighted and cannot read the Koran without wearing spectacles, so after what you said, they should not believe in what is written in the Koran when they wear glasses" (cheers from the crowd, for this was a neat thrust

—"Ah, Ah, Ah"). But the sheikh said that if a weak-sighted person could not see the writing of the Koran, his neighbor could see it and everybody knows about it, while nobody sees the microbe.

To this I answered: "The doctor sees it with the microscope, which is but extrastrong spectacles with powerful lenses, and he is a respectable learned man whom we believe and whose medicine we take when he prescribes it, so why shouldn't we believe in what he says about what he has actually seen under these lenses in the laboratory.

The sheikh answered back with a beautiful couplet, the meaning of which was the opposite of what I said and which was received by cheers from the crowd: "Ah! Ah! Ah!"

I said that the poem did not apply to the case we were discussing and that the joy of the crowd did not result from the meaning of the words of the poem but from their resonance in their ears. "It was the same magic of poetry that made the Prophet dislike poetry and poets." The crowd cheered again: "Ah! Ah! Ah!"

At last, as I thought that due respect to the old man dictated that I should give him the last word, and especially as I believed I had attained my object in sowing some seeds of hygiene which might bear fruit among the audience, I said that indeed, no matter how thorough we might think we are in taking precautions, we never reach perfection and there will always be some gap through which fate may enter. However, this fact should not stop us from doing all that is in our power to leave no room for fate, and any negligence would mean willful self-destruction rather than acceptance of fate.

At this point the ferryboat came and the discussion ended.

Third Season: *1947–48*

Iblis Implacable

In Upper Egypt, toward the end of August every year, the Nile, fed by the distant rains in Ethiopia and thick with rich and fertile mud, has risen to its maximum height and is flowing past high above the level of the fields. In the fields the summer crop of maize is nearly ripe, and the peasants are waiting to gather it before letting the river in over their land. At the beginning of September, after a few days of frantic work, the fields are ready; the gates are opened and the water is allowed to flood the fields. For two months it is held up by the dikes, while the river sinks, and then at the beginning of November it is drained back again into the Nile, leaving behind it a fresh, fertile layer of silt in which the winter crop of cereals or beans is planted. (This system of irrigation is called the "basin" or "hod" system; it is not used in Lower Egypt, where the perennial system, by canals, is in operation.)

These crops—wheat, barley, and lentils—the age-old food of Egypt, have been sown and harvested for six thousand years in the same ever-renewed black mud; they germinate, grow, and ripen in smooth accord with the seasons of the river, while other crops like sugarcane and cotton, which are newcomers to Upper Egypt, do not fit into this ancient pattern and have to be protected from the flood. Their fields are permanently enclosed by dikes and irrigated by artesian wells or pump-fed canals. Such an enclosure is called a *hosha,* and in one such hosha New Gourna is situated.

During the season of 1946 there had been rumors that some of the peasants were conspiring to bore a hole in the western dike so as to drown the village and put a stop to the project, which threatened to take away their lucrative hobby of tomb robbing. At that time I told the police, had the dike reinforced, and mounted a guard of twelve men to watch over it. The flood that year was particularly high, one of the highest ever known, and many villages were destroyed. Our precautions evidently frightened the conspirators, if they existed, and nothing at all happened.

It may be thought that to site the new village below flood level was unwise, but the hosha was very well protected on three sides by carefully maintained dikes belonging to the government: on the south side was the Farhana Canal bank, and on the east and north sides a railway embankment. Only on the western side was the dike privately maintained by Kamel Boules Bey, the present owner of the hosha, and by the Kom Ombo Sugar Company, which rents the land from him.

I arrived to start work for the third season on 3 September 1947. When I got to the village to start the new season's work, I found that none of my instructions given before leaving had been carried out. Particularly, all the bricks that had been produced the season before, and which were lying where they had been made, to the west of the village, had not been taken up and stacked in the east near the buildings where they were to be used. There were about half a million of them. Raslan Effendi, my new assistant, hadn't turned up for work; some weeks before he had come to my house in Cairo threatening to go on strike if I didn't put him up for promotion to the sixth grade.

On 8 September I received a cable from the Undersecretary of State calling me to Cairo to meet him on the 10th at 10 o'clock at his office. I couldn't guess the reason and was rather worried, for telegrams always bring bad news. By this time the water had begun to be let into the basins surrounding the Gourna hosha. Since it was really the sugar company's job to keep the dike in good order, and since the water had risen only some forty centimeters, I did no more than ask the company's guard to keep watch and tell my head foreman to put two watchmen on the dike.

The head foreman, Ahmed Abdul Rasoul, who always wanted to appoint as many men as possible to any job, immediately said that we ought to put twelve men on, as we had the year before. I explained that last year we had had a high flood, whereas this year the water was still quite low, and that last year, moreover, there had been a threat of sabotage. Furthermore, I would soon be back from Cairo and then we could see about appointing as many guards as he wanted.

As I stood on the roof of my house that evening with Abdul Rasoul, before leaving, I gazed around the village and noticed that the whole hosha was empty. Instead of the usual green sea of sugarcane, there was only a bare black plain, with no sign of cultivation. It was, of course, only the customary change of crop every third year, but the scene gave me a feeling of depression and even awe. When I asked Abdul Rasoul why it was empty like that, he said that the company had decided not to plant sugarcane because it provides concealment for robbers. This was almost an impertinent answer, for exactly this theory had been employed as a reason against transfer in a petition presented by some of the sheikhs.

I repeated my instruction to Abdul Rasoul, to mount a guard of two men on the dikes, when he came with the usual crowd of staff to see me off at the station.

I arrived in Cairo at seven the next morning and made my way to my house there. I was very displeased to find that Fatima, my maid, was not there, and that all my cats had been left hungry. This vexation increased the peculiar feeling of despondency that had been growing within me since I had the telegram. I fed the cats and started 131 to unpack. As I was hanging my clothes up in the wardrobe, Ouna, normally a very reserved, almost aloof cat, came and sat by me, holding the wardrobe door open with his front paws—a most unusual demonstration of sympathy. Someone brought a note, just before I left, from my friend Osman Rustum, head of the Engineering and Excavations Section, who had come back for a short time from Jaffa. He suggested that I call on him so that we should go together to the Undersecretary. This did nothing to comfort me, as he was certainly offering to back me up in the row that appeared to be coming. I recalled all my more recent sins and felt exceedingly uncomfortable when I thought of an article I had just published in a magazine in which I naughtily described a quite fictitious parliament building of the eighteenth dynasty that was supposed to have been built to relieve the country from the corruption described in the Leiden papyrus, which consists of the admonitions of an Egyptian 132 sage Ipuwer; the situation in his time bore a number of curious resemblances to that obtaining in 1947 in Egypt. I had no time to collect Osman, and indeed I was in such a hurry to know what I was in for that I went straight to the ministry, intending to phone him from there. I went in, feeling very apprehensive, then up the stairs, very reluctantly, and into the anteroom to the Undersecretary's office. A clerk behind a desk said: "Good morning, Mr. Fathy!" And all the staff joined in with: "Congratulations, Congratulations!" Evidently it was not my article; perhaps I was to have a medal.

It was, apparently, that my project at Gourna had attracted the notice of the king himself, and I had been summoned to Cairo to make a full report on our progress for him to read. The Undersecretary also congratulated me when I went in to see him and asked me to write the report mentioning all the hindrances and obstacles we had encountered, and to send it to the president of the Palace Court the next day.

Curiously enough, though I was very relieved not to be in trouble, I felt a little resentful at this unlooked-for aid; I had enjoyed struggling by myself, and I didn't like the idea of my path being magically smoothed out before me. It was as if I were a small boy fighting another one, when suddenly a grown-up came and helped me. It was unfair and took away the point of fighting; it even felt like cheating in an examination.

With Rustum's help I wrote the report, making few complaints in it. I showed it to the Undersecretary, who liked it, and then went home.

A Bad Omen

That night I had a most terrifying dream. Some boys—children of a relative of mine—were having a shower, but fully dressed and wearing rucksacks. The water played all over them, but only their trousers got wet and clung to their legs. A horse came, and it looked like the mare belonging to Sheikh Ahmed Abdul Rasoul. Onto its back jumped a bad man—I couldn't see his face—and the horse bolted with him. He was thrown down and the horse galloped off, and following it came black horses, galloping after it, excited and frightened, and the galloping horses brought out the people, and there was revolution in the air, and the people ran and began falling dead, but there was nobody killing them, and they fell in their robes, the bodies piling up on top of each other, so that I turned away my head and didn't look. From behind the dike came a man dressed like a Foreign Legionary, with a sword, and he struck with his sword and cut down my friend Rustum, then struck at me, and the sword went through my shoulder, and I wondered "Am I killed?" for I felt no pain—and I woke up, most upset, and got no more sleep that night.

I took my report to Hassan Youssef Bey, the president of the Court. He had previously visited Gourna, and knew something of my troubles; when he saw me he assured me that the king's interest meant that I would find things much easier in future. Once more my hopes revived and came back to me; I saw fruit trees planted, the crafts schools working, the whole village bustling with happy, purposeful, industrious life. More than that, I saw the completed village acting as an example of cheap, good housing for the whole of Egypt.

I lunched at Groppi's that day because Fatima was still absent, and over lunch I told my dream to Ramses Wassef and Dr. Charles Bachatly. We explained both the dream and my feeling of foreboding as perhaps portending some unpleasant reaction in Egypt to the breaking off in the talks at the U.N. (that Nokrashy Pasha had been conducting). There might be some sort of unrest or even revolution if, as the bolting horse in my dream had started all the others running, any irresponsible person should do anything foolish to set it off.

The Great Mire

On my way home I noticed in Ismailia Square an enormous poster advertising a film, "The Great Mire." It gave me a nasty feeling—it seemed like a bad omen, and I turned my face away from it as I went past. When I reached my house I found a note from Rustum, asking me to call as he had a telephone message from the chief inspector in Luxor saying that the whole village had been flooded and drowned. I felt dizzy, my head swam, and I dashed round to Rustum to hear more. He could add little to his note; so we phoned the inspector at Luxor. I wish no one, not my worst enemy, the agony of that hour's waiting for the phone call to come through. At last we heard him and learned that the village was in fact flooded, that the dike had been broken, and that the whole site was under water. "How deep is the water?" I said. "I didn't measure it." "But about how deep? Up to the windows? The door posts? Over the roofs? I want to know." But he didn't seem to know; so I told him we should be coming by the night train and hung up.

We left that night, and in the train I told the dream again, to Rustum. He explained it by saying that the boys were my houses, wetted from below by the water, that the man with the sword was the man who had broken the dike, and that the black horses represented the rushing waters of the flood.

Arriving at the village the next morning, I found the water had risen only about half a meter and that the eastern side was not flooded at all. But all the bricks we had prepared last season had melted away; they would have been safe if my assistant had moved them as I had told him to. Not even in this emergency, however, could Raslan forget about his promotion, and he didn't come at all to offer his help.

I hurried to the place where the dike had been pierced through, about a mile and a quarter west of the village, and found a deep wide trench dug through the dike, about eight meters across. There were about a hundred workmen there, supervised by irrigation engineers and two police officers, but to my sorrow I found that there was not one Gourni among the workmen, who had been forcibly recruited from neighboring villages to deal with the crisis. All the Gournis had refused to work on the dike, and even those who had been rounded up the night before and put to work on it had made off through the water under cover of darkness, rather than help save their new village. While working, they had contrived to widen the gap with their feet while ostensibly filling it in with their hands.

Yet in doing this they were directly hurting themselves, for they were all earning good money as laborers in the village, and the new houses were, even financially, better than their old ones which, for the most part built on government land, were virtually worthless. There is a proverb which says: "If you know the reason, surprise will stop," and here there was more than one reason. First, the patriarchal system is very strong, and everybody obeys the heads of families, who, in Gourna, were tomb robbers. They were both feared and respected by the people, and they used their power to preserve their trade. They had no intention of giving up their nice, profitable, squalid houses in the cemetery with treasure waiting to be mined under their floors, to move to a new, hygienic, beautiful village away from the tombs. Second, the Gournis are all closely interrelated, and no one would fail to support a family chief in any enterprise. Third, a kind of shame had prompted them, the shame of being considered cowards for not taking part in the sabotage.

They had chosen their time very cunningly: first, when the sugarcanes had been pulled up, which happens only once in three years; second, when I was away from the village, and, third, when the water was very low, so that no one feared or suspected any danger at all.

All the work was still concentrated on the breach in the dike, but I found that the difference in level inside and outside the hosha was only some ten centimeters. The water would not rise any further, for the outside level could be controlled by the irrigation authorities; so I turned my attention to saving the buildings in the village. As we had already lost all our bricks (those that ought to have been moved) and the water was lapping round the houses, I had a little dike built close around the buildings, only fifty centimeters high, and started pumping this area dry.

I examined the breach again, and found two large cuts, about two meters apart on the "dry" side of the dike. Clearly there had been a line of similar cuts the whole width of the breach. True, the irrigation expert, when asked by the police, had at first said that the hole could have been made naturally, but this was a hasty conclusion, based on the frightening appearance of the waves that first night and not on scientific facts at all.

The wind that comes off the mountains had whipped up quite substantial waves, which looked black and alarming in the night and wetted the trousers of the engineers, who immediately forgot all their knowledge of hydraulics, forgot that the dike was a good six meters thick at the bottom, that the water was only fifty centimeters high, that the seepage gradient would come out well below ground level—forgot, in short, that it was physically impossible for the dike to have broken by itself—and saw only an ocean of black waves that seemed able to beat down any dike.

Once our first dike was built, we put in the new pump to pump the water out from inside this barrier, and then started to construct a second dike enclosing a larger area, taking in important places such as the kilns. The built area was dry in three days. Then we shifted the pump to drain this second area, borrowing too, a second pump from the Irrigation Inspectorate. In this work *osta* Mahmoud showed great enthusiasm and goodwill. He made the new pump his special charge and worked at it tirelessly, day and night for three days, wherever it went, standing in the water, clearing it when it got blocked, and contributing very considerably to the success of our efforts. Another invaluable helper was Ibrahim Hassan. He was unbelievably strong; he could wrap his arms round an eighty-gallon oil drum that three men could hardly shift, and pick it up like a sack of feathers. He seemed to be as tough and enduring as the pump engine itself. All day and all night he was there, ready to pick it up and walk with it wherever we wanted. Without these two men, Ibrahim Hassan and *osta* Mahmoud, we could not have cleared the site in twice the time.

Within ten days we had our lorries driving onto the land round the buildings that had been flooded, and we could start bringing in materials again to go on with our building.

While all this was being done, the district attorney descended upon us to make an investigation into the flooding. He and his assistants went round asking every villager in turn: "Did you pierce the dike?" Every villager in turn replied "No," and when the attorney had filled three sheets of legal-sized paper with these answers, he went home satisfied that the affair had been investigated.

As it happened, I myself got more out of his questions than he did, for Ahmed Abdul Rasoul gave quite different names from the ones he had given me as those of the guards he had appointed, thus showing me that he hadn't appointed any at all. However, I preferred not to give him away but to deal with him myself.

My first report to the Palace, then, was at least interesting and resulted in my immediate recall to Cairo to tell the story in person. The president of the Court was most indignant with the criminals and said that arrangements would be made to send a detachment of Sudanese frontier guards—very tough and much-feared troops with big whips; I was quite horrified at the proposal and begged him to do nothing of the sort, for it would not solve the mystery and would certainly inspire so much hatred that the peasants would never be won over to the new village. "At least," he said, "let me send you some soldiers to guard the project. Let me give you arms for yourself." "Arms will only attract more arms. If anyone wants to shoot me, he has only to hide behind a door and wait till I'm not looking. No amount of guns would be of any use to me." At last I managed to persuade him that I wasn't going to be bothered with a regiment of soldiers running all over my village, and he let me go, though with evident misgiving about my fate. He did at least get the official enquiry reopened, and shortly afterward the district attorney reappeared this time with the governor and numerous important people. They went round the village, asking "Did you pierce the dike?" The villagers, understandably enough, once more answered "No," and when the investigators had filled up ten sheets of paper they went off, and that was the last we heard of them.

Sacrifice to the Gods Accepted

When he saw me so depressed after this affair, my friend Schwaller de Lubicz* told me that the flooding was my sacrifice to the gods for the village.

* The founder of a school of Egyptology that has, through the interpretation of symbols, penetrated to the mode of thought of the Ancient Egyptians. His

I felt that the gods had accepted the sacrifice and approved of the village because they revealed through the flooding an important fact that I might otherwise have overlooked. The diked hosha in which Gourna was to be built had been dry for thirty years, and its earth was hard and compact, so that it was not quite typical of the village and farmland of Upper Egypt. Generally, in this part, the hod system of irrigation is used, by which the river water is let in over the fields at flood time. This annual wetting of the soil causes it to expand, so that when, by August or so, it has dried up again, enormous cracks appear all over it, as in dried mud. The earth at this time is called *sharaki,* which means "parched."

Building on such soil presents big structural problems for the peasant, and for this reason villages in Upper Egypt are usually built on mounds raised above flood level. The mounds, though, have their own problems, one of which is that, as the waters rise, all the vermin of the fields—rats, mice, snakes, and insects—take refuge in the village, bringing a variety of diseases with them. At this time of year vast numbers of birds—storks, pelicans, and hawks—flock to the villages to feast on all these animals. Also these mounds are overcrowded with people, and one of the reasons why the villages cannot expand is this very flooding and the unstable nature of the soil in the low-lying fields. There are now projects suggested for converting the land to the perennial irrigation system with canals and for building village extensions on the flat land, but all these extensions will find themselves up against the problem of the cracks.

So when Gourna was flooded, its soil reverted to the sharaki state, like all the rest of Upper Egypt, and enormous cracks began to appear all over it as soon as it dried up. These were really alarming, going down as much as three meters and as wide as fifty centimeters at the surface, almost as if there had been a little earthquake. Since the subsoil water rises every year to within two meters of the surface, and the foundations of the houses in Gourna were of the customary strip type, made of rubble masonry and earth mortar, laid in trenches a meter and a half deep, each house would be sitting on a thin crust of soil floating on liquid mud. The cracks would allow the soil to slide laterally, and the houses themselves would certainly crack.

So I had to find a way of giving my houses foundations that would not be affected by these cracks; moreover, if I was to be faithful to my concept of a model village, the solution would have to be practicable for any peasant to copy in any village.

---

work, embodied in such studies as "Le Temple de l'homme" and "Le miracle égyptien" is no less important than Champollion's deciphering of the Rosetta Stone.

Thus the problem was not one of engineering alone, for various accepted solutions exist, such as concrete pile or raft foundations, which are all prohibitively expensive for the peasant. I denied myself the use even of a reinforced concrete bond beam, to ensure that my solution could be easily copied.

I consulted Professor Khalifa of the Soil Mechanics Department in the Faculty of Engineering at Cairo University, and was interested to see that he suggested the same solution that the Pharaohs had used. The ancient Egyptians, when they built a temple, would mark out the corners of the precinct with pegs, and then at a chosen point within this they would dig down until they came to the "secret water," which would be the subsoil water, probably choosing the winter solstice for this, when the water would be at its lowest. Then they would put a layer of sand in this hole, as sand is incompressible and does not expand when wet. On this they would plant a papyriform or lotiform column, as if it were to grow. (There is an interesting archaeological oddity in connection with this ceremony. M. Robichon, when excavating the theple Montu at Karnak, found in the foundations a layer of sand and, under that, imprinted in the mud, the impression of an august bottom left where the architect, or possibly Pharaoh himself, had evidently slipped and sat down when performing the ceremony, leaving the marks of his pleated kilt for posterity to admire; M. Robichon made a cast of this which may be seen in the Museum of Karnak.)

The problem of foundations in sharaki earth and the solutions applied in Gourna together with some others that are proposed to be tried and tested are fully discussed in appendix IV.

The Decauville

My lorries were being steadily ruined by carrying earth, which was really a job for a Decauville railway. The Department of Antiquities had a lot of Decauville equipment, but it was almost impossible to get it out of the clutches of the various archaeologists to whom it had been allotted, for all archaeologists are as jealous of their equipment as they are of the tombs they dig, and won't give it up even if it is lying idle in the stores, as much of this equipment was. When I asked Ahmed in Abydos, he referred me to Aly in Aswan, and when I called upon Aly he said he had sent all the equipment to Abydos.

It happened that near Gourna there was a large quantity of material—thousands of meters of rail and dozens of wagonettes—left over from the Metropolitan Museum's excavations at Deir el Bahari, which had long since stopped. I coveted these, but could find no one connected with the museum to apply to for them. I called on the University of Chicago's Oriental Institute people in Luxor, who said they had nothing to do with the Metropolitan Museum's excavations but advised me to try the director of the National Bank in Luxor, who was the museum's acting agent. He said that his responsibility ended with paying the guards who looked after the equipment. He did, however, give me the name of the head of the Egyptian section of the museum, Dr. Lansing; I had already written to him but had had no answer, for the poor man was gravely ill.

When the king took an interest in the project, I wrote to the Palace about the trouble I had had getting a Decauville. A committee was immediately appointed under the Secretary of State for Education. On this committee was M. Chevrier, director of the Karnak excavations, and he promised me 800 meters of rails and twelve wagonettes, for which I thanked him most gratefully. The minutes of the meeting were duly signed, the file tied up and stamped "Dealt with," and it was put in a pigeonhole. When I went back to Gourna I asked M. Chevrier for the equipment, but to my astonishment he refused to give it to me, saying that he had just expanded his work on the demolition of the third pylon of the Temple of Karnak.

I was very disappointed. My lorries were going from bad to worse, and there seemed no prospect of relieving them. I thought to myself that I had asked everyone, even the king. Where could I turn now? Only God is higher than the king; so I prayed to God and asked him to give me a Decauville.

Within a week I was visited by M. Bruyère, the director of the French Institute's excavations at Deir el Medina, who said he had heard that I wanted a Decauville. He had used up all his funds and had had to stop excavations before the end of the season; he was ready to give me all his Decauvilles on condition that I employ his men, so that they shouldn't lose their pay for the rest of the season. I was quite willing to take his men, and would even have suggested it myself, as his equipment would be safer in the hands of the men who were used to it.

I was quite ecstatic at having got a Decauville at last, but, even more, I was seized with a feeling of awe that my prayers should have been fulfilled so plainly and promptly. At once I prostrated myself in prayer to the Almighty, thanking him for his gift, which I took as a sign of approval of my work.

The Koran says that if you give thanks you will be given yet more. At the beginning of the next season I was called upon by Mr. Hauser and Mr. Wilkinson, both working for the Metropolitan Museum. They had arrived from Iran to liquidate all the assets of their museum in Gourna, and as they knew that I needed a Decauville, they were willing to sell me theirs—3,000 meters of rail, thirty wagonettes, and eleven flat trucks—at a nominal price of L.E. 100. They had had a higher offer for it in town from a commercial firm but preferred to give it to a scientific organization like ours, stipulating only that they should be paid within one month; they were well used to administrative delays. I readily promised, secretly resolving to pay for it out of my own pocket and, if the administration did not pay, to hold a ceremony when my work was finished to which all the departmental chiefs concerned would be invited, at which I would sink all the rails and trucks in the river.

Luckily the administration did pay; so the equipment did not end up in the river.

4 Finale
Gourna Dormant

An Architect in Search of a Patron

After three seasons' work on Gourna, I found it increasingly difficult to do anything against the stiffening obstruction from the Department of Antiquities. I wanted to transfer the whole project to some more appropriate department; so I tried to get it taken over by the Fellah Department. They wouldn't touch it; so I tried the Housing Department, which also declined the honor. Here, when I pointed out that the peasants couldn't afford cement, I was told, "We shall build cement works." This is wildly impracticable, a modern version of Marie Antoinette's "Let them eat cake."

The obstruction reached its climax when some changes in the department's staff brought two employees who were hostile to the project into leading posts, and my last champion, Shafik Ghorbal, the Undersecretary, moved to the Ministry of Social Affairs.

I thought that, with Shafik Ghorbal in the Ministry of Social Affairs, the project would be better off under him there, and so applied to the Fellah Department of that ministry. Before long it became clear that the Fellah Department was not very interested in the fellah—or at least not in housing him—and so once more I was told to apply to the Housing Department. Here our housing project came to a complete standstill.

Each one of these moves had made the situation worse, quite apart from involving us in interminable office work as inventories were made and stores handed over. In all three departments committees sat, apparently convened solely to find excuses for stopping the work and enabling the department concerned to wash its hands of Gourna altogether.

It was clearly impossible to go on working with such people, so when I was finally told either to return to the School of Fine Arts or to give up my chair and go permanently into the Housing Department, I returned to teaching with relief. Yet even teaching brought little reward. I felt I was trying to teach something I had failed to do myself, and grew increasingly anxious and impatient. Results took too long; it was like growing a palm tree from seed—ten years before you can pick one date.

Then a series of fresh misfortunes decided me. There was a competition for the design of the cheapest adequate peasant house. Two designs were required, and the designs I submitted won in both categories. The Minister of Social Affairs then gave L.E. 250 for the erection of one of these designs, as an experiment. A site was found on some land belonging to the Social Center in Marg, near Cairo. I worked hard on the working drawings and estimates in order to have them ready before anyone changed his mind, and finished within a week. In spite of this the Housing Department never built the house, although they had everything—designs, site, and money—because, they said, they could not decide under which heading of their budget to enter it.

At that time the government opened the Building Research Center, so I proposed to transfer the L.E. 250 to this research center and to build the house under their auspices. In this way, I hoped, a mud brick building would be subjected to an official and authoritative test, and it would be proved that mud brick was really cheap. The research center agreed, but said it would be necessary to build a second house out of orthodox materials (pre-stressed concrete beams) for comparison with mine. Eventually they built this second house (which cost them L.E. 1,000), but not mine. I had put great hopes in this experiment to prove my contentions as to the cost of mud brick and to put an end to the stories of the high cost of Gourna, but nothing came of it, and the L.E. 250 are still with the research center.

After this, when I hoped that the success of my school at Fares would at last vindicate the mud brick method, a high official of the School Buildings Department told a direct and deliberate lie to the minister, saying that the school had cost L.E. 19,000 when in truth it cost L.E. 6,000. On learning this, I understood that there was no place for me in Egypt; it was evident that mud brick building aroused active hostility among important people there. As it happened, I had recently had an adventure with two thieves who had broken into my house and stabbed me, yet it is no exaggeration to say that I felt safer with these thieves than with officials who could lie to prevent a benefit from reaching the peasants.

The Koran says to the believer who finds it impossible to carry out his mission among his people, "Then he shall go elsewhere." At this time I was asked by Dr. Doxiadis to join his organization in Athens, to work for him on rural planning in Iraq. I felt that it was more important to build than to teach; that buildings, no matter in what part of the world, would speak louder than lectures; and that if some completed project attracted international attention, it would eventually have an effect on Egypt.

I chose, then, to build rather than teach, feeling that I could entrust the theory that I had evolved at Gourna to this book, which is a contribution to the theory of ekistics. The ekistic approach, though, which should be as practical as possible, calls for some reference to the pitfalls and obstacles in the way of practical application of theory; hence this second part.

The young architects who read this book must not suppose that once they know all about materials and structures, once they are fired with a love of beautiful buildings and a determination to bring beauty into the lives of their fellow men, they are then equipped to go out and build. When an architect feels a sense of mission, he will inevitably experience a great deal of resistance to his purpose. If he wants to build for the people, he must understand from the outset that he has a bitter struggle ahead of him. He will meet many technical and artistic problems that will call forth all his training and skill, but surmounting such problems is exciting and spiritually rewarding, like climbing a mountain, and it is presumably because he likes tackling such difficulties that he ever became an architect at all.

But there are other obstacles in his path besides the straightforward technical and artistic ones, obstacles that will make him doubt even his most fundamental beliefs. As his architectural sense drives him through clear logic to more and more radical solutions, he will find within himself treacherous feelings that tempt him to give up his mission and conform to the general practice in architecture. When I found even the peasants hostile to the Gourna project, I began to question the whole principle of the mud brick vault. I thought that perhaps, although it was sound economically, aesthetically, and from the standpoint of engineering, it might carry some suggestions of the tomb, or some other discouraging associations, to put the peasant off. I was comforted in this by Schwaller de Lubicz, who assured me that although the semicircular vault was associated with Osiris and death and might have been unsuitable, any sort of pointed, parabolic, or segmental arch would not carry disagreeable symbolism. He himself visited me in the new village and found the impression of the domed madyafa very pleasant.

In fact some of the opposition may have been suggested by memories of certain squalid dwellings erected by miserly landowners (for their fellaheen) in Beheira, in the North of the Delta, which were roofed with squat, low domes and would indeed remind you of a tomb. On the other hand, vaults and domes of one sort or another are used cheerfully as dwellings in Nubia, Syria, the Aegean Islands, Sicily, and Italy without anyone thinking of the grave. But to a young architect who was proposing such unorthodox methods, self-doubt was most unsettling. Apart from this fundamental uncertainty, the architect will be oppressed by all the everyday weaknesses of the spirit. Inertia, the wish for a quiet life, considerations of material comfort, reluctance to offend others, and even plain fear all counsel the creative architect to betray his vision and become respectable like everybody else.

This inner struggle must be experienced by all creative artists, but the architect will find that in his case the struggle takes place externally too, when he tries to realize his vision in solid buildings. Then he will recognize the same enemies, inertia, the wish for a quiet life, etc., which he has overcome in himself, entrenched in the official bodies with which he must cooperate to succeed in his mission. The last temptation for him is then to become angry and contemptuous of the reluctance and obscurantism of the officials he has to deal with, and to give up all attempts to work through official bodies. To help himself ignore this temptation, the architect should remember how lucky he is to have a long technical education behind him. He should remember that for him the very excitement of solving architectural problems and seeing his buildings coming up provides the satisfaction and reward of an act of creation, which to the officials is unfortunately just another complication in their everyday routine, another headache for the overworked and poorly paid civil servant whose only motive for action is, too often, fear of the Court of Accounts. What interest can we expect a senior official to have in revolutionary proposals, to commit his department to major schemes involving untried techniques and unsound-seeming methods of finance? He has achieved his position after a lifetime's cautious progress up the hierarchy, and now sits heavily at his desk, concerned only to avoid mistakes and possibly keeping one hesitating eye on the next place up. The aspiring architect must unfortunately develop patience and a technique for working harmoniously with officialdom. Nevertheless, if solving architectural problems gives the satisfaction of climbing a mountain, cooperating with the bureaucracy is like wading through a bog—soul-destroying, nothing less.

Yet these officials and those who head their offices are ordinary men, part of the people, like all of us. Individually they are kindly, sensitive, and intelligent and, one hopes, anxious to rebuild their country. Can't they see that revolutionary ambitions need revolutionary measures? Or are we all at the mercy of a system of official procedure that everybody hates, that is universally recognized for a harmful, choking growth of weeds, and that no one is prepared to uproot? Even the peasant is slow to take an interest in proposals for bettering his condition. He is apathetic and dumb, he has no education, no conception of national affairs, no status. He does not believe that he can help himself or make himself heard.

Slander Continues

The detractors of Gourna have used a variety of lies: they have said that the Gournis would not live in the village because they didn't like houses mud-roofed with vaults and domes; they have said that to use mud brick is not progressive and that it is not a sound engineering material; but they have concentrated their attack, in the manner of Dr. Goebbels, upon the strongest claim to recognition of the techniques employed: their low cost. They have said that the method of building is very expensive.

Therefore, I must attempt to give some explanation here.

First, about the Gournis not wanting to live in the village. But why wouldn't they? Surely we should have the curiosity to ask why. We already know the attraction of the old village. The people who profited most from the tombs—the richer villagers, naturally—formed a "committee of sheikhs" to oppose the transfer. They engaged a lawyer and thought up the wildest excuses for not moving —even to saying that they would be in danger from wolves in New Gourna. This committee was composed entirely of antique dealers, dragomans, ex-guards of antiquities, and so on—clearly people with a strong interest in staying as they were—yet their voices were heard while the majority of the villagers, who accepted the move, remained passively silent.

An architect is not supposed to be a policeman to push people in and out of houses. Was it my job to see that the Gournis moved?

The government made a law expropriating the Gournis. Was it enforced? I have often heard responsible officials refer to the peasants as sons of dogs and say that the only way to handle them is to build them houses of any sort and bulldoze the old ones. The Department of Antiquities made no attempt to gain the cooperation of the peasants, and even seemed sometimes to side with them in opposing the scheme. The attitude of department personnel was one of callous brutality to the peasants in private talk among themselves, and timid procrastination in practice. I was in an unhappy in-between situation, neither properly of the government nor of the village; so I suffered from both sides.

To return to whether the Gournis liked the houses or not: I once secured the help of a young social worker, Hussein Serry, to interview the peasant families and get details of the houses they wanted. Within twenty days he had interviewed two hundred families and obtained their written and signed approvals for the broad specifications of their respective houses. These approvals I still have. And it should not be supposed that they were rushed or cajoled into accepting plans that they couldn't understand; they had opportunities to inspect actual standing buildings. In fact, when Aly Abu Bakr brought his family to see a house, the women were delighted with it; but when he went back to the village he was bitterly attacked for betraying the villagers' cause.

If only the government had let Hussein Serry stay for another month, I am sure he would have got every family in Gourna to agree to move into its own new house (except, perhaps, for the twelve sheikhs!).

I was really almost pleased that the government had left me to deal with the villagers in my own way, for of course I would never be a party to the "bulldozing" tactics favored by these officials. It suited my principles to be allowed to take each family as a private client and to build with the family's help and consent. In fact, the further away the authorities kept, the better I was pleased. I often tried to explain to the peasants that now we had an opportunity to build together, quietly, just as we wanted, before the government came in and put a stop to our self-help. I told them that in certain circles I was said to be pampering the peasants, that the Department of Antiquities had no interest but to clear them off the hill and push them anyhow into houses, and that they could never expect personal consideration from a government department. I begged them not to use the government as a weapon against me, who wanted only to serve them. I can still remember how one Friday, when I was sitting with the sheikhs after prayers and urging these pleas, one very old and holy man, deeply venerated throughout the region, Sheikh el Tayeb, said in great anger to his brother sheikhs that it is a sin to kick a man's hand when he offers it to you in friendship.

Second, it has been stated that mud brick is not an engineering material, and so no government authority should have anything to do with it; that mud brick needs frequent maintenance and repairs; and that, in short, it should be left for peasants to build with on their own.

The answer to this is that those architects who so airily dismiss mud brick are in fact not competent to judge whether it is a suitable material for engineering or not. The only science that can give us a satisfactory verdict on the strength and reliability of mud is the science of soil mechanics. Experiments have been made in many parts of the world on mud as a building material—notably in the University of California and in Texas—while in Egypt Dr. Mohammed Said Youssef, professor of soil mechanics in Cairo University, Dr.

Mustapha Yehia, professor of materials, and Colonel Debes have all investigated the properties of earth bricks.

Tests on samples of ordinary mud bricks carried out by Colonel Debes in the Engineering Faculty laboratories of Cairo University found the crushing load to average round thirty kilograms per square centimeter. As a conclusive proof of the suitability of mud bricks for engineering purposes, I refer the reader to the results of Colonel Debes's leading tests, and the results of the wetting and drying tests of mud brick walls carried out by Dr. Mustapha Yehia. These are shown in Appendix V.

From these tables it is quite clear that all types of mud brick may be trusted to support any reasonable load under worse rain than could ever be experienced in Egypt.

In Gourna no brick is subjected to a greater load than two and one-half kilograms per square centimeter which provides a safety factor of around 10.

Perhaps one of the reasons why architects are so shy of mud brick is that it is a more lively material than concrete. Concrete, once set, stays the same; mud does not, but continues to shrink until it has become dry. This might take a year or more, according to the permeability of the soil and the climatic conditions. However, there is no need to be alarmed at this behavior. It doesn't worry the peasant who builds in mud brick; he, with the experience of generations, knows how to allow for it, as for example when he builds a wall a few courses at a time, leaving the masonry to dry for some time before he continues with the construction.

It doesn't worry the soil mechanics engineer either, as he can allow for it in his calculations and manipulation. It is only the architect, without the tradition of the peasant or the knowledge of the scientist, who refuses to venture away from the concrete he thinks he knows enough about and feels so secure in using. This was brought home to me very recently.

I must explain that, after seeing my school at Gourna and another one I built at Fares, the minister of education decided to build two more experimental schools in mud brick, one at Radisseya and the other at El Bayerat. It was recently reported that these last two schools were on the point of collapse; they had been evacuated, and it had even been proposed that the carpentry should be removed and saved from the wreckage. By good luck I happened to be in Cairo just at the time when a committee was appointed to investigate this matter.

I pointed out to the minister the seriousness of the allegations and begged him to appoint some responsible scientist to the committee. Thus it came about that Dr. Mohammed Said Youssef and Dr. Michel Bakhoum, the professors of soil mechanics and structures at Cairo University, were invited to examine the suspect schools. They found that the schools reported to be collapsing were perfectly sound; what had happened was that the natural shrinkage of the walls had cracked the plaster, and this only because the architects had put hard sand and lime plaster over mud brick, whereas as an engineering principle the foundation should be stronger than what you put on top of it; any peasant could have told them what to expect. The schools at Gourna and Fares, where earth plaster was used, were quite unaffected. Incidentally, we found that one of the experimental schools, at Radisseya, had been built in the middle of a dale, and that as a result of heavy rains it had been submerged up to a height of 1 meter 20 centimeters for a whole month. Yet the structure had suffered nothing.

After all the attempts to denigrate the mud brick method that I had seen, it did cross my mind that this school might have been sited in a dale—which was known to get flooded from time to time—on purpose, so that when it collapsed someone could say "I told you so." But perhaps this is just persecution mania.

The third accusation is, as I said, the most important: that Gourna proved too costly. Now if it did, this is a most singular and interesting fact. If it is really true that mud and straw somehow cost more than cement and steel, surely this is extraordinary and calls for an inquiry. But there has been no such inquiry, because it would immediately show that the buildings in fact cost less than any comparable buildings erected anywhere else in Egypt by a government department, and that three-quarters of the cost of the permanent skilled labor went to pay a staff idle because of administrative delays.

The most convincing refutation of this claim is an analysis of where the Gourna money actually went. This I have dealt with in appendix VI. Please bear in mind that the total expenditure at the time when the project was handed over to the Ministry of Social Affairs was L.E. 94,120.36, from which at least L.E. 20,000 should be deducted for unused equipment, lorries, and materials lying in the stores. So the total expenditure was L.E. 74,120, the total amount of building done 19,301.90 square meters, and therefore the buildings, including a mosque, a market, a khan, a theater, a townhall, and two schools, cost L.E. 4 per square meter. Where else have public buildings been erected so cheaply?

As a matter of fact, the minister of social affairs, interested to compare the costs of building the then remaining 790 houses according to the two systems, as represented respectively by the contract and the method used in the project, appointed a committee to investigate this matter. The committee found that, by the contract system the cost would have been L.E. 441,864, while by the Gourna one it would have been only L.E. 237,202 (see appendix I for cost analysis).

Some people have said that Gourna was too much of a one-man show. It has been suggested that there is something peculiarly difficult and advanced in designing for mud brick, and that the method is not suitable for other architects to take up. This is complete nonsense, of course. If a village boy can be taught in three months to build a vault, then a qualified architect can presumably learn to draw one.

I have already put forward (see appendix II) a proposal for the deliberate training of a body of graduate architects, to prepare them for work in Egyptian villages. My hopes for the future of the Egyptian countryside rest with these young architects of my country. It is the architects who should now be studying rural building who will have to apply the principles developed at Gourna. The rebuilding of the Egyptian countryside will take forty years of continuous hard work, and these young people will have to see it through. I know I can trust them to devote themselves sincerely to village building, for I have always met the most enthusiastic and sympathetic response from young architects.

The government, though, must recognize the size and requirements of the task of rebuilding rural Egypt in the way I have proposed. It must accept its responsibilities to the architects who will carry through the program and who will have given up the possibility of a profitable private practice. It must guarantee these men a sufficient salary (bearing in mind that the object is to attract the best young architects in the land, and not just those who cannot make a living privately) and be considerate to them in all personal matters. Equally important, the government must let the architects do their job, and make sure that the officials in the administration do not hamper the building work. Unless the administrative machine is modernized so as to eliminate *all* holdups due to procedural and accounting processes, unless the technical staff are backed by a sufficiency of officials who are authorized and willing to take responsibility, unless the telephone call replaces the application-in-triplicate-with-fifteen-signatures-of-approval, then our rural rebuilding program will simply repeat the fiasco of Gourna on a scale involving millions of pounds, while three hundred architects grow embittered and cynical and all possible hope of a decent future for twenty million peasants is lost forever. The danger of this happening is so real that I felt it my duty to describe some of the ways in which the administrative machinery brought work at Gourna to a standstill, so that future governments may be warned and may take action to avoid such happenings.

As to the young architects who will form the dedicated group of rebuilders, they must understand too that the way of the pioneer is rocky and beset with thorns.

In the past, I have refrained from encouraging young architects to follow in my footsteps, because I felt a sense of responsibility for their material welfare. Just as one does not encourage one's son to become a poet, out of consideration for one's grandchildren, so I could not think of founding a school of mud brick architects. I had experienced all the difficulties and obstructions that such an approach to architecture must entail; so how could I see any young architect commit himself and his family, at the very outset of his career, to the certain poverty that a devotion to the interests of the peasants would mean? St. Francis at least enjoined celibacy on his followers.

Gourna Revisited

In January 1961 I visited Gourna again. The village was exactly as I had left it; not a single new building had been erected. One of the complaints against the project had been that it took too long, but in spite of all the obstacles we did manage to build quite a lot; in the ten years that it has been in the hands of the ministry, not one brick has been laid on another, while the Gournis continue to live among the tombs on the hill.

This building standstill is matched by a standstill in the crafts. The little boys who worked so promisingly under Talha Effendi have now all grown up. They are young men of twenty or so, all unemployed. The old moallem of the village weavers, Iskander, has died, and although his son has taken his place, the traditional berda and monayar weaves are dying out.

Only two things flourish. One is the trees I planted, now grown thick and strong, perhaps because they were not subject to the administration, and the other is the forty-six masons we trained, every one of whom is working in the district, using the skills he learned at Gourna—a proof of the value of training local craftsmen.

Looking over the village with its deserted theater, empty khan and crafts school, and few houses inhabited by squatters, with only its boys' primary school in use, I thought what Gourna might have been—and what it still must become, for the problem of the Gournis is still as acute as it was in 1945, and there is still no other solution proposed.

Certainly I learned more from the struggle than I would have done had my path been perfectly smooth. The Koran says that things you dislike are often good for you, and certainly a direct consequence of my disappointment at Gourna has been a great deepening of my understanding of the problems of rural housing. For the problem is concerned with more than the just technical or economic; it is primarily human, embracing systems and people, professionals as well as peasants. It is much greater than Gourna and the Department of Antiquities.

More than one research has to be conducted in more than one field and more than one pilot project to be carried out in more than one place in the country. The project should be evaluated and the results of the research should be assessed before we can give our verdict in the matter and put forward policies to be universally applied. The time seems not to have come yet for such an attitude toward the problem of rural housing. In the later years that followed the stopping of the work in Gourna, during my work abroad and after my return home—unlike the prodigal son, unrecognized by my father—I had been hunting in vain for a patron among the authorities concerned with housing and scientific research to sponsor such projects. Several experiments were started in Egypt and elsewhere, but as soon as they reached the stage of yielding any concrete results they were stopped as by some mysterious agent or by the force of destiny itself, and like Sisyphus, I had to carry the stone uphill, slide down, and carry it up again and again.

This is not to say that the authorities were not interested in the welfare of the people, but that an intrinsic incompatibility exists between the principles, aims, and procedures of the cooperative system of building and those of the contract system which is well established in the official economy and administration. The opposition to cooperation will be further understood when we know that housing in all developing countries absorbs from one third to a half of the national income allotted to development, which means several billions of pounds spent every year. I realized at last that I had to be my own patron if I wanted to continue with the struggle.

Gourna in Nabaroh

Therefore I hope my own work in future will be to apply the principles of cooperative building and to develop to the limit all the ideas outlined in this book, in a modest project in the small provincial town of Nabaroh, which gave my mother all her memories of the countryside and to which she always longed to return.

If this experiment goes forward, it is important that it should not become another isolated and unfruitful bit of model building like so much in Egypt recently.

Then clearly the experiment needs to be sponsored by a university department, by the government, or by some international body. It is already clear that a whole new community added to a provincial town cannot be a private responsibility; it will involve close cooperation with the local authorities as well as with the central government. True, the project authority should be as autonomous as possible, to avoid the frustration of working through ministries that are not intended to handle such affairs, but without official sponsorship the Nabaroh scheme cannot have the international importance it deserves.

The Gourna experiment has provided all the information it can. True, it must be finished, but the planning has been done, and the circumstances anyway are so special that the actual execution of the work would not be particularly relevant to the problems of cooperative building. Gourna has done its job, and it is in Nabaroh that I hope to see the full flowering of the ideas that germinated there. Gourna will be fully realized in Nabaroh, and from Nabaroh, let us hope, a housing revolution will spread throughout Egypt.

Appendixes

These are not intended to be a comprehensive treatment of building construction or of the organization of works. I discuss only special problems actually met with at Gourna, and problems, solutions, or suggestions arising from these, together with the problems of cooperative building in Egypt and countries with similar labor and economic conditions. Cooperative building methods, it will be remembered, were not tried out at Gourna, but they urgently need research and experiment.

Appendix I
Cost Analysis of Labor and Rates of the Execution of Works

The analysis that follows is a complete breakdown of the work included as done at Gourna. Because Gourna was a government-financed project, employing only paid labor, the final figure for each item is in Egyptian currency and represents the actual cost of the item at the prices and wage rates prevailing at Gourna between 1946 and 1950.

It will be realized, however, that the analysis is valid for any project employing the Gourna type of construction, since it shows, besides the cost, the *amount* and *type* of labor, in man-hours, for every item of construction and for the procuring and preparation of all materials. The labor that goes into an item is constant, at least for Egypt, where the skills exist and the climate is nowhere less favorable than at Gourna. Thus this analysis may be applied with confidence to any building project employing the same techniques, whatever system of labor is adopted—cooperative or otherwise—and whatever price conditions may be prevailing (i.e. whether labor, materials, or equipment happen to be dearer, cheaper, or the same price as at Gourna).

In a project designed on a cooperative basis, as any major scheme must be, it would therefore be easy to determine from this analysis what proportion of the project would be borne by the government and what by the local people.

The analysis shows clearly that a house can be built very cheaply. At Mit-el-Nasara village, where the cooperative system was to have been employed, a house would cost L.E. 84. This sum (to pay for the specialized skilled labor, carpentry and sanitary fittings, and pipes that could not be made locally) in any project might be furnished as an outright subsidy or as a long-term loan, and it is worth noting that, whereas L.E. 600—a very low figure for a contract-built house of industrial materials—represents an impossible debt for most families, there are very many that could afford to pay off L.E. 84 over ten or twenty years.

Cost Analysis of Materials and Labor Used in Gourna Village

Brick Making:

1. Only rough field tests were made for determining the composition of the soil and the resistance of bricks made.
2. Earth was dug from the piles left along the bank after the excavation of the Fadleya Canal bordering the site of the project. The soil was of Nile silt deposits, composed almost entirely of silt and clay like most of the land irrigated by the basin system in Upper Egypt.
3. The shrinkage of the bricks made of pure clay, with no straw and molded very wet in the traditional way, was about 37 percent after drying, with bad cracking which took place a very short time after molding.
4. Bricks were made of mixtures of different proportions of earth, sand and straw. The following composition gave the best results: 1 m^3 earth, ⅓ m^3 sand, 45 lbs straw. This quantity produced 660 bricks measuring $23 \times 11 \times 7$. The molds used measured $24 \times 12 \times 8$ cms.
5. Samples of bricks made with this composition were kept as a standard of comparison.

Cost Analysis of Making 1,000 Bricks

(*a*) *Earth.* It was intended to extract the earth required for brick making from the site of the artificial lake originally designed for this purpose and the other ones as explained in the chapter on this subject, but unfortunately the canal irrigating the Hosha of Kamel Boulos Bey which was to feed this lake was abandoned and replaced by an artesian well. So the earth had to be fetched from the residue of the excavation of the Fadleya Canal as mentioned previously.

It was transported along a light railway in tipping hand trucks of 0.5 m^3 capacity.

Two workmen to each truck transported 10 loads of earth from the canal bank and two loads of sand from the dumps on the site, which is the amount necessary to make 3,000 bricks per day.

The wage of each workman: 10 PT.

$\therefore$ Cost of transporting of earth and sand per 1,000 bricks $= \frac{20}{3} = 7$ PT.

(*b*) *Straw.* The price of straw fluctuated between 60 PT and 120 PT for the *hamla* (*hamla* is a unit weight measure of 555 lbs) during the whole time of the work from 1944–45 till 1952–53 except for 1952–53, when the price rose to 210 PT.

So cost is calculated at 120 PT.

$\therefore$ Cost of straw per 1,000 bricks $= 120 \times 45 \times 1{,}000 = 15$ PT.

(*c*) *Sand.* Sand was transported by lorries from the quarries about three miles to the north of the village.

Cost of 1 m^3 of sand including transportation = 22 PT.

$\therefore$ Cost of sand per 1,000 bricks $= \frac{1{,}000 \times 22}{660 \times 3} = \frac{100}{9} = 11$ PT.

(*d*) *Water.* Water is supplied to the project by a pump worked by a petrol engine. The water is used for brick making, mixing mortars, and irrigating the trees.

In the beginning this pump was operated by a mechanic, Ibrahim Hassan, who was in charge of drilling the artesian wells for the village fountains as well. His wage was 50 PT per day. (To employ a mechanic specially to run this small engine would not be justifiable.)

Later on, this mechanic was assigned to the job of drilling the boreholes for drainage and latrines, and the operation of the water pump was entrusted to the car's mechanic (Anwar), wage 35 PT per day, in addition to his duties of looking after the cars. He was helped by a simple laborer who minded the engine at 10 PT.

As there were 4 lorries besides the pump, we can consider that we had 5 mechanical units to be looked after by the mechanic.

Daily Expenditure on Running the Pump

Petrol	70 PT
Oil	5
Workman	10
Share of the wage of the mechanic in running the pump	$\frac{35}{5} = 7$
Wear and repairs	5
Total	97 PT

Accounting two-thirds of this expenditure for the water used for brick making and one-third for the water used for mortars and trees, we shall have the cost of water for brick making per day $= \frac{97 \times 2}{3}$ $= 64.3$ PT.

There were 4 teams of brick makers at that time, producing 12,000 bricks daily.

$\therefore$ Cost of water needed for 1,000 bricks $= \frac{64.3}{12} = 5.5$ PT.

The Brick Making Team

Workmanship was given to the brick makers at a global price of 25 PT per thousand.

A "team" is usually composed of two brick makers for molding and two ordinary laborers, one for mixing and the other for transporting the mortar. The team can produce normally 3,000 bricks per day. The pay of a brick maker is 25 PT and of the workman 10 PT.

Putting the Bricks on Edge and Stacking

For drying, the bricks were put on edge on the third day after molding, and they were lifted from the brick making grounds to be stacked on the sixth day. Three workmen were assigned to each two teams of brick makers at a wage of 10 PT per day, each. These three workmen could handle 6,000 bricks per day.

∴ Cost of putting the bricks on edge and stacking per 1,000 bricks $= \frac{30}{6} = 5$ PT.

Transportation of Straw

Straw was stacked in large stores after being weighed at the time of reception. The quantities withdrawn for the daily use in brickmaking were weighed as well.

One camel was hired for 20 PT per day for the transportation of the straw from the stores to the brickmaking yard, serving the four teams of brickmakers producing 12,000 bricks daily.

∴ Cost of transportation of straw per 1,000 bricks $= \frac{20}{12} = 1.6$ PT.

Supervision Charges

One supervisor at 15 PT was employed for the four teams. His job was to control the measurement of the ingredients and to supervise the mixing and molding operations. (The mixture is to be left to ferment for 48 hours at least before molding.)

∴ Supervision expenses per 1,000 bricks $= \frac{15 \text{ PT}}{12{,}000 \text{ bricks}} = 1.2$ PT.

General Expenses for Running the Light Railway

Setting the rails, maintenance, supervision, etc., required:
1 supervisor at 30 PT
1 workman at 10 PT
40 PT per day.

As this railway was used for the transportation of the ready-made bricks as well as the earth, therefore we account half the general expenses for brickmaking.

Cost per 1,000 bricks $= \frac{40}{12 \times 2} = \frac{20}{12} =$ say 2 PT.

Total Cost per 1,000 Bricks

Straw	15.0 PT
Sand	11.0
Earth	7.0
Molding	25.0
Putting on edge	4.0
Transportation of straw	2.0
Supervision	1.2
General expenses of light railway	2.0
Water	5.5
Total	72.7 PT

Cost of Stone

Most of the hills near the village are not practicable for quarrying except in two places which are more or less suitable; the one on the site of the ancient quarries of Queen Hatshepsut, to the north of the Valley of the Kings, and the other to the south of the Valley of the Queens, both at about three and a half miles distance from the village.

The first quarry was used by the Department of Antiquities for extracting the stones required for the restoration work, and permission was obtained to quarry stone for the project from this site, so long as we respected the ancient quarries and left them intact.

The surface was covered with layers of hard packed gravel and sand about 5 to 8 meters deep, which had to be removed before getting to the good stone. Soft strata were met in the formation of the mountain, too, which gave very soft and salty stone.

These layers had to be quarried away, just like the good layers, but they didn't yield any stone.

As the quarrymen's wages were calculated on the basis of their production at a unit price of 15 PT per m^3 of good stone received on the job site, they were granted the free help of 10 workmen to each team for a period of 10 to 15 days according to the time estimated necessary for the removal of the undesirable layers. Wages of these workmen were accounted for as general expenses, but the quarrymen were not paid for their work in clearing the unusable layers; the rate paid them had to be for good stone delivered and was calculated to cover the clearing work as well.

There were 4 quarries exploited with a team of 6 to 8 quarrymen working at each, helped by 8 workmen. Four of these workmen were on the charge of the project and 4 on the quarrymen's.

For the calculation of the wages of the quarrymen their production was measured every fifteen days and the wages calculated at 15 PT per m^3. The wages of the 4 workmen on the quarrymen's charge were subtracted, and the rest was divided between the quarrymen. As the system of the work was on a daily wage basis, the sum due is transformed into day wages and fractions: ¾, ½, and ¼ day wages.

Explosives and Fuses

The quarrymen drilled 4 shot-holes 1.5. m. deep per day. Each shot will produce about 9 m^3 of suitable stones. The 4 quarries utilized 5 kgs. of explosives per day costing 100 PT.

The amount of stone produced by the 4 quarries. = 40 m^3

$$\therefore \text{Cost of explosives per m}^3 = \frac{100}{4} = 2.5 \text{ PT}$$

Cost of fuses	0.5 PT
Explosives and fuses, total cost	3.00 PT

Cost of Transportation

Stones are transported by trucks, 2.5 m^3 capacity. Each truck could perform 8 journeys per day = 20 m^3 per day.

(*a*) *Gasoline*. Six gallons per 8 journeys = 102.5 PT.

$$\therefore \text{Cost of gas per 1 m}^3 \text{ of stone} = \frac{102.5}{20} = 5.1 \text{ PT.}$$

(*b*) *Oil*. One-half kg. of lubricating oil for each car daily = 5 PT.

$$\therefore \text{Cost of oil per m}^3 = \frac{5}{20} = 0.25 \text{ PT.}$$

(*c*) *Drivers' wages*. Daily pay of a driver = 63 PT including the allowance for high cost of living.

$$\therefore \text{Cost of truck driving per m}^3 = \frac{63}{20} = 3.15 \text{ PT.}$$

(*d*) *Loading and unloading*. Five porters were assigned to each truck at a daily wage of 15 PT each.

$$\therefore \text{Cost of loading per m}^3 = \frac{5 \times 15}{20} = 2.15 \text{ PT.}$$

(*e*) *Amortization of cars and repairs*. Cars are calculated to last 10 years. Each car costs L.E. 1,000. Depreciation per year = L.E. 100.

$$\therefore \text{Depreciation per day} = \frac{10{,}000}{300} = 30 \text{ PT.}$$

$$\text{Charge of depreciation per m}^3 = \frac{30}{20} = 1.5 \text{ PT.}$$

Forge

A blacksmith and his helpers were employed for sharpening the tools.

(*a*) Blacksmith	35 PT per day including furnace rent
(*b*) Assistant blacksmith	15

(c) An apprentice	8
(d) Coal: 5 kgs × 10 PT =	50
Total	108 PT

Forge expenses per m³ = $\frac{108}{40}$ = 2.6 PT

General Expenses

(a) 4 workmen on charge of the project (4 × 10)	40 PT
(b) Foremen	45
(c) Ganger	15
(d) Watchmen (2 × 18)	36
(e) Share of the quarries in the expenses of the mechanic and assistant:	
mechanic	35
assistant	15
	50 PT

Quarrying share in transportation ¾ of the total.

∴ Cost per day = $\frac{50 \times 3}{4}$ = 37.5 PT.

Three quarries only out of the four could be calculated as working regularly, producing 30 m³ per day.

∴ The general expenses per m³ will be:

$$40 + 45 + 15 + 36 + 37.5 = \frac{173.5}{30} = 5.8 \text{ PT, say } 6 \text{ PT.}$$

Cost of Removal of Aggregates

Ten workmen were assigned to each team for a period of ten to fifteen days, at the beginning, and every time the soft strata were reached. The cost of this operation could be calculated only from the actual working.

As the work was not going on regularly all the time, a period of three months during which quarrying was uninterrupted has been chosen for calculating the expenses due to the removal of aggregate and soft strata.

The total output during these three months was:

April	775 m³
May	928 m³
June	568 m³
	2,268 m³

Wages paid to workmen in charge of the project for the removal of aggregate = L.E. 93.800.

Share of one m³ in this cost = $\frac{9.380}{2.268}$ = 4.12 PT.

Cost of Explosives Used for Removing the Aggregate

The number of days of quarrying suitable stones and those of removing the aggregate are shown in following table:

Month	Quarry no. 1 Aggr.	Quarry no. 1 Stone	Quarry no. 2 Aggr.	Quarry no. 2 Stone	Quarry no. 3 Aggr.	Quarry no. 3 Stone	Quarry no. 4 Aggr.	Quarry no. 4 Stone
April	15	10	0	25	13	14	16	11
May	7	16	5	24	14	16	13	16
June	0	15	0	26	0	15	0	15
Total	22	41	5	75	21	45	29	42

∴ Number of days of removal of aggregate = 77
Number of days of quarrying good stone = 203

Ratio of days of removal of aggregate to quarrying good stone is about 1:3 as the quantities of explosives used for the removal of aggregate are bigger than those used for quarrying stone due to the loose consistency of the former. Therefore we might calculate the ratio to be 1:3, which means that the amount of explosives used for removing aggregate was ⅓ of that used for extracting good stone.

∴ Cost of explosives to be added to the cost of 1 m^3 of stone = 2 PT.

Stacking

Stones are stacked in piles of regular shapes immediately after they reach the job. Cost of this operation is 1 PT per 1 m^3.

∴ Total cost of stones:

(1)	Cost of stone received on the job site	15.0	PT
(2)	Explosives and fuses	3.0	
(3)	Petrol	5.1	
(4)	Oil	0.25	
(5)	Driver	3.15	
(6)	Loading	2.15	
(7)	Amortization	1.50	
(8)	Forge	2.60	
(9)	General expenses	6.00	
(10)	Cost of labor for the removal of aggregate	4.12	(wages)
(11)	Cost of explosives and fuses for removal of aggregate	2.00	
(12)	Stacking	1.00	
		45.75, say 50 PT	

Sand

One car performs 7 journeys to the sand quarries per day.

Load = 2.5 m^3.

∴ Quantities of sand transported by one truck = 7 × 2.5 = 17.5 m^3.

Expenditure

(1) Gasoline (6 gallons)	112.50 PT
(2) Driver	63.00
(3) Oil (½ kg.)	5.00
(4) Porters (loading) 5 men at 15 PT	75.00
(5) Guard	18.00
(6) Amortization of cars	30.00
	303.50 PT

Cost of 1 $m^3 = \frac{303.50}{17.5} =$ 17 PT

General expenses:

(1) Removal of surface gravel	2 PT per m^3
(2) Share of wages of mechanic and assistant	1 PT per m^3
Total cost per 1 m^3	20 PT

Construction

Rubble Masonry below the D.P.C. Width More than 0.70 m. in Stabilized Earth Mortar

Production and labor expenses of one team of masons:

Item	Labor	No.	Fee	Total	Total Production	Remarks
1	Mason	2	40	80		
2	Workman	2	10	20	8 m^3	Handling the bricks
3	Helper (boy) for mortar	4	8	32	per day	Carrying the mortar
4	Workman for stone	½	10	5		Carrying stones for 2 teams
5	Workman for mixing mortar	1	10	10		
6	Apprentice mason	1	10	10		Trainee helping to fill in the core of walls.
				157	8 m^3	

General Expenses:

(*a*) Foreman serving 10 teams — 10 PT

∴ Share of 1 team $= \frac{10}{10} =$ 1 PT

(*b*) Water for mortar mixing = ⅓ total expenses of running the pump. (See item of water in brick making expenses.) $= \frac{97}{3} = 32⅓$

Average number of teams working: 15

$\therefore$ Cost of water per one team $= \frac{32.5}{15} = 2$ PT.

Maximum number of teams working on the project was 30 and minimum 10; the average is calculated as 15 instead of 20 because the periods in which the work was going slowly were much longer than those in which it was going at a high rate. Economy would dictate that the rate should not be less than a certain amount to be determined by the following factors:

1. The sum allotted in the budget to the project in the financial year and its balanced distribution over the working months. (The working period was supposed to be 10 months, the heat in July and August being intolerable—80°C in the sun. Actually a working period did not exceed four months due to delays of routine and somnolence of officials in the administration section.)
2. The maximum possible capacity in producing building materials, especially bricks and stones, and the availability of tools and equipment.
3. The rate of transportation of building materials with the existing means; trucks, rail trolleys, camels, donkeys, etc.

For example, there were 4 trucks in the project; 2 used for the transportation of stone and the other 2 for the transportation of sand and earth.

Each truck transported 20 m³ per day.

The two working in the transportation of stone could supply 40 m³.

$\therefore$ The maximum output in masonry for foundations will be 40 m³ per day, unless some stone is stored in advance. So here transport capacity is the limiting factor.

Mortar

Mortar for the rubble masonry of the foundations was composed of earth and sand in the proportions of 2:1. One m³ of rubble masonry required 0.20 m³ mortar. Cost of mortar = cost of sand and water only as the earth was taken from the excavation of the foundations.

1 m³ sand + 2 m³ earth gave 2.5 m³ of mortar.
Cost of sand = 20 PT.

$\therefore$ Cost of mortar per 1 m³ of rubble masonry $= \frac{20}{2.5 \times 5} = 1.6$ PT.

Total cost of rubble masonry for foundations will become:

Workmanship and labor	157 PT
General expenses	3
Total for 8 m³	160 PT

$\therefore$ Cost of workmanship + general expenses per 1 m³ $= \frac{160}{8}$

$= 20.0$ PT

Cost of mortar per m³	3.5
Cost of stone per m³	50.0
Total cost of rubble masonry for foundations more than 0.7	73.5 PT

Cost of Rubble Masonry Less than 0.70 m. Width.

Item	Labor and Materials	No.	Wage PT	Total PT	Daily Output	Cost per 1 m³	Remarks
1	Mason	2	40	80	4 m³	20.0	
2	Workman	2	10	20		5.0	
3	Helper (boy)	2	8	16		4.0	For transp. of mortar
4	Workman mixing mortar	½	15	7.5		2.0	One for each 2 teams
5	Trainee (youth)	1	10	10		2.5	
6	Foreman	1/10	10	1		0.25	For 10 teams
7	Water					2.00	
8	Stone					50.00	
9	Mortar					3.5	
						89.25 PT say 90 PT	

Cost of Masonry in Stabilized Sun-dried Bricks above D.P.C. up to the Level of Windowsills (1.20 above Ground Level of the Floor).

Item	Labor	No.	Wage PT	Total PT	Daily Output	Cost per 1 m³	Remarks
1	Mason	2	40	80			
2	Workman	2	10	20			To handle bricks
3	Helper (youth)	2	8	16			
4	Trainee	1	10	10			
5	Light rly. foreman and workman	1/15	20	20/15 = 1.3			Workman to lay the rails
6	Workmen for trans. of bricks	2	10	20			
7	Water						
8	Workman mixing mortar	½	10	5			
				154.3	6 m³	26 PT	

Cost of bricks = 400 × .075 = 30 PT

Cost of mortar $\frac{8 \times 1}{3}$ = 3 PT

Cost of workmanship and labor = 26 PT

Total 59 PT, say 60 PT

Cost of Brick Masonry from +1.2 m. Level to the Top of the Ground Floor: Workmanship and Labor:

Item	Labor	No.	Wage PT	Total PT	Daily Output	Cost per 1 m³	Remarks
1	Mason	2	40	80	5 m³		Handling bricks
2	Workman	2	10	20			Handling mortar
3	Helper	2	8	16			
4	Trainee	1	10	10			
5	Light rwy. foreman and workman	20/15		1.3			
6	Workmen	2	10	20			Transporting bricks from stacks
7	Workman (mortar)	½	10	5			Mixing the mortar
8	Water	—		2			
9	Scaffolding mounter + 3 workmen	—	50/15	3.3			One mounter + 3 laborers serve 15 teams
	TOTAL			157.6	5 m³	32 PT	

Cost of 400 bricks = 30 (400 bricks to the m³)

Mortar 3

Workmanship and labor 32

Total 65 PT

Cost of brick masonry for the 1st floor:

a) Workmanship and labor (as previous item) 157.6 PT

b) One more workman for transporting bricks 10.0

c) One youth for carrying mortar 8.0

175.6 PT

Output 4 m³ ∴ cost of 1 m³ = $\frac{175.6}{4}$ = 44 PT

Cost of bricks (400 bricks) 30

Cost of mortar 3

Total 77 PT, say 80 PT

Number of Bricks Required in the Different Works

1. *Walls:*
   1 m^3 of brick masonry 23 × 11 × 7 cms. requires 400 bricks.
2. *Vaults:* Bricks 25 × 15 × 5 cms.
   (*a*) One m.l of vault span 3 m (17 rings × 20 bricks) = 340
   (*b*) " " " " 2.75 m (17 " × 18 ") = 306
   (*c*) " " " " 2.50 m (17 " × 61 ") = 272
   (*d*) " " " " 2.00 m (17 " × 12 ") = 204
   (*e*) " " " " 1.50 m (17 " × 9 ") = 153
   (*f*) " " " " 0.90 m (17 " × 6 ") = 102
3. *Byzantine Domes:*
   (*a*) B. dome span 3 m. takes 1,400 bricks including pendentives.
   (*b*) B. dome span 4 m. takes 2,000 bricks including pendentives.
4. *Domes on Squinches:*
   (*a*) Span 3 m 2,000 bricks.
   (*b*) Span 3 m 3,000 bricks.
5. *Arches:*
   Pointed 1:5 arch span 3 m, three rings .60 thickness of arch takes 540 bricks.
   Pointed 1:5 arch span 3 m, three rings .60 thickness of arch takes 360 bricks.
   Segmental arch span 1 m, three rings .6 thickness of arch takes 150 bricks.
   Circular arch span 1 m, three rings .6 thickness of arch takes 192 bricks.
   Circular arch span .70 m, three rings .6 thickness of arch takes 90 bricks.

Concrete for Foundations and Floors, Composed of Broken Stone and Sand, Lime and Crushed Brick Mortar

(*a*) Workmanship (global price including mixing, transport, pouring, ramming, etc.) 16 PT
(*b*) Cost of broken stone (same cost as sand) 20 PT
(*c*) Mortar:

1 m^3 lime	152 PT
2 " sand	40
1 " crushed bricks	40
	232 PT gives 3 m^3 of mixture.

1 m^3 mortar $= \frac{232}{3} = 80$ PT

Cost of mortar per m^3 concrete $= \frac{80}{2} = 40$ PT

Cost of transportation of stones from dumps to site of work inside the project = 3.5 PT

Cost of 1 m^3 concrete = 16 + 20 + 40 + 3.5 = 79.5 PT

Cost of Baking Lime

Item	Labor and materials	No.	Wage PT	Days of Employ ment	Total PT	Output	Cost per m^3
1	Stacking	1	30	2	60		
2	Workman for stacking	1	10	2	20		
3	Youth for stacking	2	8	2	32		
4	Youth (breaking stones)	2	8	2	32		
5	Workman for firing	1	15	1	15		
6	Supervisor for firing	1	10	1	10		
7	Unloading workmen	4	10	1	40		
8	Solar oil fuel, barrels	2			510		
	Total				719	6 m^3	120 PT
	Cost of stone						30 PT
	Total cost of 1 m^3 of quicklime =						150 PT

Cost of Making Baked Bricks

Item	Labor and Materials	Job	No.	Wage	Days of employ- ment	Total PT	Produc- tion	Cost of 1,000 bricks
1	Mason	Stacking bricks in kiln	1	30	2	60		
2	Asst. mason	Stacking bricks in kiln	1	30	2	34		
3	Workman	Stacking	4	10	2	80		
4	Workman	Trans- porting bricks from stack	2	10	2	40		
5	Workman firing	Night work	1	15	1 night	15		
6	Ordinary workman	Night work	2	10	1 night	20		
7	Workman	Unloading	6	10	1 day	60		
8	Solar oil fuel, 4 barrels kgm each x 1.5					1020		
						1329	10,000	132.9
	+ Cost of raw bricks							50.0
	Total cost of 1,000 baked bricks =							PT 182.9

Construction of Arches:
Span 2.50 to 3 m, 3 Rings 0.6 Width

Item	Workers and Materials	No.	Wage PT	Total PT	Daily Output	Cost of Unit
1	Mason	2	40	80	1½ arch	
2	Workman	1	10	10		
3	Youth for mortar	2	8	16		
4	L.rwy exp.	—	—	1.5		
5	Transp. of bricks	—	—	7.5		
6	water	—	—	2.0		
7	Workman for mixing mortar	½	10	5.0		
				122 PT	$\frac{122 \times 2}{3}$	= 82 PT

Plus: Cost of bricks 540 × .08 = 43.2
Cost of mortar 0.25 × 8 = 2.0

Total 127.2 PT
Say 130 PT per piece

Construction of Arches from 0.9 to 1.2 m Span

The same team as before building 3 arches per day.

(*a*) Workmanship $\frac{122}{3}$ = 41 PT
(*b*) Cost of bricks (200 × .08) = 16
(*c*) Cost of mortar $\frac{1 \times 3}{8} \times 8$ PT = 1
(*d*) Centerings 2

Total 60 PT per piece

Construction of Arches from 1.5 to 2.0 Span

The same team as before building 2 arches.

(*a*) Workmanship $\frac{122}{2}$ = 61 PT
(*b*) Cost of bricks (360 × .08) = 24
(c) Cost of mortar = 1
(*d*) Cost of centerings = 4

Total 90 PT per piece

Domes

(*a*) *Byzantine Dome—Diam. 3 m*
The same team will build one dome in 2 days.
Cost of workmanship 122 × 2 = 244 PT

Cost of bricks (1,400 × .08)	=	122
Cost of mortar	=	8
Cost of straw $\frac{45 \text{ lbs} \times 120}{555}$	=	10
Total		374 PT per piece

(*b*) *Byzantine Dome—Diam. 4 m*

The same team will build the dome including the squinches in 3 days.

Cost of workmanship 122 × 3	=	366 PT
Cost of bricks (2,000 × .08)	=	160
Cost of mortar (1.5 m^3 × 8)	=	12
Cost of straw $\frac{70 \text{ lbs.} \times 120}{555}$	=	10
Total		513 PT per piece

(*c*) *Dome on Squinches—Diam. 3 m*

The same team will build the dome including the squinches in 3 days.

Cost of workmanship 122 × 3	=	366 PT
Cost of bricks (2,000 × .08)	=	160
Cost of straw $\frac{70 \text{ lbs.} \times 120}{555}$	=	15
Cost of mortar 1.5 m^3 × 8	=	12
Total		553 PT per piece

(*d*) *Dome on Squinches—Diam. 4 m*

The same team will build the dome in 4 days.

Cost of workmanship and labor 122 × 4	=	488 PT
Cost of bricks (3,000 × .08)	=	240
Cost of mortar 2 m^3 × 8	=	16
Cost of straw $\frac{100 \text{ lbs.} \times 120}{555}$	=	22
Total		766 PT per piece

Vaults

(*a*) *SPAN 0.9 m*

The same team will build 9 m.l. per day.

Cost of workmanship per m.l. $\frac{122}{9}$	=	15 PT
Cost of bricks 100 × .08	=	8
Cost of mortar $\frac{1}{16}$ × 8	=	5
Cost of straw	=	1
Total		29 PT per m.l.

(*b*) *Vault Span 1.5 m*

The same team will build 6 m.l. per day.

Cost of workmanship $122 \times 1/6$	=	20.5 PT
Cost of bricks $(150 \times .08)$	=	12.0
Cost of straw	=	2.0
Total		34.5 PT, say 35 PT per m.l.

(*c*) *Vault Span 2.0 m*

The same team will build 5 m.l. per day.

Cost of workmanship $\frac{122}{5}$	=	24.5 PT
Cost of bricks $(200 \times .08)$	=	16.0
Cost of mortar and straw	=	3.0
Total		45.5 PT per m.l.

(*d*) *Vault Span 2.5 m*

The same team will construct 3 m.l. per day.

Cost of workmanship $122 \times 1/3$	=	41 PT
Cost of bricks $(280 \times .08)$	=	18
Cost of mortar and straw	=	4
Total		63 PT, say 65 PT per m.l.

(*e*) *Vault Span 3 m*

The same team will construct 2.5 m per day.

Cost of workmanship $\frac{122}{2.5}$	=	49 PT
Cost of bricks $(350 \times .08)$	=	28
Cost of mortar and straw	=	6
Total		83 PT, say 85 PT per m.l.

Appendix II *In-Service Training*

				Grade Cost			Repayment		
Stage	Week	Activity	Grade	Wage PT	No. of days	Total	V-A	No. of days	Total
A	1, 2	Learns to square layout, dry brick walls, 1, ½, 2	Helper	8	12	96	—	—	—
B	3, 4	Works on job, handling materials and watching	Helper	8	12	—	0	12	0
C	5, 6	Learns to do above work, but using mortar. Also partitions	Helper	8	12	96	—	—	—
D	7, 8	Works on job, helping 2 masons by filling cores of walls. Does ¼ work of two masons	Apprentice	12	12	—	8	12	96
E	9	Learns to build segmental arches	Apprentice	12	6	72	—	—	—

Stage	Week	Activity	Grade	Grade Cost			Repayment		
				Wage PT	No. of days	Total	V-A	No. of days	Total
F	10	Works on job as assistant mason with one master mason (40 — 18 = 22)	Asst. mason	18	6	—	22	6	132
G	11	Learns to build vaults and a Byzantine dome	Asst. mason	18	12	216	—	—	—
H	12 14	Works on job as mason	Mason	25	12	—	12	180	
I	15 16	Learns to build domes on squinches, vaults on unparallel walls	Mason	25	12	300	—	—	—
J	17	Practices stone building on the job	Mason	25	6	—	15	6	90
			Master mason	30	24	—	10	24	240
						780			738

Appendix III
Organization of Work

An estimate of cost of materials and labor is to be worked out showing cost breakdown for each bit of work.

Before any work is started, the architect will issue an assignment of work in which will be defined the work to be done, the time for its execution, the labor to be engaged, and the materials needed to carry out this work.

From this "assignment of work" the secretary or supervisor of works will fill out two forms which we can call "Order for Labor" (form A below) and "Order for Materials" (form B below). Both forms will be kept in small books and done in duplicate. The original will be detachable and the copy fixed in the book.

The Order for Labor will go to the supervisor of works, who, in turn, will give orders to the foreman to supply the labor wanted. After having made the necessary plans, the supervisor of works will hand over this order to the secretary, or to whoever is responsible for filling in the usual labor sheets which go to the agency.

The Order for Materials will go to the storekeeper, against which he will fill in the usual issue vouchers, according to the general system of administration used in the agency. The object of this system is to ensure that the labor engaged and the materials issued have been judged necessary for the work by the responsible architect on the spot, and will serve for control at the end of every period as to the veracity of the issue vouchers and labor sheets, which he will not approve except against the presentation of these forms. Thus we shall have created a link between the technical and administrative work in a simple way which will not hinder the technical men by requiring them to go into the administrative routine work while on their technical jobs.

In order to keep in continuous touch with the progress of the work, the financial situation, and the stock in store as well as the rate of expenditure of the materials in general, and to have a clear view of the whole situation in an easy way, so as not to be short in materials or to exceed the time limit given for the work, three forms have to be filled out daily.

Form No. 1. Control of Progress of the Works

As will be seen from the accompanying sample, all the different kinds of work and labor are included in the form of a checklist. The entries needed are reduced to signs or numbers. By these forms one can easily detect any deficiencies in the progress of the work, for they are worked out almost like graphs. If there is any delay, it will be easily found out whether it is due to the small number of laborers, which must therefore be increased, or, if their number is judged to be sufficient according to the accepted norms which are determined beforehand and agreed upon by both parties, the agency and the workmen, whether the delay is due to the laborers' negligence.

Form No. 2. Daily Stock Sheet

This sheet will be filled in daily or at least after every issue from stores. The purpose is to have, with reference to all materials, a clear picture of

(a) stock in store, (b) rate of daily expenditure, and (c) stock on hand. In this way, we can estimate for how long the different materials will last, and fresh orders can be made in due time to avoid stopping the work for lack of materials.

Form No. 3. Wages Balance Sheet

On this sheet will be entered all the wages of the labor engaged every day and for the whole period to date, so as to have the balance of all expenditure and the actual situation compared with the allotted budget.

The storekeeper will be responsible for filling out this form. It is to be noted that this sheet is different from the "Wages Sheet" used by the agency. It does not concern the general accounting of the agency except as a check, and its purpose is limited to each site so as to indicate the financial situation accurately.

Form A.

ORDER FOR LABOR

AREA ....

SITE ....

Labor	No.	Wage	Duration	Date on which to start	Actual date of starting	Remarks

Director of Works ....Supervisor ....

Clerk of Works ....

Form B.

ORDER FOR MATERIALS

DATE ....

SITE .... *Date* .... *19*....

Specifications	Quantities	Unit	Purpose	Particular Applicant	Remarks

Applicant ....

Supervisor of Works ....

Director of Works

....

Storekeeper

....

Form No. 1

CONTROL OF PROGRESS OF THE WORK

Building No. *Date* . . . . *19*. . . .

DESCRIPTION OF WORK	NATURE AND NUMBER OF BUILDINGS	REMARKS
Excavations		
Concrete for Foundations		
Masonry " "		
Rubble Masonry		
Mud Bricks Masonry		
Roof } Domes		
Roof } Vaults		
Fixing Rafters		
Boarding		
Tiles		
Reeds & Mud		
Plastering Exterior		
Plastering Interior		
Carpent. Doors & Wind.		
Sanitary Fixtures		
Flooring		
LABOR ENGAGED		
Masons 1st Class		
Masons 2nd Class		
Assist. Mason		
Laborer Man		
Laborer Boy		
Carpenter		
Assist. Carpenter		
Plasterers		
Laborers		
Plumbers		
Assistant Plumber		
Laborers		

Form No. 2.

DAILY STOCK SHEET

AREA . . . .

SITE . . . . Date . . . . 19. . . .

Material	Quantity received today	Quantity received before today	Total receipt to date	Quantity issued today	Quantity issued before today	Total issue to date	Stock on hand

Storekeeper . . . . Architect . . . .

Form No. 3.

WAGES BALANCE SHEET

AREA ....

SITE .... Date .... 19....

Description of Labor	Number	Daily wage L.E. Millims	Total L.E. Millims	Sum Total L.E. Millims	Remarks

Sum total of the day ....

Total of the previous days in the period of payment ....
(week or fortnight)

Total sum of the wages from the start of the work ....

Total sum of all wages to date ....

Architect ....

Accountant ....

Appendix IV
Foundations

Foundations and roofing are the two biggest technical and economic problems in cheap rural housing.

There are several technical solutions to the problem of foundations—pile foundations, concrete raft foundations, etc. Our problem, though, is not merely technical; we need a suitable foundation *that we can afford*. Ekistical efficiency[1] demands a foundation that is within the means and skill of peasant builders.

There seem to be three possible solutions to the problem of building firm foundations on cracked soil.

A type of pile foundation can be used, in which auger holes are sunk at the corners of each room to below the depth of the cracks (say 3m). These are filled with earth concrete consisting of gravel, broken stones, broken pottery, broken baked bricks, or any such aggregate, bound with sand-stabilized earth mortar. In orthodox practice, piles are tied together with a horizontal concrete bond beam. This is too expensive; so the bond beam is replaced by a relieving arch. The main load of the wall and roof is carried to the pile by this arch built into the wall from the ends to just below windowsill level. Such an arch is easy to build, using the lower courses of the wall itself as a centering, and in conjunction with the piles will effectively transmit the load of the building to the compacted soil below the cracks.

Another solution, which also involves getting below the cracks, is to dig the trenches for the foundations down to a sufficient depth and then, to economize in masonry filling, to fill them with sand or sand-stabilized earth, rammed in layers of 20 cms each, to the normal depth for foundations of 1.2 meters. This method involves considerably more digging, the labor ramming, and the transport of sand, so it might in practice prove to be ekistically expensive in some districts where sand quarries are not close by.

1. If the cost of local labor provided by the peasant reckoned in man-hours and converted to cash, plus cost of materials obtained freely $= L$, and cost of hired labor and imported materials $= E$, then the ekistical efficiency K of the building is represented by $K = \frac{L}{L + E} \times 100$

The criterion must always be, What method involves the least importation of materials and plant from outside the area?

The third method is to compact the soil artificially. We noticed that in Gourna the buildings erected before the flooding were not affected by the cracks when they appeared later. Even our first house, which was intended to be temporary and was built on precarious baked brick foundations, suffered no damage after the flooding. The explanation is that the weight of the building compacted the soil, and that this effect was distributed over a larger area than that of the foundations, according to the lines of equal pressure. The pressure within the zone prevented cracks from occurring inside it. A building erected on previously cracked land, however, could not compact the soil in the same way, because the cracks would prevent the lines of equal pressure from developing naturally, and the whole weight of the building would be taken on a much smaller area of soil.

Thus, if the ground could be compacted with a heavy roller before building, it should be possible to build in the original Gourna fashion safely. This operation might be performed actually in the foundation trenches of each building, with a hand roller, or on a large scale over a whole site with a mechanical roller. Again, this method would have to be compared with the others for ekistic efficiency. Finally, there is always the alternative of accepting the cracked walls and repairing them. Mud brick is very easy to repair, and even if cracks appear again and again, they can be filled up. The material is always there, labor is available, and anyone can do the job. It might be that the most efficient way of building, ekistically speaking, would be to design in the expectation of cracks and to allow for their continuous repair. Within a year or two no further cracks would appear in a house, because it would have compacted the soil beneath it and lateral movement of the soil would stop.

Of these alternatives, the last is that used by peasants, and the second—deep trenches with the masonry resting on sand—I tried out at Gourna. All these methods need very careful assessing, to decide which is ekistically the soundest for any given district. We need to find the minimum effective depth for foundations and piles; we need to test the effectiveness of pre-compacting the soil, and we need to find out the economic and social effects of designing for repairs. These alternatives are only suggestions, and the relative merits of each have yet to be actually determined by research.

Once properly conducted experiments have provided us with a number of proved methods of building foundations, we can decide which would suit any particular locality best. It may be that experiments will lead to the evolution of some quite new alternative. The important point is that we already know how to solve the engineering problem, and all our research must be directed to solving the economic problem of a foundation that peasants can build using their own resources and a minimum of outside help.

In Lower Egypt the soil has become compacted because the perennial irrigation system is used and there is no periodic flooding. Thus the surface cracks do not appear. The fluctuation of subsoil water is not as great as in Upper Egypt. Thus the physical state of the soil is more stable than in Upper Egypt.

Hard aggregate is not to be found within reach in the Delta, and stone and gravel, which exist in the desert, are too far away for the peasant to be able to transport them. Thus peasant houses in Lower Egypt are usually built with no foundations in the usual sense. Walls are built in a shallow trench about twenty to twenty-five centimeters deep, mud brick being laid straight on the soil and close to the surface—a most unsound constructional procedure. The ground swells, shrinks and settles down, and all such walls soon crack. However, as they are in mud brick, they can easily be repaired. After two or three successive repairs a crack will disappear for good as the earth becomes fully compacted under the weight of the walls. Fortunately the extensive lateral movement of soil common in Upper Egypt, caused by the very deep cracks that appear, is uncommon in Lower Egypt, though there is some vertical movement due to the swelling of the soil as the waters rise. The main problem here is the capillary attraction of underground water into the walls and the consequent deterioration of the lower parts of the walls through repeated wetting and drying. The recognized practice in professional structures of concrete, masonry, brick, etc., is to put a damp-proof course in the wall about fifteen centimeters above the level of contact with any wet soil.

Appendix V
Brick Making

The composition and properties of soil vary widely from place to place. The variation is likely to be reflected in the quality of sun-dried earth bricks made from the soil, a fact that has caused architects and engineers to be reluctant to use such bricks.

Because of the variability of soils, it is essential that at any given site the soil to be used for brick making be carefully analyzed, chemically and physically.

Experiments and laboratory tests on sample bricks and a sample wall (full size in each case) must be made to determine the shrinkage, bearing power, behavior under wetting and drying, and other physical properties.

In large-scale projects tests should be made on complete architectural units, such as alcove, dome, vault, stairs, etc., separately, and on one complete room. The most important tests in this latter case are on loading and on wetting and drying.

Specifications should be drawn up as a result of these tests, for the composition of the soil (proportions of sand, clay, silt, etc.) granular graduation, the method of mixing the soil, and the method of making bricks (molded, hand-pressed etc.). It is important to understand that no general specifications can be laid down in this matter, as they can be for steel or concrete. Each case, each site, is different and a specification must be drawn up to suit the soil there.

A warning here. Expensive methods of stabilization are unnecessary. Once a sufficiently strong brick has been made, leave well alone.

Research is needed on the effect of straw in bricks and external plaster. It has been observed that bricks and plasters made according to the peasant fashion in Egypt and the Sudan, by which straw and cow dung are added to the mud and left to ferment for a long time, seem to resist water well.

It is known that clay bricks need straw as a binding agent or to be stabilized with sand—at least 30 percent; without this they will crack.

The straw fibers seem to hold the brick together while it is shrinking during the process of drying. In the case of mud plaster made with straw, it would be interesting to see whether its observed water-repellent properties are due to a simple binding effect, or whether to some chemical change such as the formation of lactic acid during fermentation or whether to the water-repellent property of the straw itself, some of which is exposed on the surface of the plaster. It has been noticed that after rain the clay surface of such plaster is washed away and the straw is left exposed over much of the surface.

Extract From Colonel Debes's Experiments

No mechanical pressure has been applied in the making of the bricks, which were cast in iron molds using simple tapping to fill in the mold as is done in common practice. The bricks were left to dry in the laboratory room for seven days and then taken out to dry in the open air.

Three types of the bricks tested are chosen here:

Group A. Composed of silty clay soil and sand of different grades.

Group B. Composed of silty clay soil, sand of different grades, and straw.

Group C. Composed of same as *A* with bitumen.

Brick Type *A*

		Stresses kg/cm²			
	% sand	7 days	30 days	90 days	180 days
Fine sand	20	44.00	56.90	55.70	52.00
	40	38.30	44.00	38.50	34.20
	60	22.90	28.30	25.25	24.00
	80	6.12	6.12	4.60	4.45
Small sand	20	42.19	61.30	50.96	47.00
	40	33.40	42.40	36.30	29.00
	60	20.90	29.45	22.67	21.00
	80	11.26	11.70	13.13	13.50
Medium sand	20	37.76	48.73	41.90	41.30
	40	27.43	35.40	29.80	26.20
	60	18.53	20.75	25.10	17.00
	80	12.39	11.54	11.79	12.00
Large sand	20	32.84	36.36	26.86	32.20
	40	17.58	19.08	21.96	17.00
	60	8.47	13.06	11.88	7.35
	80	6.09	8.52	4.70	4.70

Brick Type *B*

% sand	% straw	Stresses kgs/cm² 7 days	30 days	90 days	180 days
5	1.0	34.2	53.6	48.0	47.30
	1.75	33.0	48.0	43.3	45.90
	2.5	30.0	45.0	40.0	42.20
	5.0	28.5	40.0	37.0	35.55
20	1.0	32.4	44.1	40.3	40.50
	1.75	37.0	48.4	46.5	47.50
	2.5	32.0	44.6	37.6	39.00
	5.0	25.0	27.0	35.0	34.20
40	1.0	30.6	36.6	34.5	35.40
	1.75	32.0	37.0	36.0	35.80
	2.5	34.0	39.8	38.2	36.00
	5.0	22.0	32.0	30.0	28.15

Extract From Dr. Mustapha Yehya's Experiments

So as to be able to utilize such an economical material as earth in building, tests were made on small walls built of mud bricks—of which some were treated with stabilizers—coated with different kinds of plaster and using various kinds of damp-proof coursing. The foundations of these walls were built of red burned bricks as this part is more exposed to wetting and drying and other mechanical and chemical factors.

The walls were built, coated with a plaster, and left to dry. The same mixture of earth was used for the mortar in all cases, after which the walls were exposed to continuous cycles of wetting and drying for six weeks. The wetting was done by two daily, half-hour showers similar to rain, once in the morning and the second six hours later.

Observations were made on all the walls during this period, and then they were loaded to 110 kgs/m.l, and the wetting cycles were continued until the walls collapsed.

Remarks

Tests were made on two groups of walls. The first group consisted of four walls built of mud brick made with straw, one brick thick (25 cms), one meter long and one meter high, as follows:

1. A wall with a diatol-treated plaster and an asphalt damp-proof course.
2. A wall with an untreated earth plaster and an asphalt damp-proof course.

3. A wall with an untreated earth plaster and a coat of diatol mix as a damp-proof course.
4. A wall with an untreated earth plaster and no damp-proof course.

The second group consisted of three walls of the same dimensions as the last, built of mud bricks made with straw and diatol, as follows:

1. A wall with a damp-proof course of diatol mix.
2. A wall with a damp-proof course of asphalt.
3. A wall with a diatol plaster and a damp-proof course of diatol mix.

These walls were exposed to the same cycles of wetting and drying as before, which were continued until the walls collapsed.

The fourth wall of the first group collapsed first.

The tests started on 11 December 1955, and the wall with untreated plaster and no damp-proof course collapsed on 16 February 1956. The rest of the walls collapsed consecutively, starting 19 February 1956.

In most cases the walls collapsed due to the eccentricity of the loading and consequently due to bending.

Record of Experiment

Date 1. Wall with diatol treated plaster and an asphalt D.P.C.	2. Wall with an untreated plaster and an asphalt D.P.C.	3. Untreated plaster and a diatol mix D.P.C.	4. Untreated plaster and no D.P.C.
11 Dec. No visible change after shower for ½ hour.	No visible change after ½ hour shower.	No visible change.	No visible change.
12 Dec. Wall dried completely. No erosion and shower continued ½ hour.	Wall dried—no erosion—plaster holding well—shower continued for 1/ hour.	Straw started to show on the surface. Plaster started disintegrating but was dry.	Straw showed more than the previous day. Plaster disintegrated sensibly. The wall stayed wet.
13 Dec. Same as the previous day.	As the previous day.	As previous day.	Stayed wet unlike the rest of the walls.
15 Dec. No change.	Plaster disintegrated a very little.	Disintegration of plaster continued, but wall was dry.	Plaster almost totally crumbled and the wall stayed wet. While all the rest were dry.
16 Dec. No change.	The wall dried and no perceptible change from the previous day.	The wall dried but disintegration of plaster increased.	The plaster collapsed totally and the bricks themselves started disintegrating.

19 Dec. Wall dried and plaster intact.	Wall dried but bricks started to become bare at parts as a result of disintegration of plaster.	Bricks started showing out as plaster disintegrated.	Wall wet and apparent disintegration of bricks.
20 Dec. As previous day.	As previous day.	Plaster almost completely dissolved and all bricks were exposed.	Disintegration of bricks continuing and wall stayed wet.
22 Dec. No change.	No change.	No change.	Wall wet and disintegration of brick continuing.
23 Dec. No change.	No change.	Bricks started to disintegrate slightly when scratched with the finger.	" "
26 Dec. No change and shown to be best of all walls.	Disintegration of plaster stopped and wall dried. Remaining parts of plaster resisted scratching.	Bricks disintegrated more markedly. Rubbing caused falling off of parts.	Wall wet, bricks disintegrated more readily when scratched by finger.
27 Dec. " "	" "	Wall started to keep some of the dampness.	" "
29 Dec. No change and best of all.	" "	Lower parts of wall stayed slightly wet.	" "
30 Dec. " "	" "	" "	" "
2 Jan. " "	" "	Wall dried.	" "
3 Jan. " "	" "	" "	" "
5 Jan. Here the wall was loaded by a uniformly distributed load of 100 kg/m run.			
6 Jan. Very small cracks started to show in the plaster but stayed firm and will dry	Plaster started disintegrating by scratching.	No change.	Wall started to lean slightly.
9 Jan. " "	Wall dry and exposed parts of bricks solid.	Wall leaning slightly but dry.	Leaning increased and wall wet.
10 Jan. Very small cracks started to show in the plaster but stayed firm and will dry.	Wall dry and exposed parts of bricks solid.	Wall dry but bricks disintegrated with slight scratching.	Leaning increasing continuously and wall wet.

12 Jan. ” ”	” ”	” ”	” ”
13 Jan. ” ”	” ”	” ”	” ”
16 Jan. ” ”	” ”	” ”	” ”
17 Jan. Cracks stopped and continued to be best of all.	Plaster disintegration increased.	Wetting of wall and disintegrating with scratching increased.	Wall always wet and bricks disintegrating.
19 Jan. Cracks stopped and continued to be best of all.	Plaster disappeared increasingly.	As previous day.	Wall always wet and bricks disintegrating.
20 Jan. ” ”	Plaster nearly disappeared.	More disintegration of bricks and same parts stayed wet.	” ”
23 Jan. ” ”	Wall dry—Plaster almost completely disappeared but bricks stayed intact.	Disintegration of bricks increased and parts stayed wet.	” ”
24 Jan. ” ”	Wall dry and brick intact.	Inclination of wall increased and partly wet.	” ”
26 Jan. No change.	As previous day.	Wet parts increased bricks disintegrating.	Wall always wet and bricks disintegrating.
27 Jan. ” ”	Bricks were not affected in spite of loss of plaster.	Nearly one-third of wall com-completely wet, and only wet patches in the rest.	” ”
30 Jan. No change.	Bricks started disintegrating slightly.	Leaning of the wall increased and the wet parts did not dry up.	Wall always wet and bricks disintegrating.
31 Jan. ” ”	Wall dry and disintegration is slight.	Disintegration continues.	” ”
1 Feb. ” ”	” ”	Disintegration reached the stage of wall No. 4.	” ”
7 Feb. Continued to be best—cracks in plaster did not increase—and plaster firm.	Wall leaning but dry, and bricks almost intact.	Wall did not dry and disintegration increasing.	” ”
9 Feb. ” ”	Wall dry no change.	” ”	” ”

10 Feb.	”	”	”	”	”	”	”	”
11 Feb.	”	”	”	”	”	”	”	”
16 Feb.	”	”	”	”	”	”	Wall collapsed.	
19 Feb.	”	”	”	”	”	”	”	”

N.B. The three first walls stayed in the state described in the date of 11 February 1955 with no perceptible change until they collapsed on 5 March 1956 as a result of eccentric loading and the strong winds which were blowing on that day.

Appendix VI
Cost Analysis at the Moment When the Project Was Handed Over to the Ministry of Social Affairs

Area of houses built	9,499.7 m^2
Area of public buildings	9,802.20
Total	19,301.90 m^2

The public buildings included:

a. the mosque
b. the boys' primary school
c. the craft school
d. the khan
e. the market place
f. the village hall
g. the theater

The dispensary and social center, the hammam, the small church, and the permanent exhibition of village crafts were not built at the time of this estimate.

List of expenditure from the beginning

a. Permanent labor on the job	5,159.469
b. Casual labor	52,610.608
c. Purchases of materials and equipment	23,551.096
d. Purchases of lorries and fuel	10,752.004
e. Travel	916.985
f. Rent of rest house and ferryboat	552.400
g. Special duty allowances of the supervising architects	577.800
	94,120.362

If we evaluate the equipment, the lorries and the unused materials lying in the stores at L.E. 20,000, then the actual expenditure is: L.E. 94,120.362 – L.E. 20,000 = L.E. 74,120.362.

Therefore the cost of building p.m. in public buildings and houses

$$= \frac{\text{L.E. } 74{,}120.362}{\text{L.E. } 19{,}301.900} = 3.8, \text{ say L.E. } 4.$$

Glossary

Adze. Cutting tool with thin arched blade sharpened on concave side and set at right angles to handle.

Amiri. Style of architecture introduced by the khedive or the amir for palace and government buildings.

Badana. Tightly related group of ten to twenty families living in neighboring houses, with recognized patriarch.

Ballas. Jar used for fetching water from fountain.

Birka. Pit left after earth has been dug for brick making, often containing stagnant water.

Brise-soleil. Screen to block off unwanted sunlight.

Cavetto. Concave molding whose curve approximates a quarter circle.

Centering. Timber or other fabric used to support the parts of a masonry arch during construction.

Claustra(work). Moldings and tracery in mud used to decorate doors and windows.

Dorka'a. Central square of house, roofed with dome.

Dirham. An old coin, worth one piaster (1 PT).

Extrados. Exterior curve of an arch or outer surface of a vault.

Hammam. Public bath house.

Hammamgi. Bath attendant.

Hosha. Dyked area of agricultural land, irrigated by basin system.

Iwan. Recessed area of room.

Ka'a. Main hall in house.

Khan. Inn for foreign merchants arriving in town.

Madyafa. Guest house or guest room.

Maktoub. "It is written"; "It is ordained."

Malakan. American.

Malkaf. Device for catching wind at highest point of house.

Maziara. Alcove for water jar.

Moallem. Master mason.

Morda. Swimming place.

Mushrabiya. Oriel window with latticework screen.

Osta. Master craftsman.
Pendentive. Triangular, spherical section of vaulting serving to support dome.
Sabras. Door constructed by nailing together many small boards in an original pattern.
Salsabil. Kind of marble fountain in hall of house.
Shadûf. Bucket and lever machine used by peasants for irrigating.
Sharaki. Dry (earth), having large cracks.
Squinch. Support (arch, lintel, or other) carried across corner of room under superimposed mass.
Tambour. "Archimedes' screw," machine used by peasants for irrigating.
Tesht. Large laundry basin.
Voussoir. One of a number of tapering or wedge-shaped pieces forming an arch or vault.
Zeer. Large unglazed jar for storing water.

Illustrations

Queen Hatshepsut making mud brick

1. Village of Dahmit, Nubia
2. Doorway with claustrawork in Dahmit

3. Fatimid Necropolis, Aswan

4. Monastery of Saint Simeon, Aswan

5. Granaries of the Ramesseum in Old Gourna, nineteenth dynasty

6. Vault supporting a staircase in Touna el Gabal, Ptolemaic period

7. Masons outline a parabola on the end wall with mud plaster

8. Trimming plaster with an adze

9. The first brick is laid against the end wall

10. The second course starts with a half-brick

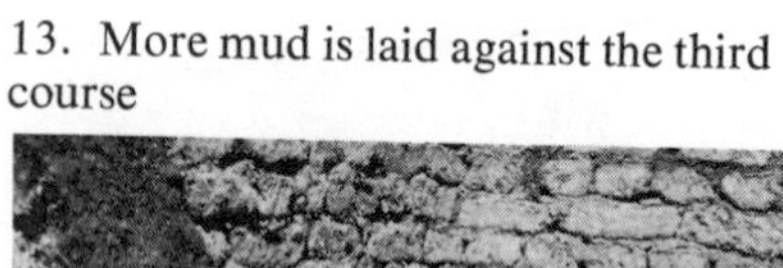

13. More mud is laid against the third course

14. The fourth course

11. A third brick completes the second course

12. The third course leans more sharply from the vertical

15. The fifth course is completed

16. The first inclined ring is completed

17. Masons insert dry packing in the interstices

18. The inclined face of the rings gives support to succeeding courses

19. Vaults supporting a staircase in Bahtim

20. Society of Agriculture farm in Bahtim

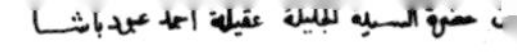

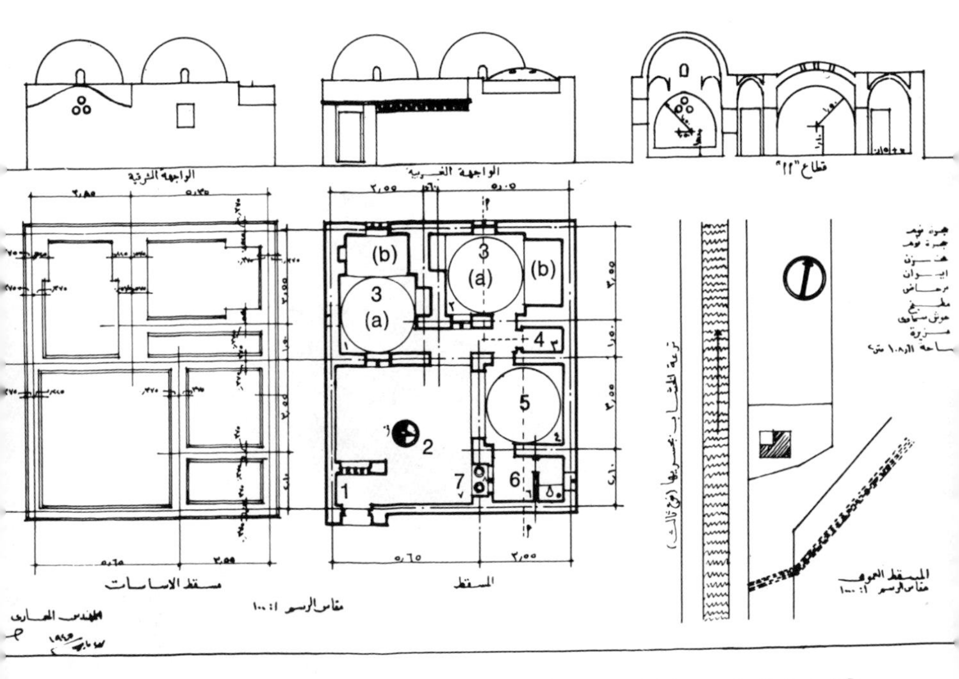

1. House of Hamed Said in Marg

22. Plans of mud brick model house in Ezbet el Basry. Legend: (1) Entrance. (2) Courtyard. (3) Bedrooms: (a) dorka'a, (b) bed alcove (iwan). (4) Storage. (5) Cooking and living loggia. (6) Bathroom. (7) *Maziara*

23. Mud brick model house in Ezbet el Basry

24. Loggia of model house

25. Façade of model house

26. Row of concrete houses in Ezbel el Basry

27. Colossi of Memmon

28. Old Gourna: peasant houses on Necropolis

29. Map of Gourna

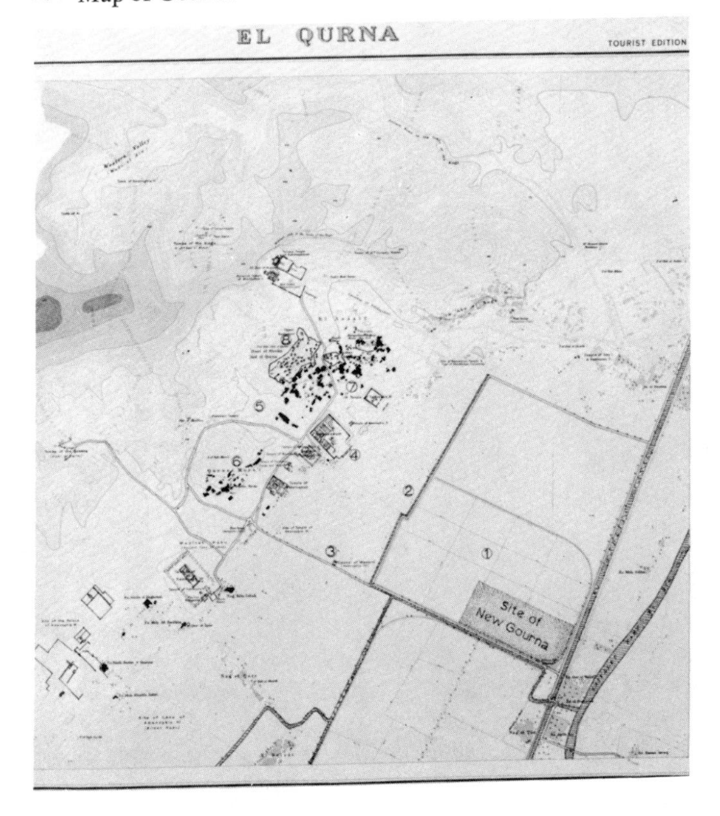

30. Sabras door of mosque
31. Sabras door of primary school

32. Interior sabras door of crafts school

33. Sabras door of exhibition hall

34. Sabras door of theater

35. Another sabras door of exhibition hall

36. Claustrawork in marketplace

37. School at Fares

38. *Beit el agrab* (mud bed designed to protect from scorpions)

39. Bed of Odysseus

40. House at Gornet Moraï

41. Pigeon tower in Old Gourna

42. Pigeon tower in New Gourna

43. *Maziara* (alcove for water jar) in Old Gourna

44. *Maziara* in New Gourna

45. Mosque in Old Gourna

46. Mosque in New Gourna

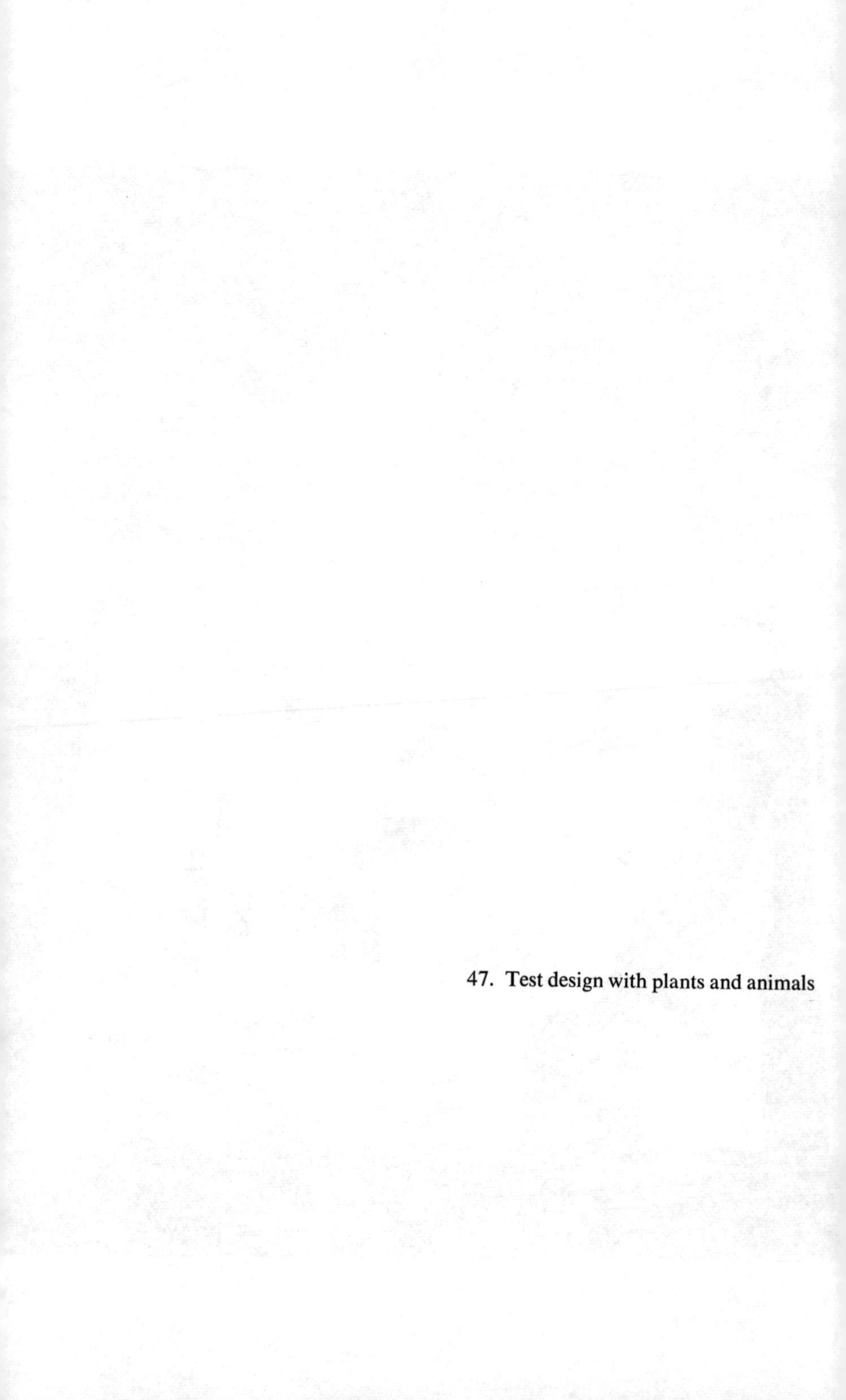

47. Test design with plants and animals

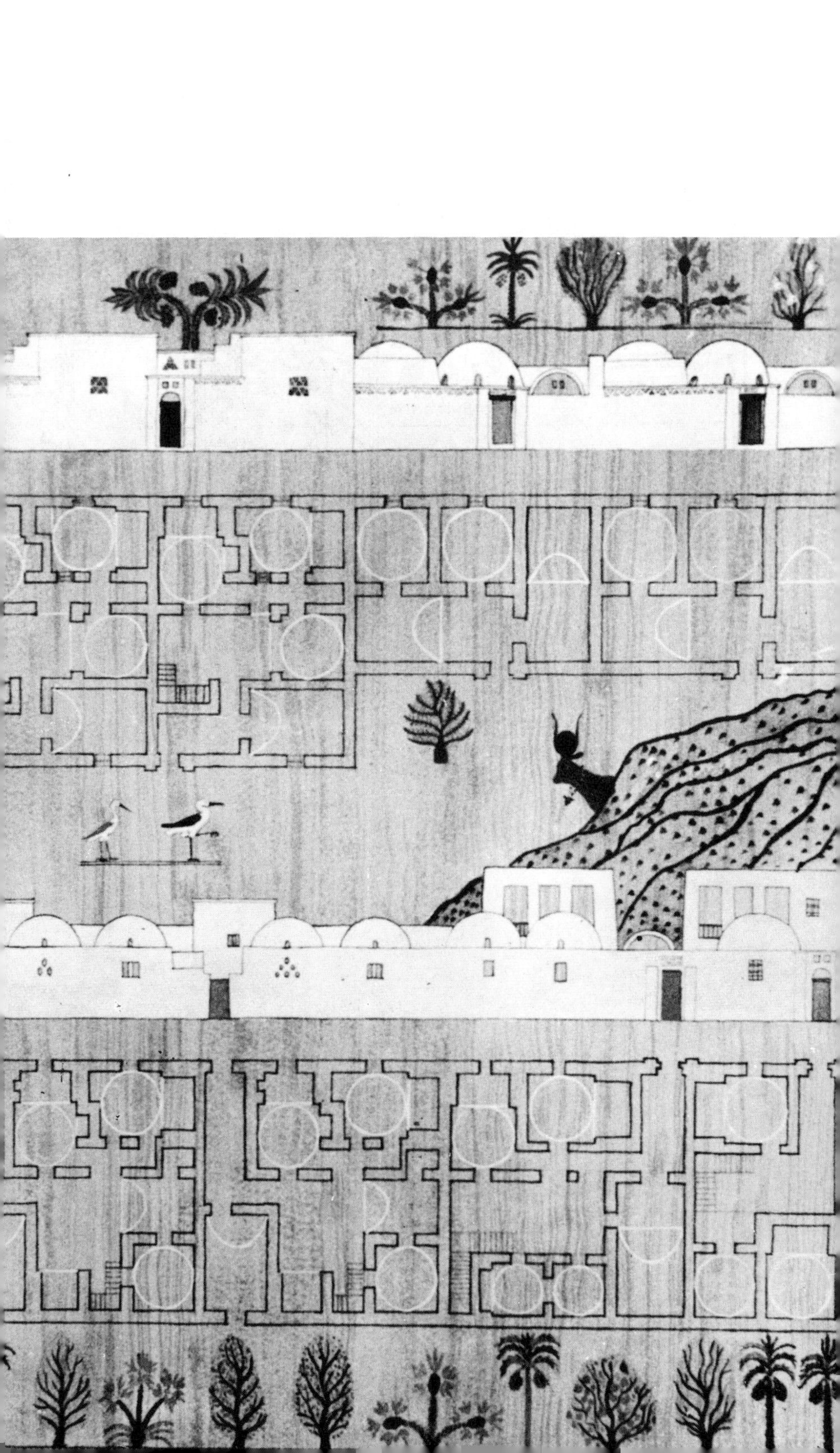

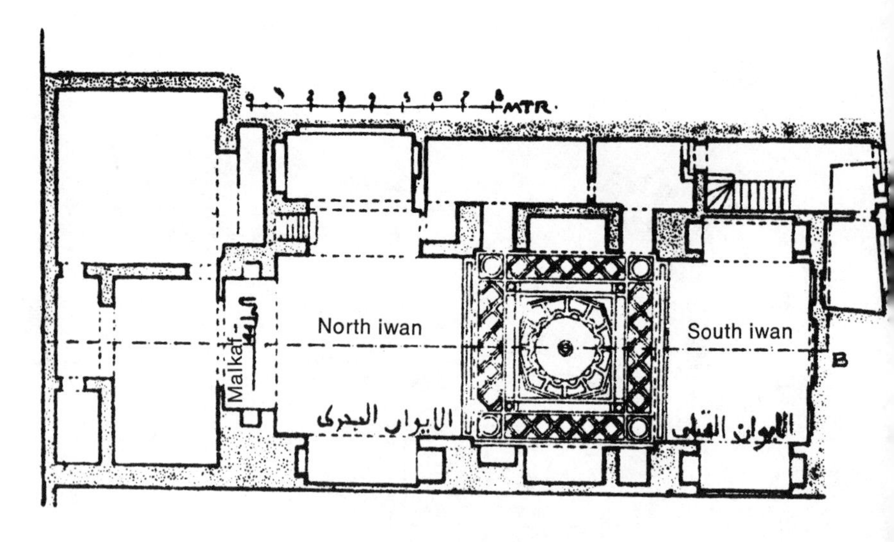

49. Plan of *Malkaf* (wind catch) in Katkhoda, fourteenth century

48. Loggia wall with openings to the windward side

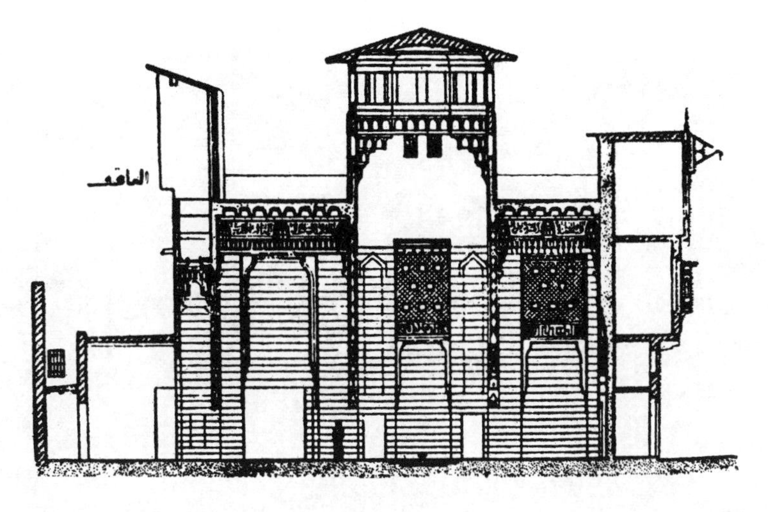

50. *Malkaf,* section

51. *Malkaf* in Katkhoda

52. *Mushrabiya* (oriel window with latticework screen) at Sehem House

53. Ahmed Abdel Rassoul family neighborhood, view of *madyafa*

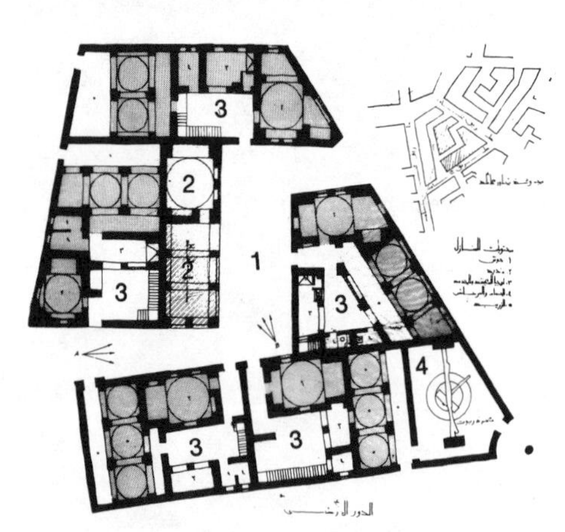

54. Family neighborhood, ground floor plan. Legend: (1) Private square. (2) Guest house. (3) Houses. (4) Mill

55. Detours dissuade strangers from using narrow streets as thoroughfares

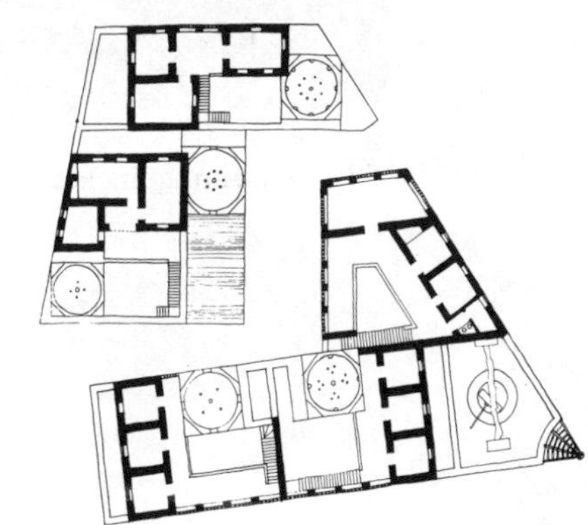

56. Family neighborhood, upper floor plan

57. Dome on squinches

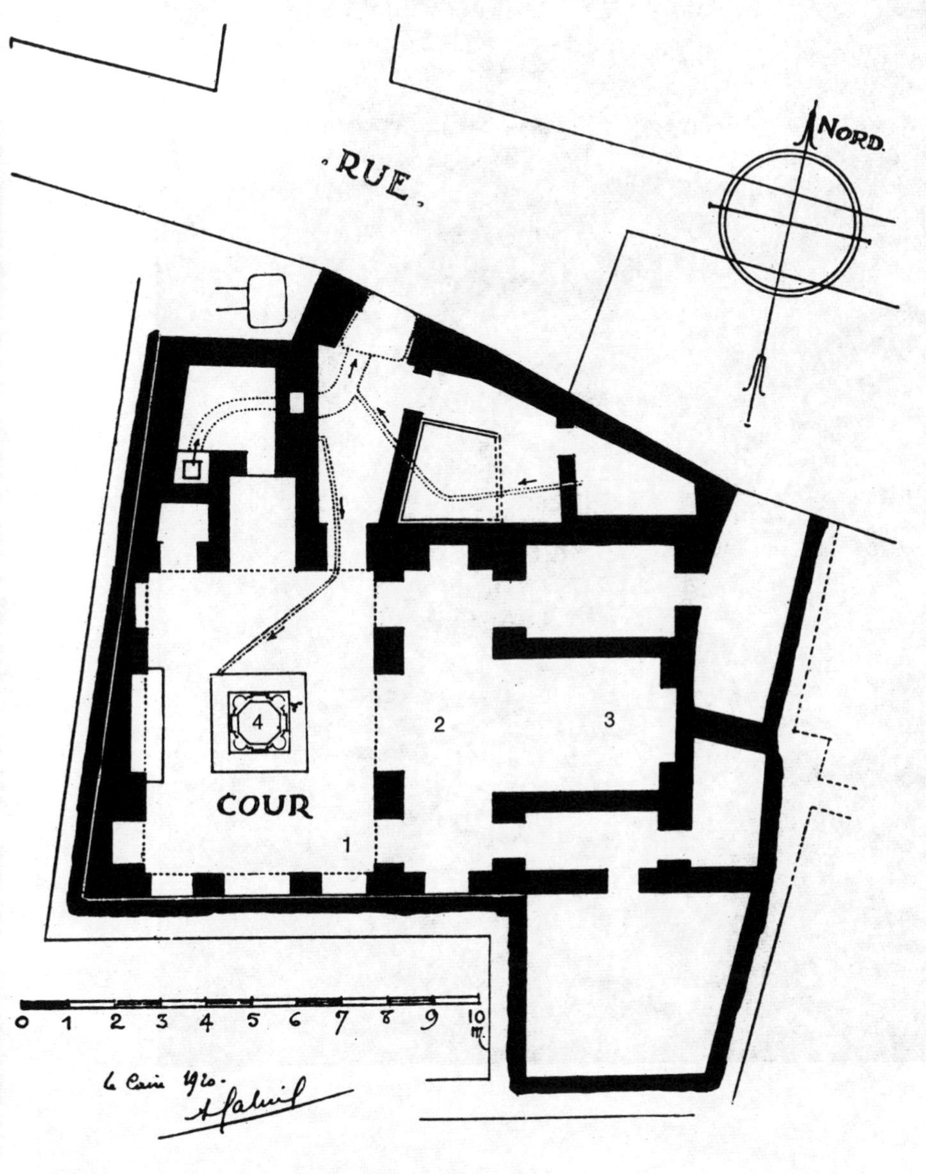

58. Fountain in courtyard of house in Fostat. Legend: (1) Courtyard. (2) Loggia. (3) Iwan. (4) Fountain

59, 60. Courtyards of houses in New Gourna

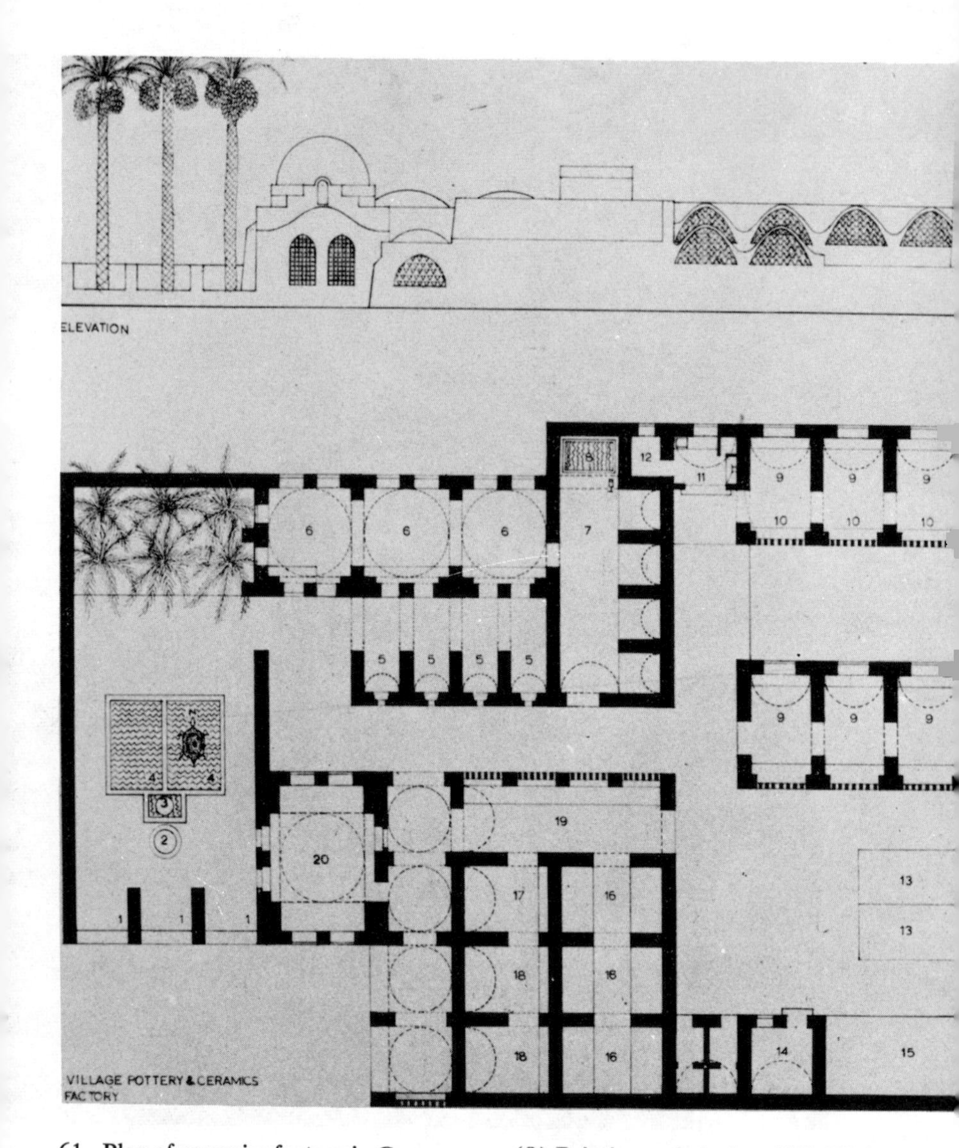

61. Plan of ceramics factory in Garagos. Legend: (1) Arrival of raw clay. (2) Sieve. (3) Mixing. (4) Sedimentation basins. (5) Kneading clay and deposit. (6) Potter wheels hall. (7) Drying room. (8) Wind catch with water basin underneath for humidifying the air (very dry in Garagos (9) Painting and glazing. (10) Dining. (11) Kitchen. (12) Food store. (13) Kilns. (14) Mechanic. (15) Fuel storage. (16) Store of ready-made ceramics. (17–18) Packing and straw cases storage. (19) Exhibition room. (20) Manager

62. Plan of khan

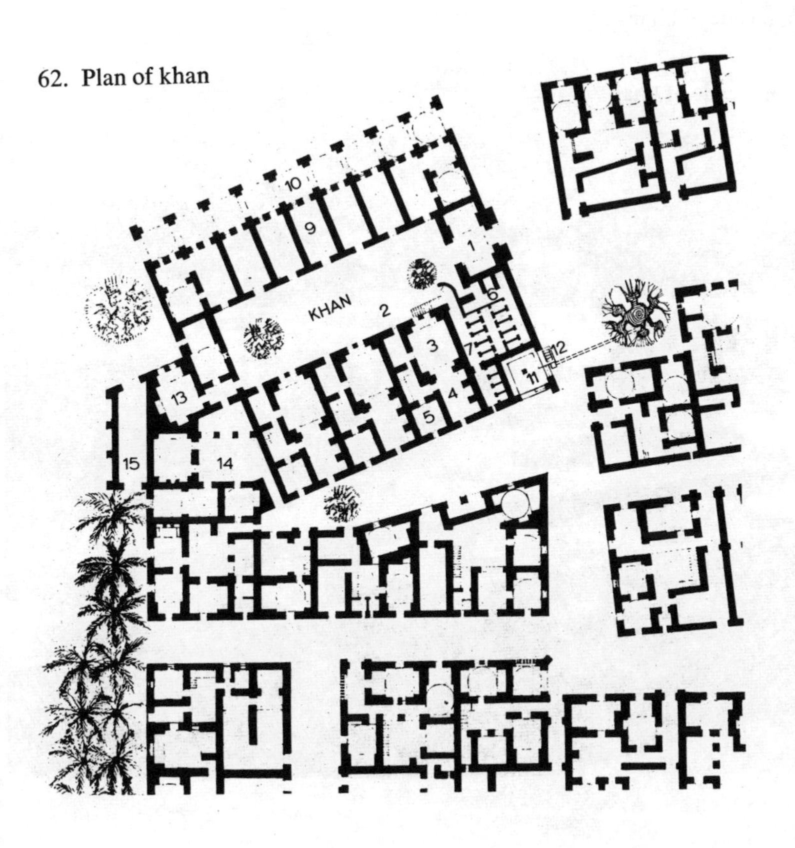

63. East façade of khan

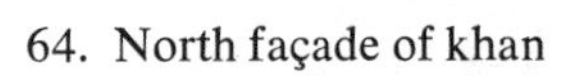

64. North façade of khan

65. Exhibition hall

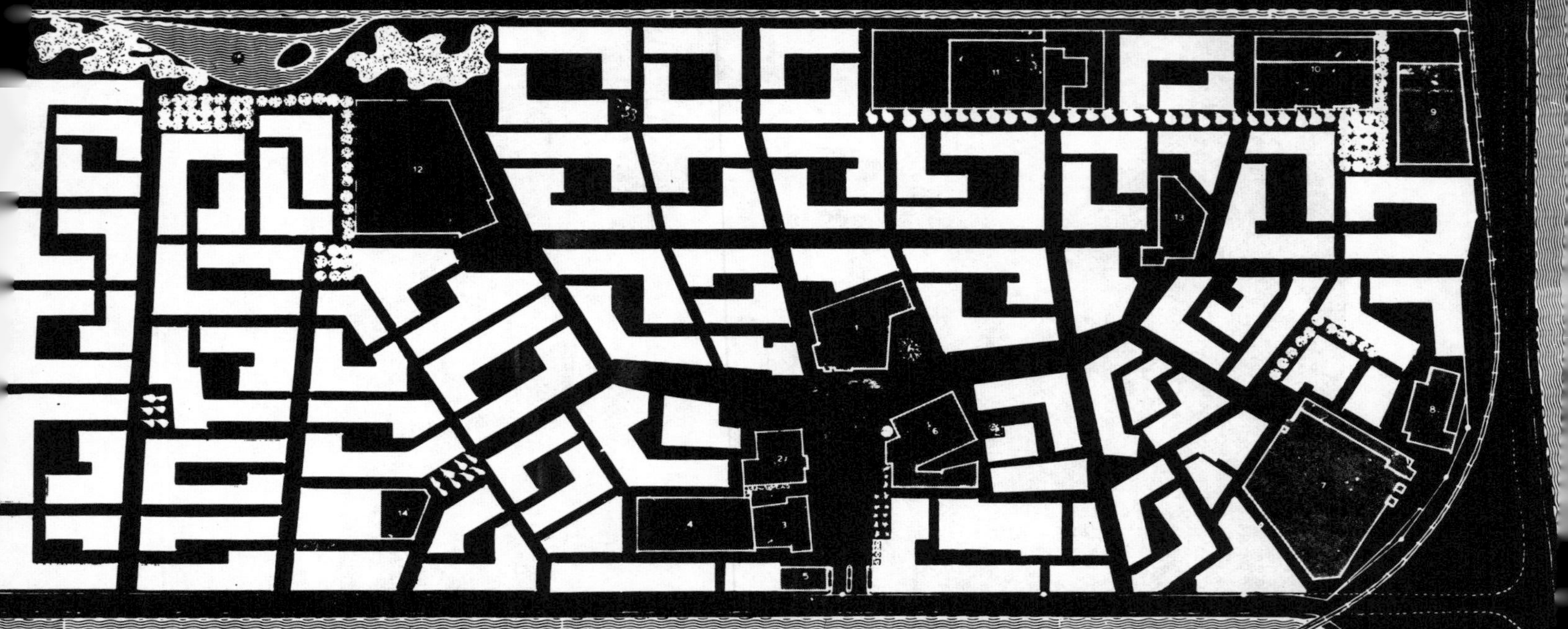
GOURNA VILLAGE
GENERAL LAYOUT
N
E
W
S
FARHANA DRAIN
OSQUE
4 SPORTING RURAL CLUB
7 MARKET — PLACE
10 DISPEUSA
& WOMEN'S SOCIAL CENTRE
13 HAMMAM
PUBLIC BUILDINGS

66. Plan of New Gourna
67. Street in New Gourna

68, 69. Streets in New Gourna

70, 71. Streets in New Gourna

73. Main square

72. Northwest corner of khan on main square

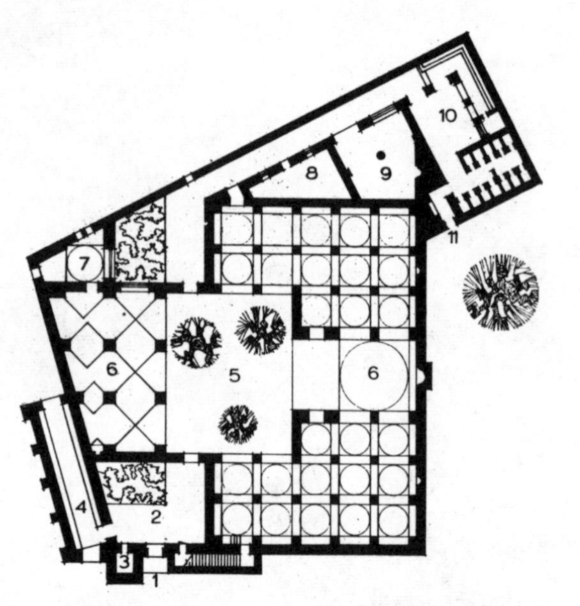

74. Plan of mosque. Legend: (1) Entrance. (2) Forecourt. (3) Store. (4) Vaulted gallery for passers-by. (5) Courtyard (6) Praying iwans. (7) Sheikh's room. (8) Store. (9) Small chapel. (10) Ablutionary. (11) Ablutionary entrance

75. The mosque in 1948

76. The mosque in 1968

77. Plan of marketplace. Legend: (1) Public entrance. (2) Supervisor. (3) Open-Air restaurant. (4) Café. (5) Wares exhibition booths. (6) Grain area. (7) Cattle exhibition. (8) Entrance into village. (9) Dovecote

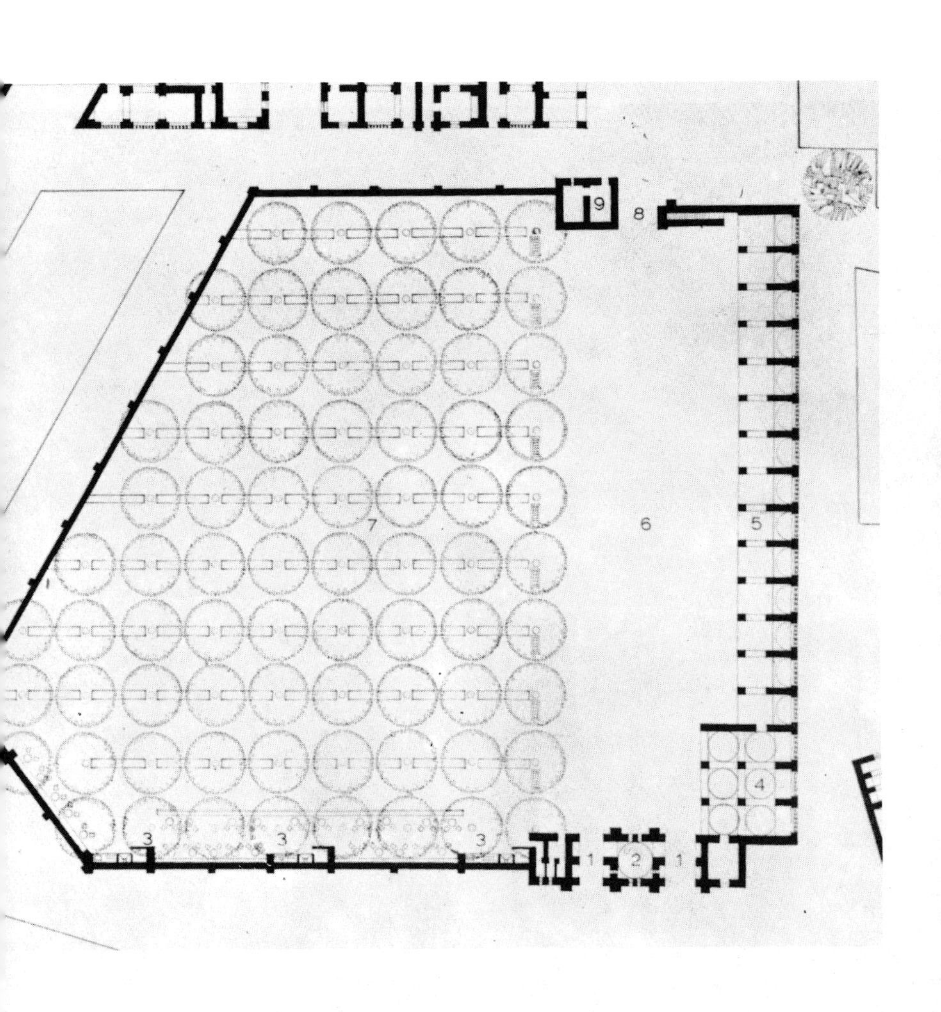
9
8
7
6
5
4
3
3
3
1
2
1

78. Entrance to marketplace

79. Marketplace in New Gourna

80. Peasants in the Old Gourna marketplace

82. Arcade in the marketplace

81. Vaults in the New Gourna marketplace

83. Bas-relief at Deir el Bahari: animals in the shade of trees

84. Shaded area for animals at New Gourna marketplace

85. Merchandise area

86. Marketplace at Nagada

87. Quarterstaff contest

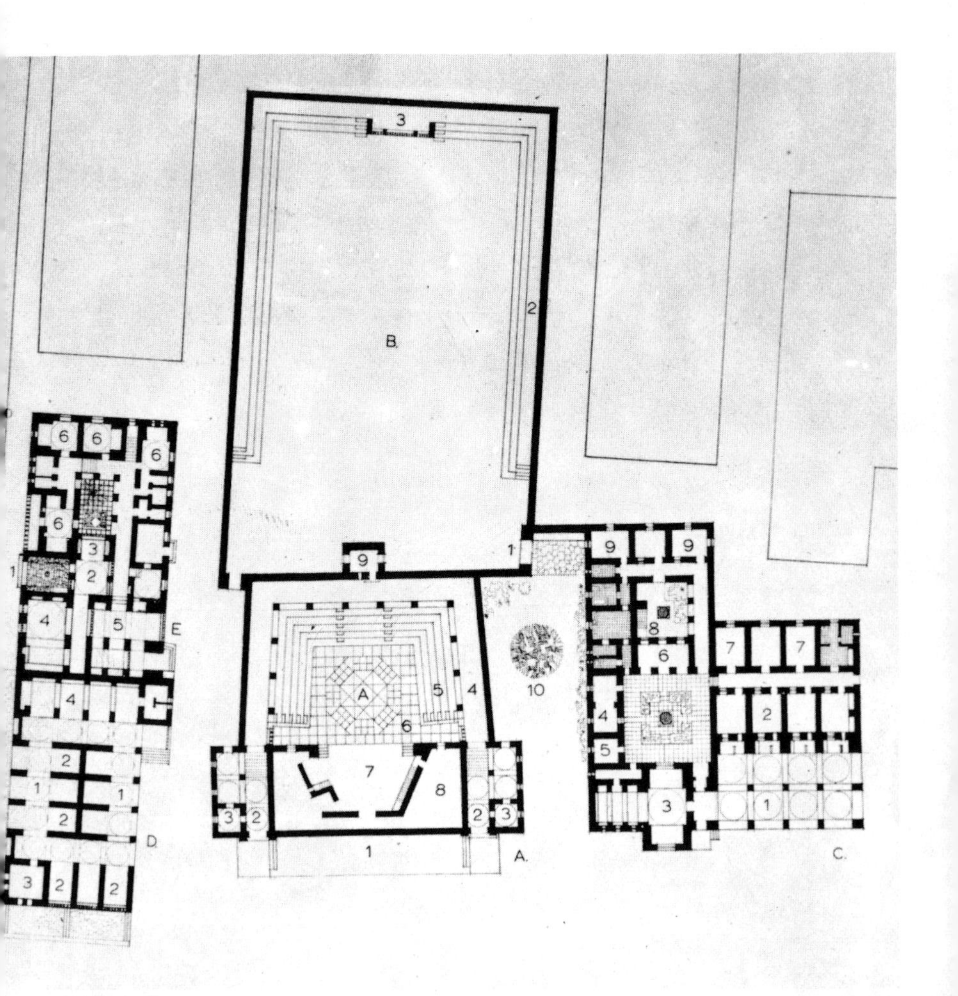

88. Plan. Legend: (A) Theater: (1) raised seating platform for open-air performances in village square; (2) entrance; (3) booking; (4) gallery; (5) seating; (6) chorus; (7) stage; (8) backstage; (9) cinema projection room; (10) open-air foyer. (B) Gymnasium: (1) entrance; (2) seating; (3) box. (C) Village hall. (D) Crafts exhibition hall. (E) Abdel Rassoul family neighborhood

89. Façade of theater

90. Theater, elevation

92. A performance

91. Auditorium

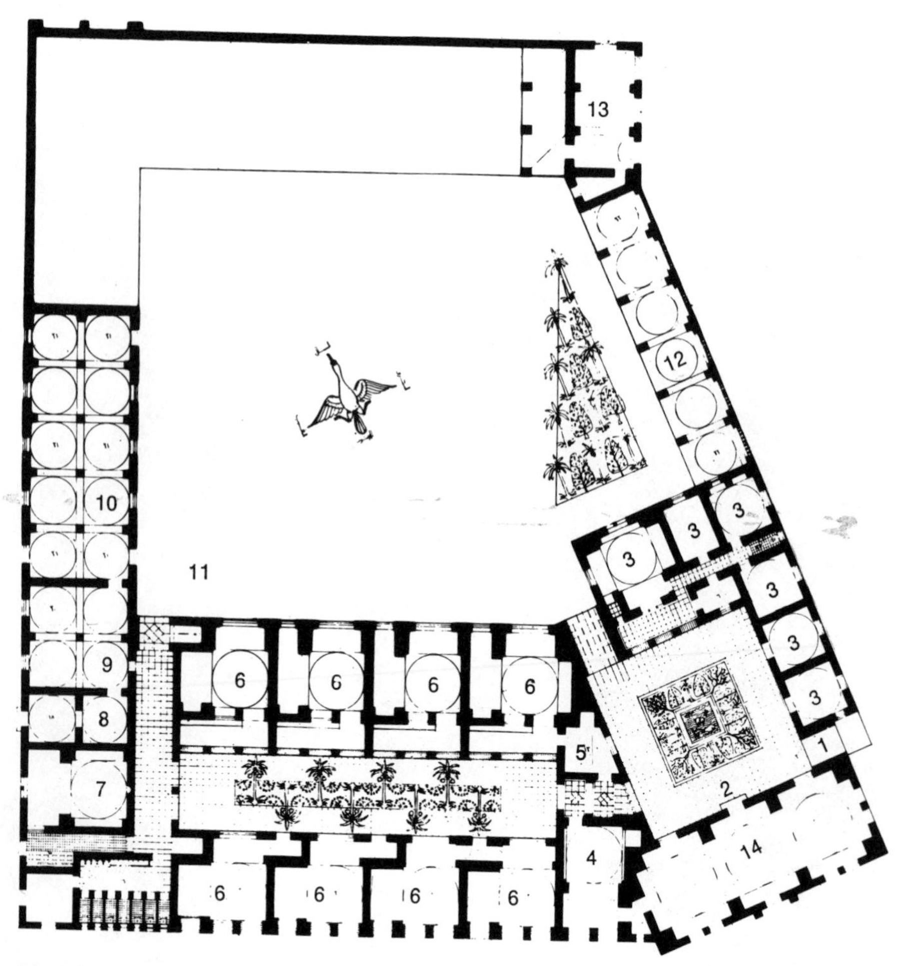

93. Plan of boys' primary school. Legend: (1) Entrance. (2) Entrance courtyard. (3) Headmaster and administration offices. (4) Masters' room. (5) Supervisor's room. (6) Classroom. (7) Mosque and ablutionaries. (8) Storage. (9) Kitchen. (10) Dining room. (11) Main courtyard. (12) Shed. (13) Manual works workshop. (14) Assembly-lecture room

94. Boys' primary school

95. Entrance courtyard of boys' primary school

96. Classroom courtyard of boys' primary school

97, 98. Classroom

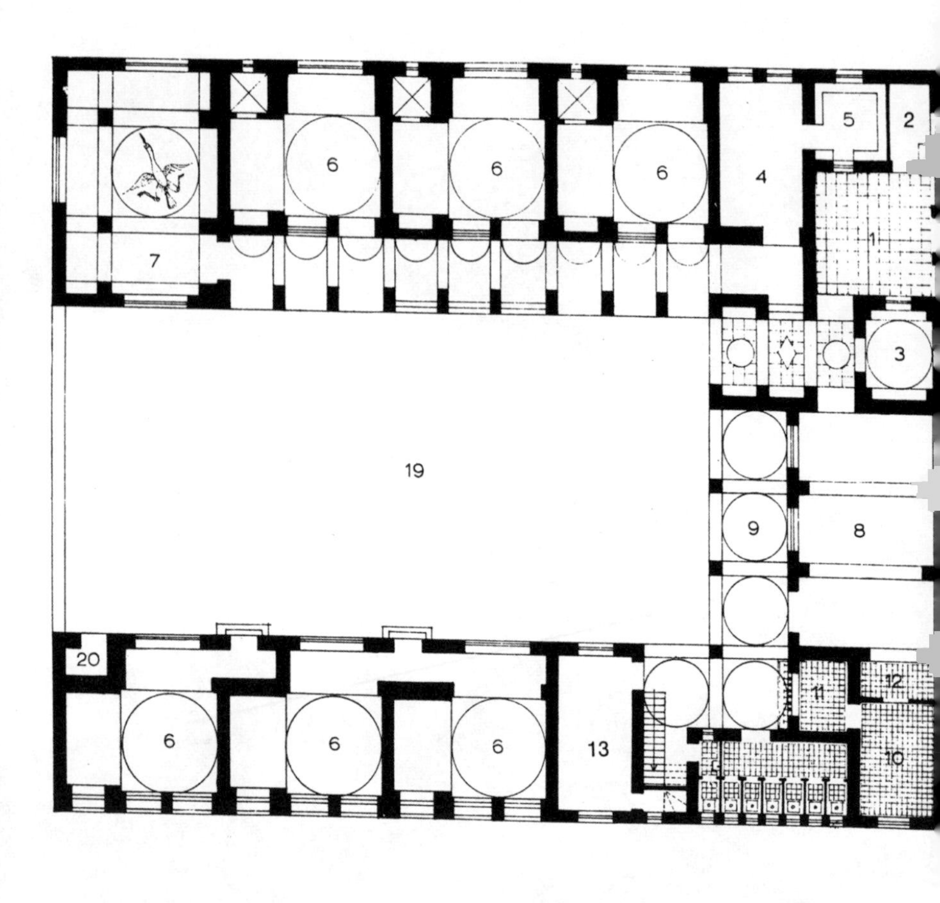

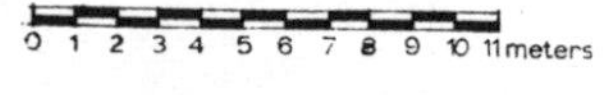

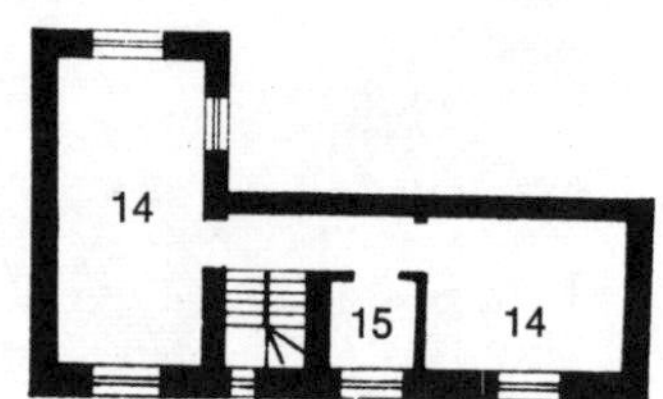

99. Plan of girls' primary school. Legend: (1) Entrance. (2) Porter. (3) Supervisor. (4) Book storage. (5) Book distribution. (6) Classroom. (7) Art room. (8) Dining-exhibition room. (9) Shed. (10) Kitchen. (11) Storage. (12) Serving. (13) Mistresses' room. (14) Mistress's bedroom on upper floor. (15) Bathroom

100. Ventilation system at girls' primary school

101. Courtyard of girls' primary school

102. Courtyard of crafts school

103. Façade of crafts school

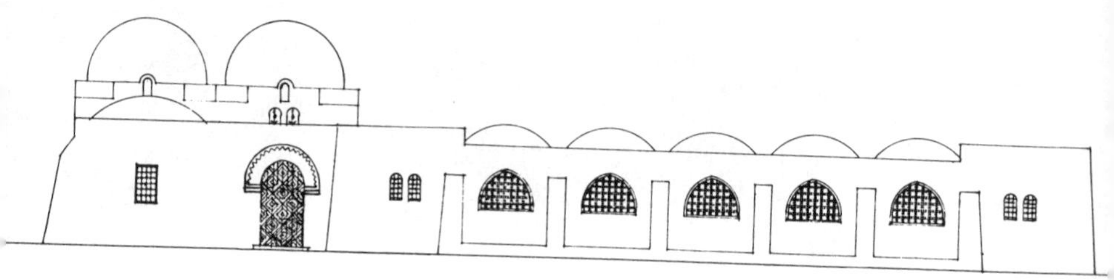

104. Exhibition hall

105. Plan of brickyard. Legend:
(A) Brickmaking ground. (B) Mixing troughs. (C) Canals. (D) Decauville rails. (E) Stacking area

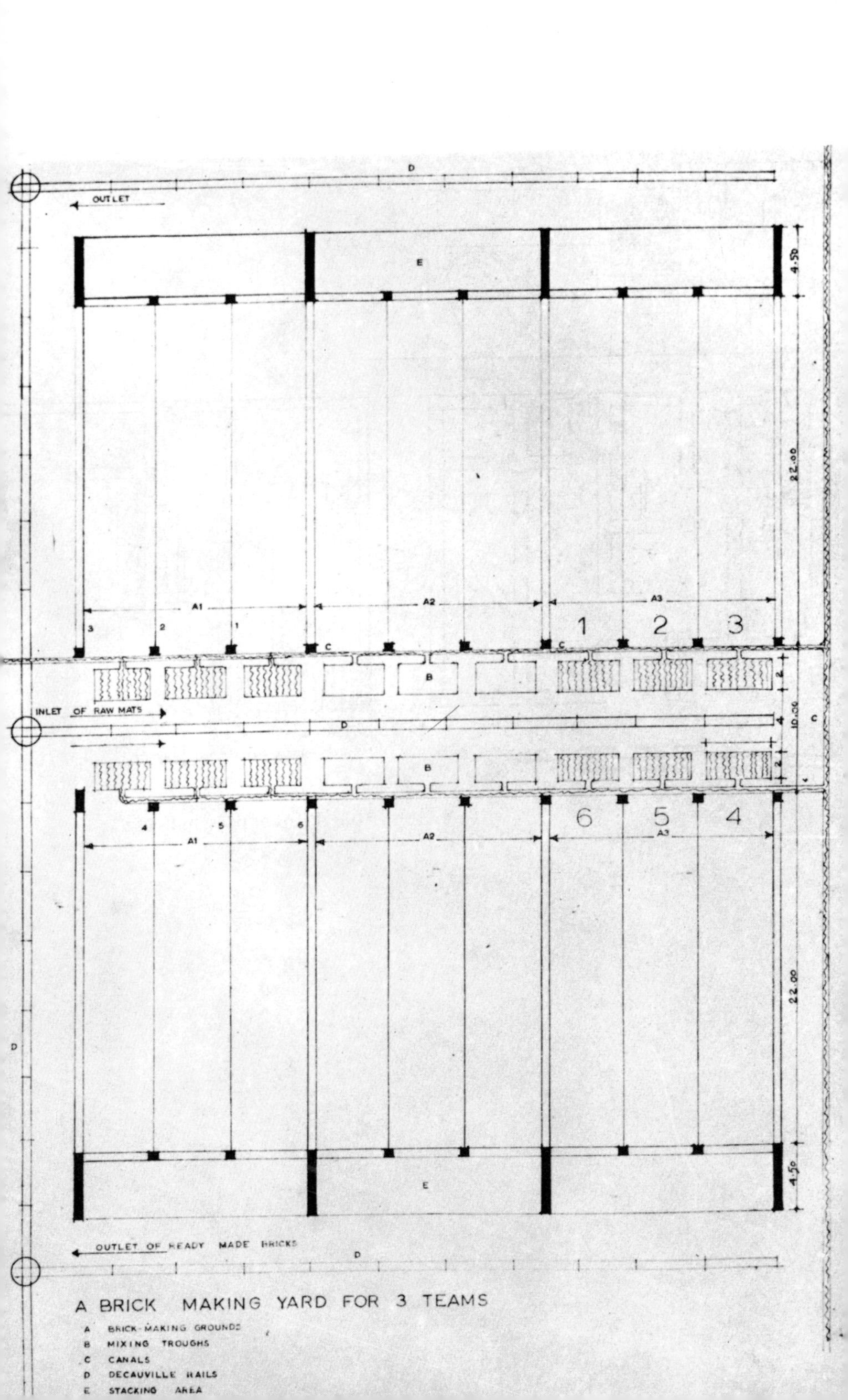
D
OUTLET
E
4.50
22.00
A1
A2
A3
3
2
1
1 2 3
C
B
2
INLET OF RAW MATS
10.00
6
5
4
6 5 4
OUTLET OF READY MADE BRICKS
A BRICK MAKING YARD FOR 3 TEAMS
A BRICK-MAKING GROUNDS
B MIXING TROUGHS
C CANALS
D DECAUVILLE RAILS
E STACKING AREA

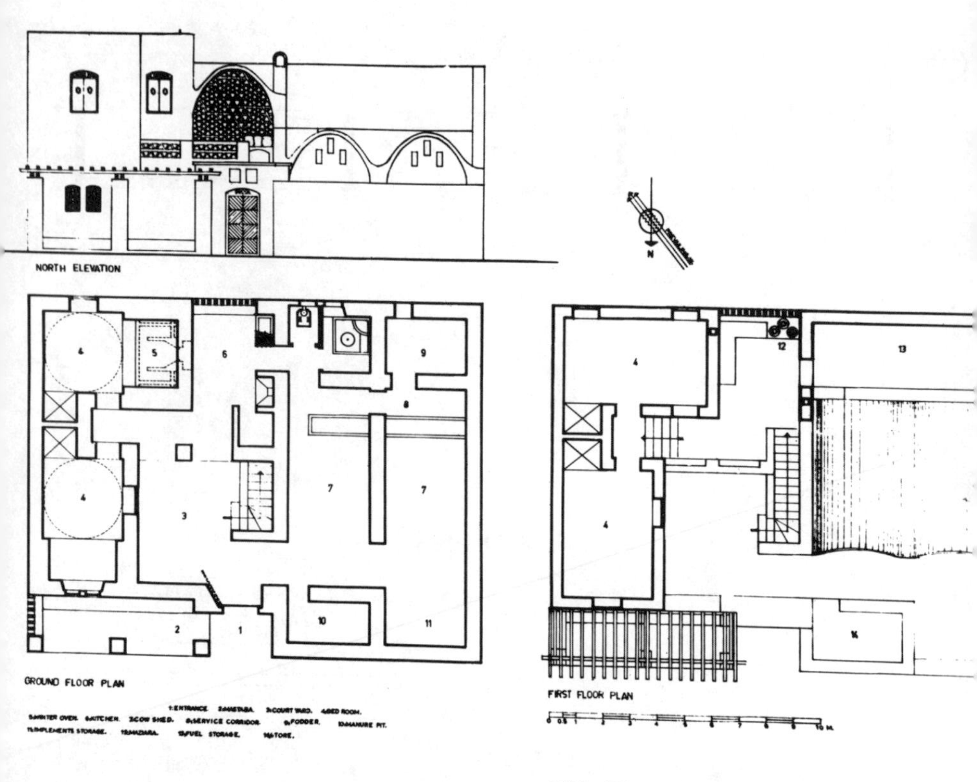

106. Plans of peasant house

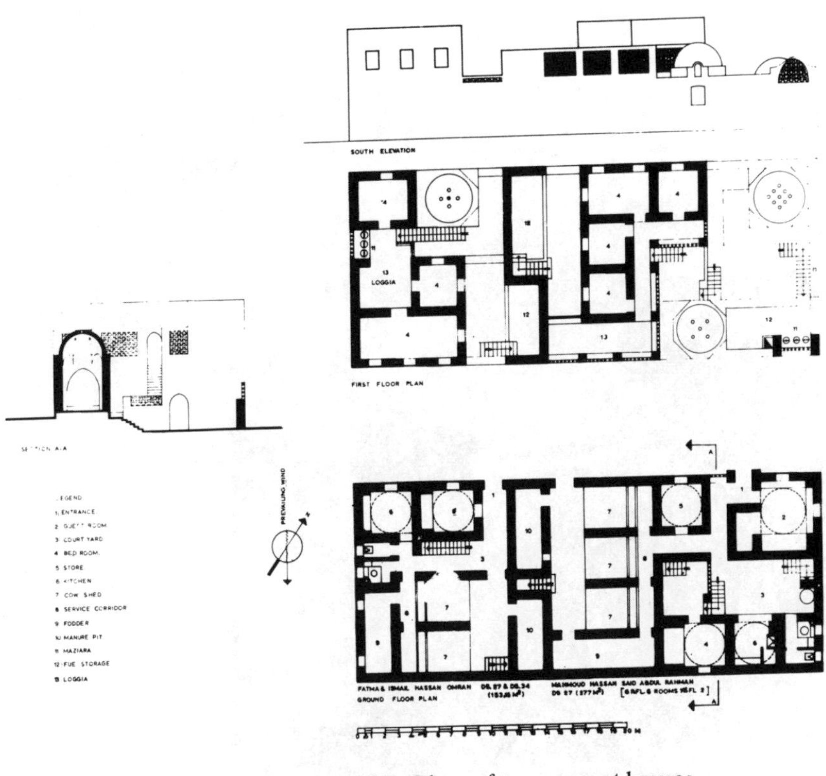

107. Plans of two peasant houses

108, 109. Mud brick houses

110. Mud brick house on stone foundation

111. Terraces

112. Roofs

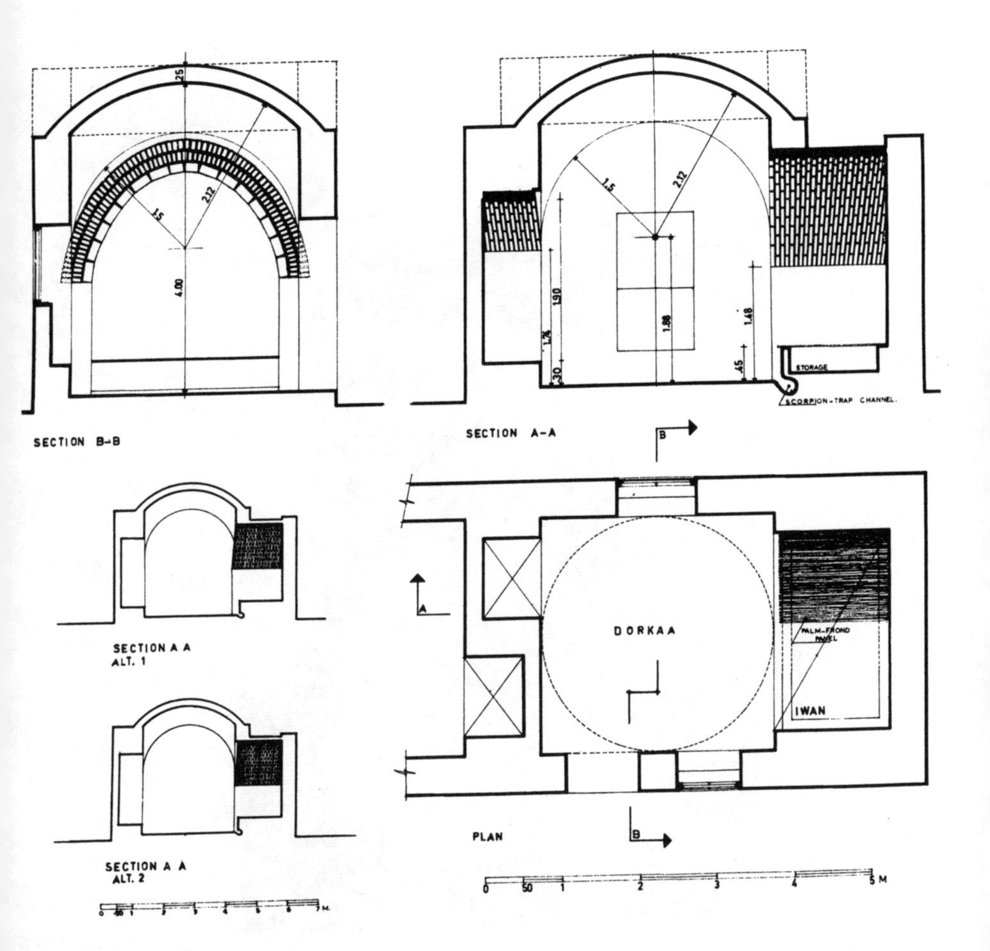

113. Plans of bedroom

114. Austrian kachelofen

115. Austrian kachelofen, sections

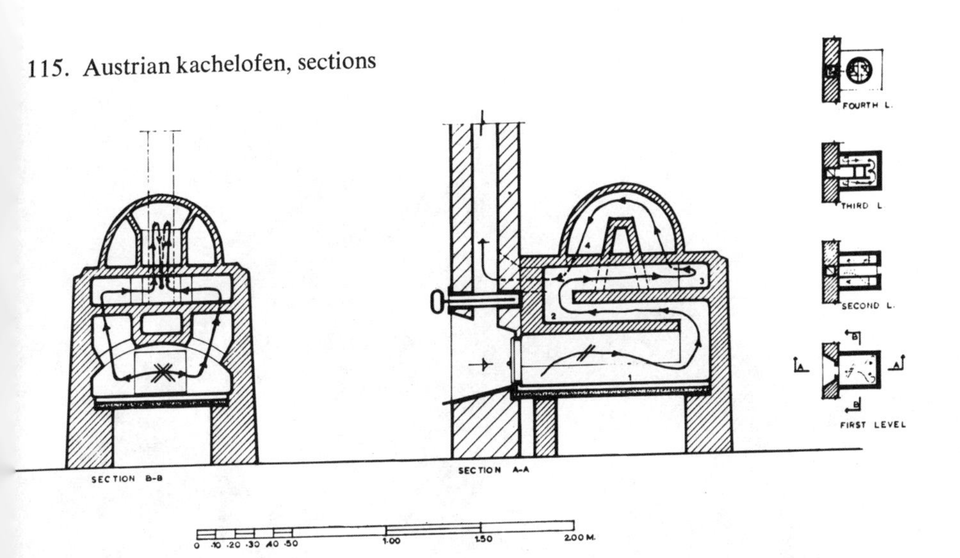

116. Mud brick kachelofen made in Gourna, sections

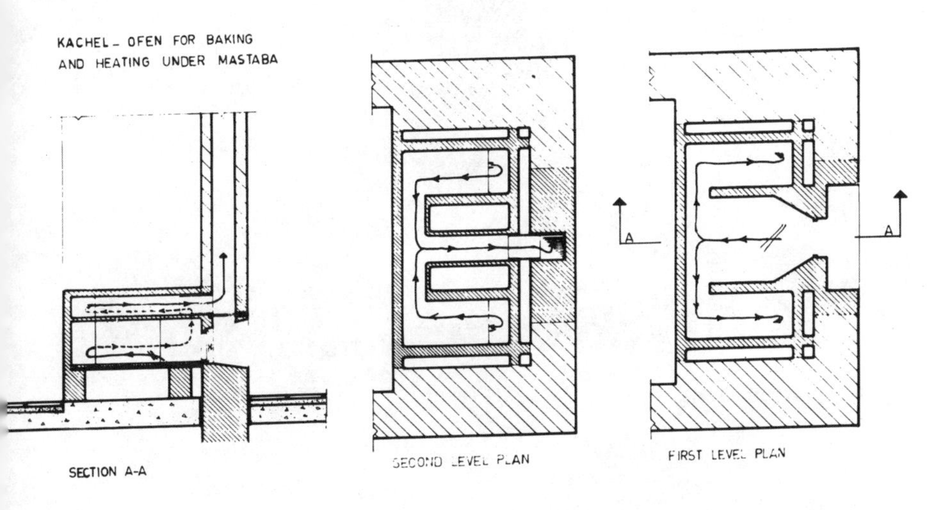

117. Fireplace in alcove

118. Peasant way of cooking

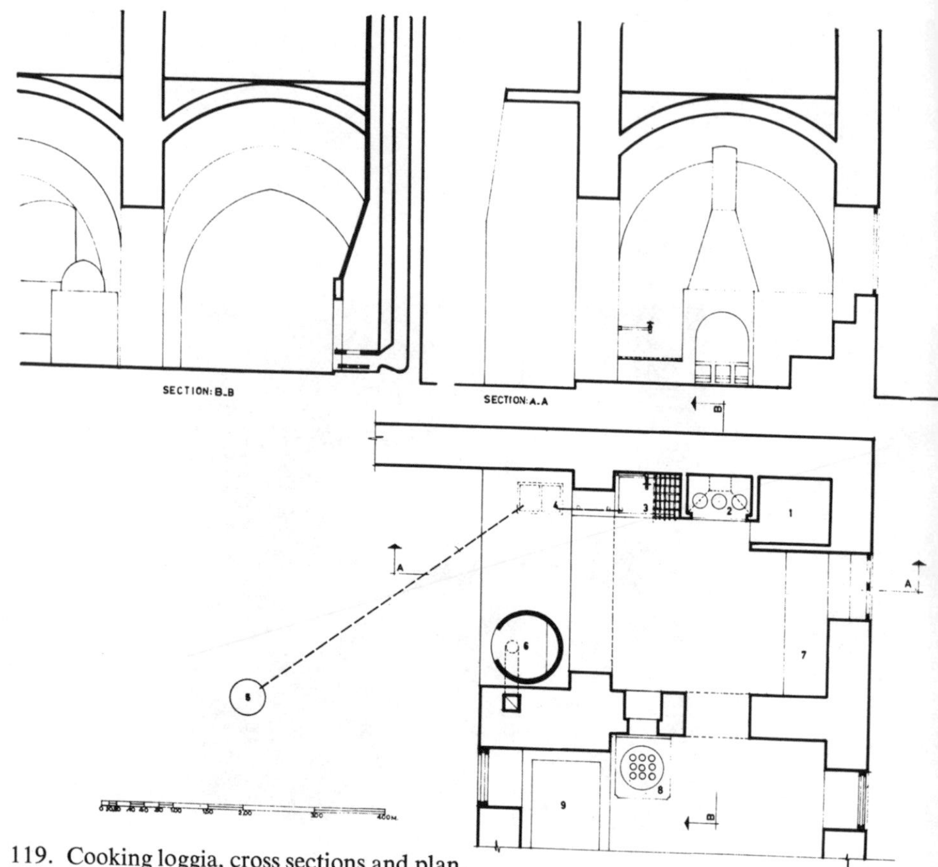

119. Cooking loggia, cross sections and plan. Legend: (1) Fuel bin. (2) Stove. (3) Sink. (4) Grease trap. (5) Bore hole. (6) Summer oven. (7) Seat. (8) Kachelofen–baking oven. (9) Bed

120. Water point, section

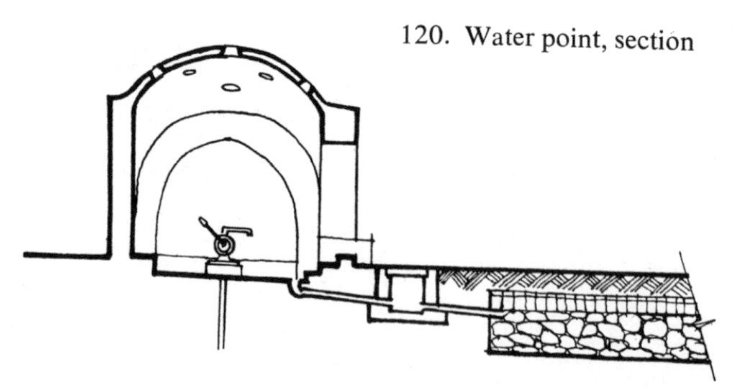

121. Water point

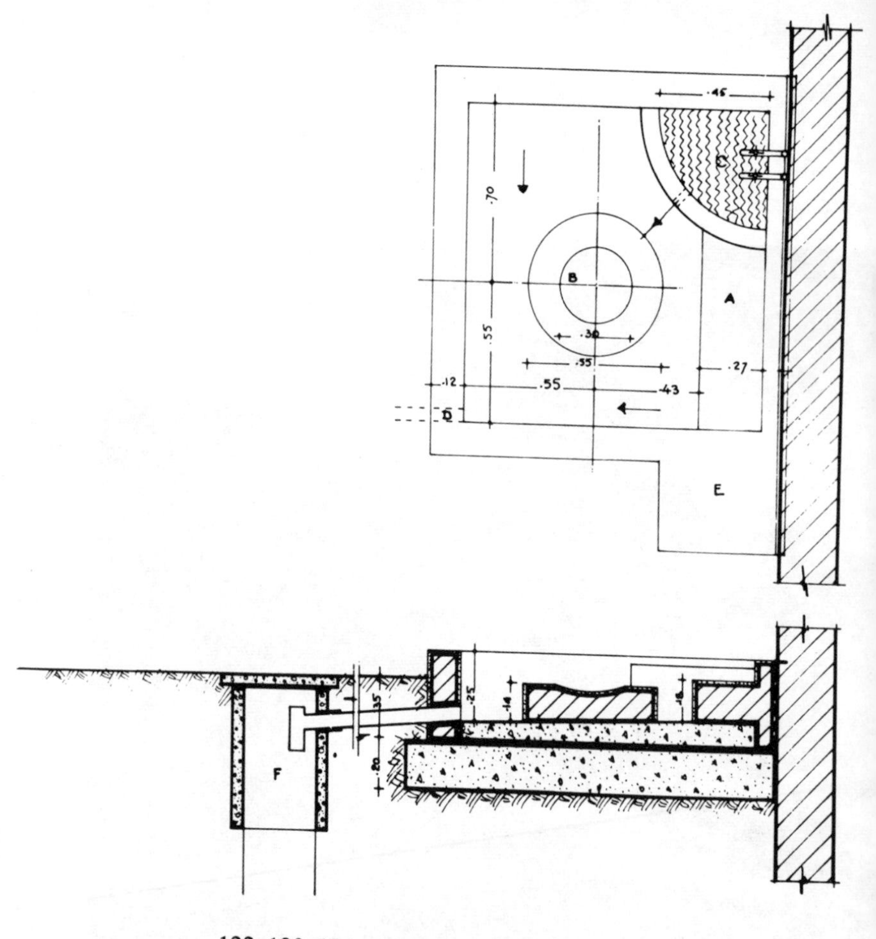

122, 123, 124. Laundry area. Legend: (A) Seat. (B) Disk supporting washing basin. (C) Basin for soaking laundry. (D) Drain. (E) Block for rinsed laundry. (F) Bore hole

125. Children in infested canal

126. Plan of artificial lake

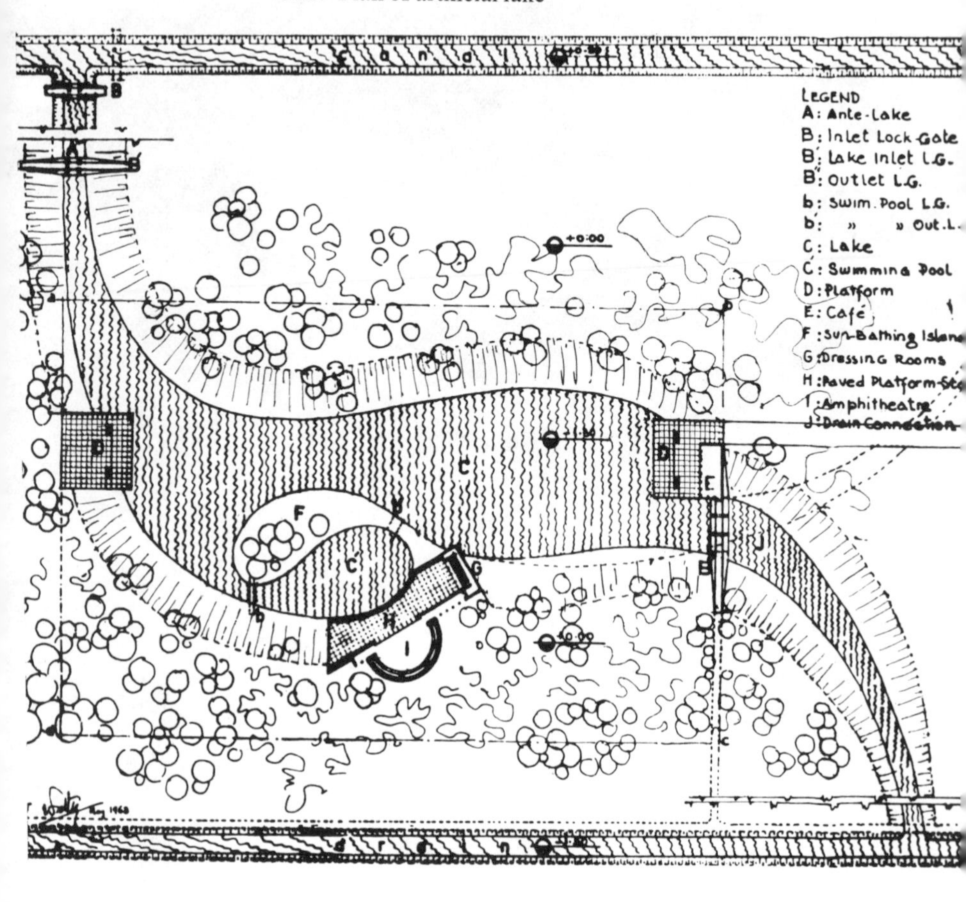

127. The demon Bill Harzia

128. Training center for masons

129. Vaulted room in Gharb Aswan, Nubia

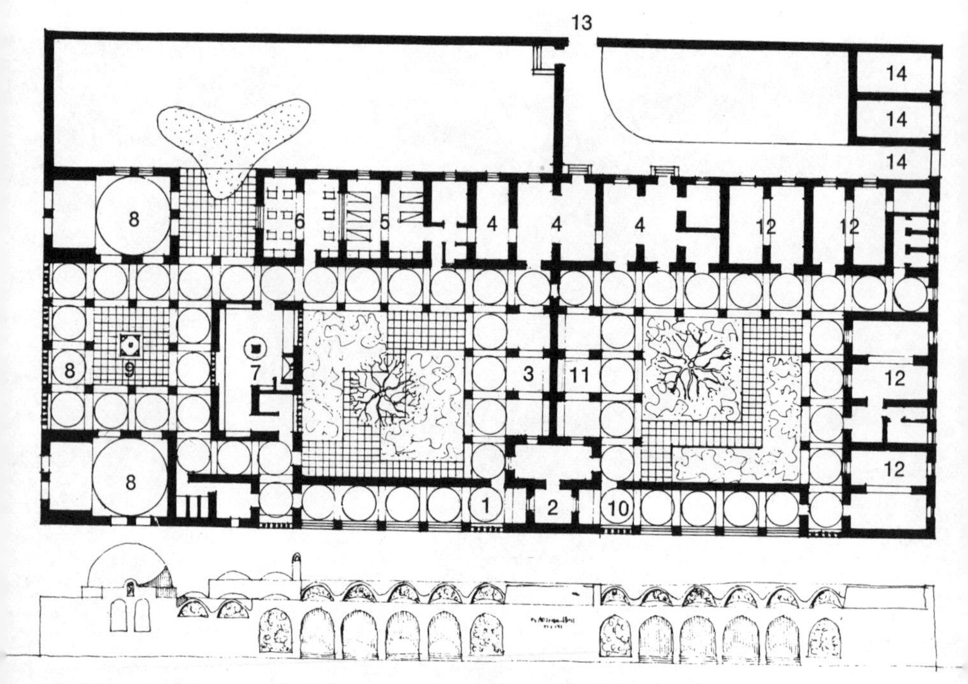

130. Plan of hygiene center. Legend: (1) Women's entrance. (2) Supervisor. (3) Waiting room. (4) Clinic. (5) Mothers' room. (6) Babies. (7) Kitchen. (8) Nursery and handwork workshops. (9) Patio. (10) Men's entrance. (11) Men's waiting room. (12) Doctors' and nurses' quarters. (13) Ambulance entrance. (14) Ambulance garages

131. Ouna
132. Parliament of the Pharaohs

The photographs are by Hassan Fathy, with the exception of the following: numbers 21, 31, 36, 38–41, 44, 45, 59, 63, 72, 78–80, 86, 91, 94, 102, 108–110, 117, 118, by Dimitri Papadimou; numbers 30, 32–35, 42, 46, 53, 55, 60, 64, 68–71, 73, 82, 87, 92, 104, 112, by Hassia; numbers 27, 65, 67, 76, 96–98, by Roger Viollet; number 81 by Selim Bahari.